Israel Getzler
NIKOLAI SUKHANOV
Chronicler of the Russian Revolution

Arturo J. Cruz, Jr
NICARAGUA'S CONSERVATIVE REPUBLIC, 1858–93

Pamela Lubell
THE CHINESE COMMUNIST PARTY AND THE CULTURAL REVOLUTION
The Case of the Sixty-One Renegades

Mikael af Malmborg
NEUTRALITY AND STATE-BUILDING IN SWEDEN

Klaus Gallo
GREAT BRITAIN AND ARGENTINA
From Invasion to Recognition, 1806–26

David Faure and Tao Tao Liu
TOWN AND COUNTRY IN CHINA
Identity and Perception

Peter Mangold
SUCCESS AND FAILURE IN BRITISH FOREIGN POLICY
Evaluating the Record, 1900–2000

Mohamad Tavakoli-Targhi
REFASHIONING IRAN
Orientalism, Occidentalism and Historiography

Louise Haagh
CITIZENSHIP, LABOUR MARKETS AND DEMOCRATIZATION
Chile and the Modern Sequence

Renato Colistete
LABOUR RELATIONS AND INDUSTRIAL PERFORMANCE IN BRAZIL
Greater São Paulo, 1945–60

Peter Lienhardt (*edited by Ahmed Al-Shahi*)
SHAIKHDOMS OF EASTERN ARABIA

St Antony's Series
Series Standing Order ISBN 0–333–71109–2
(*outside North America only*)

You can receive future titles in this series as they are published by placing a standing order. Please contact your bookseller or, in case of difficulty, write to us at the address below with your name and address, the title of the series and the ISBN quoted above.

Customer Services Department, Macmillan Distribution Ltd, Houndmills, Basingstoke, Hampshire RG21 6XS, England

The Long Search for a Third Way

The British Labour Party and the Italian Left since 1945

Ilaria Favretto
Senior Research Fellow
European Research Centre
Kingston University

macmillan

in association with
St Antony's College, Oxford

First published 2003 by
PALGRAVE MACMILLAN
Houndmills, Basingstoke, Hampshire RG21 6XS and
175 Fifth Avenue, New York, N.Y. 10010
Companies and representatives throughout the world

PALGRAVE MACMILLAN is the global academic imprint of the Palgrave Macmillan division of St. Martin's Press, LLC and of Palgrave Macmillan Ltd. Macmillan® is a registered trademark in the United States, United Kingdom and other countries. Palgrave is a registered trademark in the European Union and other countries.

ISBN 0–333–97714–9

This book is printed on paper suitable for recycling and made from fully managed and sustained forest sources,

A catalogue record for this book is available from the British Library.

Library of Congress Cataloging-in-Publication Data
Favretto, Ilaria, 1971–
    The long search for a third way: the British Labour Party and Italian Left since 1945/Ilaria Favretto.
        p. cm. – (St Antony's series)
    Includes bibliographical references and index.
    ISBN 0–333–97714–9 (cloth)
        1. Socialism – Great Britain – History. 2. Socialism – Italy – History. 3. Labour Party (Great Britain) – History. I. Title. II. Series.
HX244 .F38 2002
324.24107´09´045–dc21   2002075493

10   9   8   7   6   5   4   3   2   1
12   11   10   09   08   07   06   05   04   03

Printed and bound in Great Britain by
Antony Rowe Ltd, Chippenham and Eastbourne

To the 'House' of 83 Victoria Park Road

Contents

Acknowledgements

I am immensely indebted to Donald Sassoon, who encouraged me to start this research work and to whom I would like to express all my gratitude for the friendship and invaluable advice he has offered me since then.

I would also like to express my grateful thanks to Mike Newman and Toby Abse for their valuable and very constructive comments on some sections of the manuscript.

I want to thank all the members and friends of the various institutions in which this book was written: the Department of History of the Queen Mary Westfield College in London and the European Studies Centre of St Antony's College in Oxford. I am very grateful to Anthony Nicholls, Richard Clogg, Antonio Martins, Avi Shlaim for the encouragement and support they offered me throughout my stay in what proved to be a unique intellectual milieu and veritable 'Heaven' for thinking and exchanging ideas. I am also especially indebted to Anne Deighton and my late dear friend Mikael Af Malmborg who in May 1999 enthusiastically helped me to organise the conference 'Is There a European Third Way?' from which I drew very useful insights for this project.

I also want to thank the University of Milan and the precious encouragement and advice of Giulio Sapelli whom I respect immensely, not only from an academic but also from a human point of view. Lastly, I would like to thank the members of the European Research Centre of Kingston University in London and particularly my colleague and friend, Vassilis Fouskas. I will always be grateful to him for his long-term vision, the energy and resources he put into the Association of Southern Europe and the Balkans (ASSEB) that we founded together with other friends in 1994. The latter eventually turned into the *Journal of Southern Europe and the Balkans* that we decided to establish a few years later. Both experiences have provided me with the invaluable opportunity for meeting scholars working on similar research topics to mine and whose expressions of interest, suggestions and disagreements greatly benefited me throughout the past years.

I want to thank Geoff Andrews for carefully reading some sections of this work and for the interesting and useful comments he gave me; I also want to thank Amy Rosenthal, David Felsen and the Palgrave Macmillan editorial team for the patient editing work they did on the manuscript.

I would also like to thank the Italian National Archive, the Fondazione Pietro Nenni and the Fondazione Istituto Gramsci in Rome; the Fondazione di Studi Storici Filippo Turati in Florence; the Fondazione Giangiacomo Feltrinelli in Milan; and the Labour History Archive and Study Centre in Manchester for the kind and helpful assistance they provided me with when I visited their institutions. I am also grateful to the Italian Ministry of Foreign Affairs, the British Council and the British Academy whose financial support made this research possible.

Lastly, the friends with whom I shared the 'House' of 83 Victoria Park Road in London during the five years of this research work deserve a special mention: to begin with, Giovanni, with whom my London 'venture' began; and then in 'order of appearance' Michaela, Gabriele, Marcella, Raffaele, Susanna, Rocio, Jordi and Claudia. Not only did I have a wonderful and happy time with them, but they also created around me an extremely stimulating and supportive atmosphere which I will never forget.

Last, but not least, special thanks goes to my parents. Together with my beloved sisters Marina and Marcella, they offered me invaluable encouragement and support for which I will always feel grateful.

ILARIA FAVRETTO

Note that quoted passages from the Italian sources are the author's translation from the Italian original.

List of Abbreviations

AES	Alternative Economic Strategy
AN	Alleanza Nazionale
CBI	Confederation of British Industries
CDS	Campaign for Democratic Socialism
CGIL	Confederazione Generale Italiana del Lavoro (the communist–socialist Italian trade union)
CIPE	Comitato Intergovernativo per la Programmazione Economica (Intergovernmental Committee for Economic Planning)
CISL	Confederazione Italiana dei Sindacati dei Lavoratori (the Italian Catholic trade union)
CND	Campaign for Nuclear Disarmament
CNR	Centro Nazionale di Ricerca
CPSU	Communist Party of the Soviet Union
DC	Democrazia Cristiana (Christian Democratic Party)
DEA	Department of Economic Affairs
DS	Democratici di Sinistra (Democrats of the Left)
ENI	Ente Nazionale Idrocarburi (the Italian state hydrocarbon company)
FIOM	Federazione Italiana Operai Metallurgici (the CGIL's organisation for metal-workers)
GL	Giustizia e Libertà
IPPR	Institute of Public Policy Research
IRC	Industrial Reorganisation Corporation
IRI	Istituto per la Ricostruzione Industriale (Institute for Industrial Reconstruction)
ISPE	Istituto per la Programmazione Economica (Institute for Economic Planning)
MUIS	Movimento Unitario Socialisti Indipendenti (Independent socialists unity movement)
MUP	Movimento di Unità Proletaria (Moviment of Proletarian Unity)
NATO	North Atlantic Treaty Organisation
NEDC	National Economic Development Council
NFRB	New Fabian Research Bureau
NUGMW	National Union of General and Municipal Workers

NUM	National Union of Mineworkers
OECD	Organisation for Economic Cooperation and Development
PASOK	Panellinio Sosialistiko Kinima (Pan-Hellenic Socialist Movement)
PCF	Parti Communiste Français (French Communist Party)
PCI	Partito Comunista Italiano (Italian Communist Party)
PDS	Partito Democratico della Sinistra (Democratic Party of the Left)
PLI	Partito Liberale Italiano (Italian Liberal Party)
PRI	Partito Repubblicano Italiano (Italian Republican Party)
PSDI	Partito Social-Democratico Italiano (Italian Social-democratic Party)
PSI	Partito Socialista Italiano (Italian Socialist Party)
PSIUP (1943)	Partito Socialista Italiano di Unità Proletaria (Italian Socialist Party of Proletarian Unity)
PSIUP (1964)	Partito Socialista Italiano di Unità Proletaria (Italian Socialist Party of Proletarian Unity)
PSOE	Partido Socialista Obrero Español (Spain)
PSRI	Partito Socialista Riformista Italiano (Italian Socialist Reformist Party)
PSU (1922)	Partito Socialista Unitario (Socialist Unity Party)
PSU (1966)	Partito Socialista Unificato (Unified Socialist Party)
RAI	Radiotelevisione Italiana (the Italian state broadcasting system)
SI	Socialisti Italiani
SDP	Social Democratic Party (Britain)
SFIO	Section Française de l'Internationale Ouvrière (French socialists)
SPD	Sozialdemokratische Partei Deutschlands (German Social Democratic Party)
SPÖ	Sozialistische Partei Österreichs (Austrian Socialist Party)
TGWU	Transport and General Workers Union
UIL	Unione Italiana del Lavoro (the social-democrat/ republic Italian trade union)
UP	Unione Popolare (Popular Union)
USI	Unione Socialista Indipendente (Independent Socialist Union)
USL	Unità Sanitarie Locali (National Health System)

Introduction

The 'Third Way' has been for some time now a buzz word of European left-wing politics. Although enthusiasm for the idea varies considerably, there are now few documents, speeches or manifestos produced by the parties of the Socialist International that do not refer to it.

Talk of a 'third way' is certainly not new to the European Left. Since the Russian Revolution, a never-ending search for third ways lying somewhere between communism and capitalism has occupied socialist thinking. This resulted in the formulation of gradualist and parliamentary forms of socialism, such as the most famous model, that of social-democratic Scandinavia, or notions such as Austro-Marxism during the inter-war period that postulated 'slow revolution', the idea that a peaceful revolution could be carried out through 'structural reforms'. The latter, incidentally, powerfully influenced the number of 'Italian roads to socialism' that both the Italian socialists and communists elaborated throughout their history.

It goes without saying that the content of today's third way differs quite substantially from the number of third ways that the European and, in particular, the Italian, Left formulated over the last hundred years. While in the past the search for a third way was always intended to be between communism and capitalism, today's third way is inside the capitalist model and is now conceived as something between neo-liberalism and old social democracy. This shift towards the capitalist model sets the neo-revisionism of the 1990s apart from any previous brand of socialist revisionism. While in the past the parties of the Left dedicated themselves to directing their respective economies, they also maintained the goal of an alternative system. Today the Left has renounced any such goal, and has fully embraced the principles of the market economy. Capitalism is no longer considered a transitory phase, destined to disappear sooner or later and leave the way free for a socialist society. Instead, it has become a system of production destined to last in the foreseeable future: a system that can be tempered, but not changed.

One should not, however, ignore the degree of continuity that exists between today's and yesterday's revisionism. Particularly when emerging from long periods of crisis and electoral decline, political parties tend to overemphasise the novelty of their renovated policies and identity. Electorates need to receive a clear message that something completely new is now out in the political market. This is what the British Labour Party has been doing over the last few years, symbolically adding the adjective 'new' to its party's name while never formally changing it. The deeper the crisis, the fiercer is the iconoclasm shown by parties towards their past history; a sense of 'new beginning' has to be created. However, in spite of the efforts devoted by politicians to make the electorate forget the past, the task of historians is the one of keeping it alive. It is only by knowing where we come from that we can reach a greater and fuller understanding of where we are.

Socialist parties, as all other political parties, have always confronted the need to adapt their policies and theories to altered socio-economic circumstances. The implementation of universal suffrage in the late nineteenth century challenged their belief in revolution as the unique way to socialism. Long waves of capitalist expansion, such as the one that occurred at the turn of the century, called for some reconsideration of the idea of the inevitable collapse of the system; Bernstein attempted this in 1899 in *Evolutionary Socialism*.[1] The response of capitalism to the Great Slump of the late 1920s and the subsequent transformed role of the state, laid the foundations for further reinterpretations of Marxism in the 1930s, such as Austro-Marxism and neo-socialism. Last but not least, post-war boom economies posed a serious blow to deep-rooted Marxist dogmas such as the 'pauperisation' theory, or the creed that professed the imminent and inevitable collapse of capitalism. Capitalism, by contrast, proved quite resistant and, most significantly, far more 'generous' in redistributing its 'fruits' than previously expected.

Neo-revisionist politics, while no doubt signalling an important and far-reaching break in the socialist tradition and challenging long-cherished and consolidated 'totems', is in fact very much a continuation of many attempts made in the past by socialist and social-democratic European parties to adjust their policies and agendas. The profound transformation embarked upon by socialist parties over the last two decades is not, in other words, a 'last minute' conversion but should be regarded instead as a further step towards the reassessment of issues which left-wing parties had long been confronted with and addressed. This is just another step within a continuous long journey that did not start yesterday; nor, despite all the talk of 'end of history' over the last fifteen years, has it come to its 'last stop'.

By focusing on the Italian and the British left, this book will compare and contrast the earlier wave of revisionism that occurred in the 1950s and 1960s, whose far-reaching repercussions for socialist parties equalled in importance that of today's neo-revisionism. Post-war revisionism represented a veritable ideological overhaul: the nationalisation of the means of production, which had been central to European socialists' policies since the inter-war years, came to lose relevance to socialist objectives. The existence of forms of private ownership was no longer seen as an obstacle to the establishment of socialism. Furthermore, it had a broad impact that the precursors of the 1950s' revisionists had been denied. It was only with the 'golden years' and the prosperity Western countries experienced in the decade following the end of the war that the right conditions existed for revisionism to make a real breakthrough in socialist thinking.[2]

The depth and scale of change which characterises both waves of revisionism in the 1950s–1960s and the 1980s–1990s, reflect the depth of crisis that European socialism plunged into in both historical periods. As was the case in the 1950s when revisionism was elaborated within a context of conservative hegemony and a wake of a successive electoral setbacks, it was during a long period of opposition (the British Labour Party and the German SPD in the 1980s and 1990s experienced fifteen and eighteen years of opposition respectively) that European socialists were forced to thoroughly rethink their position and condition. This process led to a new series of 'Bad Godesberg': the ditching of the notorious Clause Four from the British Labour constitution in 1995, the SPD's replacement of the 1959 Bad Godesberg declaration with the Berlin Programme in 1989;[3] the Italian Communist Party's decision in 1991 to change its name and symbol which came as the obvious conclusion to a thorough process of reappraisal which the party embarked upon in 1989.

As had been the case in the post-war years, repeated electoral defeats throughout the 1980s gave strength to proponents of 'modernisation'. Change was also facilitated by the long political 'exile' experienced in the 1980s. The history of socialism shows that the most fertile periods for elaboration of new ideas correspond to periods in opposition; it is only when out of office that parties can afford inner debate and dissent and, most of all, have time to produce ideas and new policy documents. Once back in power, any long-term perspective becomes subordinate to short-term and immediate solutions.

One further similarity between the two phases of revisionism is the climate of major socio-economic changes they both stemmed from. The years from 1950 to 1973 were years of unprecedented high rates of growth and productivity and dramatic qualitative advances for the whole Western world. For those who still had a vivid memory of the Great Slump, there was a widespread feeling that a new era was opening up which required political parties to rethink their past assumptions and creeds. The same applied to the 1980s and 1990s: mounting globalisation and increasing economic interdependence, the contended end of the national state, the collapse of 'really-existing socialism' and the end of the Cold War, all contributed to a sense that 'nothing will be the same again' which has, in fact, acted as a further impetus to change.

Similarities between the two revisionisms are not confined to the context within which they were elaborated. In considering the neo-revisionist debate, it is clear some of its most distinctive elements were already present in the 1950s and 1960s: the downgrading of nationalisation and a far more pragmatic and flexible approach to the question of public ownership, the redefinition of equality as equality of opportunities, the transformation into catch-all parties and a greater electoral orientation, were all issues at the centre of a reappraisal by European socialist parties in the wake of the booming post-war years.

Before going any further, however, I should make some qualifications as to what will, and will not, be included in my account. It is always much better to disappoint readers in the preliminary pages instead of dragging them through the entire book, desperately searching for something they will not find.

The focus of this work will be almost exclusively on domestic policies. This is not to deny that, in the years considered, foreign policy issues, no less than domestic ones, were objects of intense controversy in both parties' debates. Suffice it to mention the contentious issue of unilateral disarmament for the Labour Party and the no less controversial conversion to Atlanticism and Europeanism of the PSI in the 1950s and of the PCI a few years later. These issues were as much a source of dissent and inner-party tensions as were questions about the nationalisation of the means of production. Nevertheless, two considerations should be made: first, as far as the 1950s and 1960s are concerned, the debate on foreign policy was, in some respects, a matter apart from the revision of domestic policies which European socialist parties carried out. The 'road to socialism' they elaborated was, in other words, a *national* one which paid little regard to the global interdependence that was developing. Labour's opposition to European integration up to its return to power in 1964 clearly shows the large degree of confidence then still attached to national solutions to the problems Britain's economy suffered from. Second, if some room for manoeuvre existed as far as the elaboration of domestic policy was concerned, far less room for manoeuvre existed for a 'socialist' management of foreign policy. Labour foreign policy that emerged in 1964 had hardly altered since 1951. More significantly, it was fully in line with the Conservative Party's foreign policy: the special relationship with the USA remained a sacred cow, unilateral disarmament was discarded, the commitment to overseas territories was unaltered, and although distinct in tone and emphasis if compared with the Conservatives, a hostile attitude towards European integration was reasserted.

PSI foreign policy meanwhile underwent a profound reassessment: anti-Atlanticism was dropped, and Europe was enthusiastically endorsed. Nevertheless, far from being distinctively 'socialist', these moves represented the PSI's realignment with its future coalition partners: acceptance of NATO and the positive stance towards European integration were the preconditions for Italian socialists to be allowed to enter the centre–left government. The same pattern was to be followed by the communists ten years later.

As far as domestic policies were concerned European socialist parties established true theoretical hegemony by the early 1960s. However, the opposite was the case when it came to foreign affairs: the 'consensus' in this area revolved around Atlanticism – *alias* an unconditional support for American foreign policy, and, in some respects, Europeanism. Moving to the present, in spite of the strong emphasis on 'humanitarianism' which the Left has been making in relation to its foreign policy, once back in office parties like New Labour and the Italian DS have shown quite clearly that this is a sphere where, more than any other, a number of powerful constraints make promises for an 'ethical' approach hard to fulfil. Foreign policy has always been an area where European socialist parties' 'distinctiveness' and specificity could barely emerge. The pursuit of the 'national interest' since World War I, when most socialist parties supported the war, has always been the prerequisite for them to earn the necessary legitimacy within their countries as national parties. Admittedly, once in power they have always adhered to their opponents' foreign policy, sometimes with even greater commitment. Consider, for instance, the uncritical attitude towards the Vietnam War adopted by most European socialist parties. Every breach with long-established foreign policies has always come exclusively from the Right, which is the only one in a position to do so: the anti-USA stance of de Gaulle's foreign policy, in other words, would never have been accepted from a socialist party, whose 'national' credentials always had to be continually proved and reaffirmed.

The focus of this book will be exclusively on revisionisms occurring within the socialist and the social-democratic tradition. As far as Italy is concerned, the analysis for the years up to the 1980s will therefore be mainly confined to the Italian socialists, specifically to the PSI's autonomist (*autonomista*) course; this is the strategy which the autonomist faction forced through the PSI after 1956 that entailed a distancing from the PCI and brought Nenni's party into line with other Western European socialist parties. It was this move that made possible the formation of the first centre–left government in December 1963. The Italian Communist Party will be considered systematically only for the period of the 1980s and 1990s; that is, when it formally broke with its communist past, moved closer to European socialism and transformed itself into a fully-fledged social-democratic party. It is for this reason that Eurocommunism, one of the most famous 'third ways' elaborated in the post-war years, will be mentioned only briefly.

One final clarification I would like to make relates to the decision to focus my analysis on ideas, debates, and the relatively marginal attention paid to so-called 'high politics'. The literature regarding the histories of individual European socialist parties' suffers greatly from an imbalance between the weight accorded to politics in the narrow sense of the term and the ideological and theoretical process that preceded it. Nenni's 'autonomist' course after 1956 and the transformation which the PSI underwent in the years leading up to the formation of the first centre–left government have been usually regarded in Italian history as a series of tactical expedients which the Italian socialists developed when confronted with the possibility of entering a coalition government with the Christian Democrats. Post-war British Labour revisionism has received greater attention; however, not only is it often dismissed as the ideological cover of the inner party power struggle between the Right and the Left which occurred after the end of the Attlee government, but few works have dealt with it systematically. Similarly, if one looks at assessments of more recent neo-revisionism, commentators' attention has often focused more on the political context and constraints which debates within individual socialist parties have stemmed from than with analysing the debate itself, its distinctive features and above all its actual influence on the policy-making process. What is probably needed is a 'third way' between a rational choice theory approach which dismisses any relevance of ideas and beliefs to explain political outcomes and events, and a blind acceptance of parties' rhetoric, as if values were the only driving force inspiring their action. This is the methodological assumption which underlies the whole work which, while not ignoring the importance of electoral and political 'exogenous' factors, also aims at placing developments in a wider intellectual and theoretical milieu.

Let me now sum up briefly the structure of the book. In the first part attention will be paid to Labour's revisionist course in the years that followed the end of the Attlee government up to the first Wilson government (1964): that is, from the initial dominance of Keynesian socialists in the mould of Crosland and the Gaitskellites' grip on the party until the early 1960s, to the increasing disillusionment with Keynesian measures in the face of a growing awareness of the decline of the British economy, the revival of more 'socialist' measures and the capture of the party by the centre–left technocratic group led by Harold Wilson. As far as Italy is concerned, attention will focus on the PSI's 'social-democratisation' course which the party embarked upon in 1956 and the intellectual foundations of the first centre–left government in Italy.

In both the Labour Party and the Italian socialists it is possible to identify some groups from those years that were quite similar, although not necessarily organised factions (all the more so, given that until 1957 the PSI's internal rules prevented the formation of any organised faction within the party). There were also distinctive elements related to cultural and ideological background which lead me, in some cases, to bypass parties' boundaries in the narrow sense of the term. This is why the British New Left will be included in my account.

I use the term 'Old Left' for the Bevanites and the group within the PSI around Vecchietti and Valori that, from 1956 onwards, were dubbed the *carristi* ('tankists') due to the support they gave to the Soviet invasion of Hungary. The differences between the Bevanites and the *carristi*, as far as their ideological background is concerned, are quite substantial. The former were marked by a remarkable ideological heterogeneity and members included socialist fundamentalists inspired by Keir Hardie, Christians and pacifists following in George Lansbury's footsteps, former radical Liberals, Marxists who admired Lenin and Stalin, or Trotsky.[4] The latter were made up of Trotskyites and Stalinists who clung tightly to orthodox Third International Marxism. However, they will be treated together because of their similar resistance to any form of revisionism, either neo-Marxist or technocratic, and the common nature of unreconstructed wings in their individual parties. They both failed to grasp the extent of the profound modifications capitalism underwent in the post-war years and, until the very last, rejected any reconsideration of socialist ideology and their parties' strategies.

If we now consider the revisionists, the word itself is quite deceptive. Revisionists are all those who attempt a revision of political parties' doctrine and policies. However, the sort of revision put forward can vary to a considerable extent. Crosland, Wilson, the British New Left, Nenni and the autonomists, were all 'revisionists' while, at the same time, embodying conflicting and, in some respects, antithetical visions of their parties' future direction. In order to avoid any confusion and misunderstanding, I will stick to the common practice of labelling the centre–right revisionists as the 'revisionists', and use different labels for the other groups. That said, it has to be added that British revisionists (in the mould of Crosland) do not have any equivalent in the PSI.

Their identification with Keynesian measures and the emphasis put on democracy as the indispensable element of socialism combined with an almost exclusive concern with redistribution, would make the PSDI (*Partito Socialista Democratico Italiano* – Italian Social Democratic Party), which split from Nenni's socialists in 1947, their closer Italian *alter ego*. Nevertheless, the leading role played by British revisionists in European revisionism makes any comparison with Giuseppe Saragat's Italian social democrats quite arbitrary. The PSDI always was a party without any 'intelligentsia' behind the scenes, and its voice was always marginal to any theoretical debate. It made no contribution to theory and very little thinking was devoted to theoretical issues. Shortly after its birth, concern with cabinet seats and ministerial positions became the most salient feature of the party.

If no Italian 'Crosland' could be found in the socialist ranks, things were different when considering the centre–left technocratic socialists, namely the centre–left group which split from the Bevanites in the mid-1950s and which counted among its most prominent members Richard Crossman, Thomas Balogh and, of course, Harold Wilson. The emphasis put on planning, and the concern displayed by this group with more markedly 'structural' forms of intervention in the economy than those conceived by the centre–right are only a few of the many elements which allow for an immediate comparison between them and the autonomist faction led by Nenni in the PSI. One of the key arguments of this book, namely the convergence of the Labour Party and the Italian Socialist Party on a common political agenda in the 1960s after many years of substantial differences, rests on this resemblance.

One further parallel should be mentioned, namely the one between the British New Left and the PSI's left-wing group, which rallied around

Renato Panzieri. Indeed, the fact cannot be ignored that while the Panzieri group was inside the PSI, the British New Left was a group of intellectuals formally detached from any political party. Nevertheless, they represented, in both Italy and Great Britain respectively, neo-Marxism, the process of reassessment of some Marxist tenets that was undertaken throughout Europe from the early 1950s. Even the autonomist group's analyses relied heavily on neo-Marxist arguments, particularly in the first years of their revisionist process. However, from the late 1950s, once the autonomists came to formulate their policies and programmes for future co-operation in government more specifically, some of the most salient features of neo-Marxism disappeared from their discourses. For example, the initially strong commitment to industrial democracy and new forms of workers' control was dropped. After a clear distinction between Nenni's group and Panzieri's revisionism emerged in 1957, the real and genuine champions of neo-Marxism remained the group gathered around Panzieri and the journal *Quaderni Rossi*.

In the second part of this book the focus will shift to the new wave of revisionism – that is neo-revisionism in the 1980s and 1990s. The new course taken by the British Labour Party since the mid-1980s will be addressed and dealt with in comparison with the Italian Communist Party's contemporaneous overall reassessment of its policies and identity, which resulted in its 'social-democratisation' and transformation into the Democratic Party of the Left (*Partito Democratico della Sinistra*, PDS) in 1991 – re-named Democrats of the Left (*Democratici di Sinistra*, DS), in 1998. After the collapse of the Berlin Wall, and the resulting process of homogenisation and convergence which has characterised European socialism over the last ten years (both between East and West and North and South), parties like New Labour and the Italian DS, two parties whose histories could not be more different, now find themselves surprisingly close. Following the demise of the PSI at the 1994 elections, the PDS/DS became the main social-democratic force in the Italian political landscape, with the paradox that it was down to the heirs of Gramsci to accomplish the realignment of the Italian Left along neo-revisionist politics, which the Italian socialists had begun in the earlier years but left half-finished.

Craxi's takeover of the PSI's leadership in 1976 paved the way for a wide-ranging reappraisal of the party's policies. However, by the end of the 1970s day-to-day pragmatism rather than fixed rules and principles were to become the driving force of the party. Some aspects of Craxi's political agenda were indeed neo-revisionist: fiscal orthodoxy; a more confrontational attitude towards the unions; the emphasis on privatisation and deregulation; a more libertarian élan. However, neo-liberal policies went hand in hand with old style interventionism in the South, which was crucial for the party's electoral support and consensus. Furthermore, social provision was left unchanged. Not only did public spending grow steadily throughout the decade but welfare expenditure remained redistributive in kind: the mini boom which Craxi's 1983 five party coalition government presided over was a jobless growth with no significant reduction of unemployment rates. As was the case with Felipe Gonzales in Spain, while endorsing neo-liberal monetary policies, Craxi's party failed, beyond some cosmetic rhetoric of modernisation, to devise a distinctive and innovative set of policies in the area of welfare and employment which could have at least earned him the label of true moderniser if not that of a 'new' socialist.[5]

The decision to compare the British and Italian Left might raise some doubts due to the considerable differences in the history and background of British Labour and the Italian socialists and communists. Nevertheless, a number of factors make it more relevant than it might seem at first glance. First, as far as the 1950s–1960s period is concerned, it is undoubtedly the case that the Labour Party represented a real point of reference for Nenni's 'autonomist' course after 1956. The Italian socialist press closely followed Labour revisionism in the years after 1951. Not as much attention was paid to any other European socialist party as to their British counterparts. Many reasons accounted for this: on the one hand, the richness of Labour's theoretical debate in that period, British Labour's undisputed leadership within the Socialist International up to the 1970s (this was due to the important international role played in those years by Great Britain and the prestige gained by Labour as a result of the Attlee government), and the increasingly intense relationship which grew between Labour and the PSI after Nenni's U-turn in 1956; it is worth remembering here that Labour played a crucial intermediary role in the process of reunification between the PSI and PSDI.[6] On the other hand, as Antonio Giolitti put it,[7] very few in the party were then fluent in German, which made any contact with the SPD difficult. The SFIO, in turn, certainly could not provide a source of inspiration: the French socialists failed in these years to produce any new ideas and did not experience anything comparable with the British, the SPD or the PSI's revisionist courses. The decision to distance themselves from the PCI and the efforts made by Nenni's party to reconstruct their 'socialist' identity thus made Labour an obvious interlocutor. Furthermore, the Labour Party not only represented a real source of inspiration but also a source of legitimisation. Italian political parties have always tended to search for external legitimisation: the PCI owed their success soon after the war largely to their link with the USSR; Christian Democrats always stressed their 'special relationship' with the USA, and when the PSI split from the PCI it was of the greatest urgency to find a new international reference point which assured it international and internal legitimisation. This was sought in the Labour Party. No other parties but the moderate and gradualist Labour Party could furnish the Italian socialists with the legitimacy and the credibility they needed to earn their passport to the centre–left government.

Considering the 1980s and 1990s, it is clear the German SPD exerted a great deal of influence in the early phase of the PCI's 'post-communist' course. Peter Glotz's *Manifesto per Una Nuova Sinistra Europea* (Manifesto for a New European Left) published in Italian in 1986[8] and the 'European Left ideology' he devised were a key point of reference at the 1986 XVII Party Congress when Eurocommunism was formally dropped. However, particularly since the mid-1990s, and especially after its electoral success of 1997, Blair's party has become the model which most European socialist parties, the Italian DS included, look to. New Labour, more than any other party, has been undergoing over the last few years a great deal of change and has demonstrated, at least relative to its European counterparts, the capacity to generate new ideas. As was the case in the 1950s and 1960s, when British Labour held an undisputed leadership within the Socialist International, riding on the wave launched by the Attlee government, today New Labour is the symbol of a new, modernised, electorally successful left-wing party, which political parties embarking on a similar process of rethinking and modernisation of their policies are more than keen on being associated with. Furthermore, as was the case in the 1950s, the growing interest and reference to New Labour is also supposed to help silence once and for all the anti-communism which is still the favourite trump card of the Italian Left's electoral adversaries.

Comparing the Italian and the British Left does indeed present some difficulties. The profound differences, political, economic and social, which exist between Italy and Great Britain mean that the constraints and obstacles that the two Lefts confront are of a fairly distinct nature. First, the very different electoral system within which elections are contested means that while British Labour has always been in power on its own, the Italian left-wing vote has, by contrast, always been split between numerous parties, resulting in forms of power-sharing and coalition-building once in office. When Labour returned to power in 1964, it formed a government on its own, and after the March 1966 elections, could count on a comfortable majority of 97; by contrast, the PSI was only a junior partner in a multiparty coalition. When Nenni's party entered the Moro government in December 1963, its electoral weight was 13.8 per cent in contrast to the DC's 38.3 per cent.[9] After the breakaway of its extreme left wing, in January 1964 which became the PSIUP, its bargaining power was further weakened. The electoral decline that took place in the following years finally confined the PSI to an increasingly subordinate position (in the 1972 elections the PSI reached its lowest point since 1892, 9.6 per cent).[10]

The position of the DS today is similarly weak if compared to Blair's single-party government that commands a clear parliamentary majority. When New Labour entered office in 1997 it had a majority of 179 and a Conservative opposition with fewer seats than the party had known since the 1830s. The majority gained at the 2001 elections, although slightly reduced, was still massive. By contrast, the DS today has the lowest electoral share when compared with their European sister parties. As opposed to the 27–34 per cent enjoyed by the Italian Communist Party in the years from the late 1960s to the 1980s, in the 1990s the DS's electoral share ranged from 16.1 per cent in 1992, 20.3 per cent in 1994, 21.1 per cent in 1996, dramatically declining again at the 2001 election to a sorry 16.6 per cent,[11] ten points less than the French PS's vote when it returned to office in 1997. When in 1996 the centre–left coalition won the elections, the situation was not directly comparable with those created by the almost contemporaneous victory of the Left in France, Britain or Germany. While the PDS was the largest single party in the governing coalition, far ahead of the *Partito Popolare*, the Greens and Dini's *Rinnovamento Italiano*, its share of the vote (21.1 per cent) was not sufficient to confer upon it the kind of automatic hegemony possessed by the French Socialists or the German Social Democrats, let alone Blair's Labour Party.

One further factor which should not be forgotten is that, unlike Labour, which has never had any rivals on the left (this was challenged by the rise of the Liberal Democrats in the 1980s and 1990s whose electoral share, however, still remains strongly penalised by the first-past-the-post system), the Italian socialists in the 1950s and the PDS/DS in the 1990s have both had to struggle with competing left parties seeking to capitalise on their move to the centre ground. As Nenni's party had to look over its shoulders from the strongest Western European communist party, the heirs of the PCI still have to find a way of coming to terms with Communist Refoundation – the party which split from the PCI in 1991 at the time of the formation of the PDS. Although Communist Refoundation is a small party (it passed from 6 per cent in 1994, 8.6 per cent in 1996 and back to 5 per cent in the 2001 election),[12] it is an alliance partner that, like it or not, is essential to the electoral success of the centre–left coalition. This fact was demonstrated in the 1994 and 2001 elections when the failure to reach an agreement with Communist Refoundation resulted in the defeat of the whole coalition. It should also be remembered that the first centre–left government led by Prodi fell in 1998 following the decision of Bertinotti, Communist Refoundation's leader, to withdraw his party's support from the government.

The differences between the two contexts in which the Italian and the British Left operate are not restricted to the two countries' political and electoral systems. Significant differences also exist between the Italian and British domestic environments in terms of size of their public sectors, welfare provision, and the legal framework for industrial relations. The Labour Party has always operated in a context which, in many respects, sets it apart from most other European countries. Differences with continental Europe were further exacerbated by eighteen years of conservative dominance in the 1980s and 1990s. It is well known the extent to which the Thatcher years greatly facilitated New Labour's job once they returned to power. Against a background of drastically reduced trade union powers, a heavily curtailed welfare state and the privatisation of much of the public sector, Blair and his ministers' tasks were fairly easy compared with their European counterparts. The challenge facing neo-revisionist parties today is that of adapting both the welfare state and the system of industrial relations, formerly tailored on the Fordist model, to a new post-Fordist reality. In other words, to destroy in order to then reconstruct. Unlike continental socialists, New Labour could move straight to the reconstruction phase. This is well reflected in the fact that criticism which surrounded the first Blair government did not revolve around what socialist parties are normally accused of, such as cuts in public spending, but the hesitation and delay in giving back to the British citizens – even if in a revised or updated 'third' way – a more equal society than the one left by the 'Iron Lady'.

Thus we face two quite distinct contexts in which the two Lefts operated. This cannot be ignored and will be taken into full consideration when comparing them.

For all the efforts made by social scientists to classify and pigeonhole socialist parties into all-encompassing stereotypes, if the history of European socialism over the entire twentieth century is considered, it becomes clear that specific histories and national constraints have always impinged profoundly on the development of socialist movements. The end result of this is a wide range of 'national roads to socialism' where talk of 'deviances' should be replaced with talk of 'variations'. However, recognising differences need not prevent us from seeing analogies. Historians have largely neglected systematic comparisons between the revisionisms adopted by most of the Western European socialist parties in the post-war period, with the great majority of books on the European Left being nothing other than collections of essays on national case studies. However, truly comparative works in kind can be extremely useful to counter the 'exceptionality' rhetoric which often characterises national judgements. These can stem from either self-conceited pride (here one thinks for example of British Labour and its sense of distinctiveness as something apart from ideological and 'dogmatic' continental counterparts) or self-defeatist tendencies such as those by the Italian Left. Having long been afflicted by a 'black sheep' syndrome, the latter has often ignored the fact that 'diseases' like radicalism and fragmentation, far from being unique to it, also applied to other European counterparts like the French – which where second to none in keeping revolutionary rhetoric alive until recently – or the unlikely example of the Dutch Left which hold the record for the highest fragmentation of the European Left with regards to its number of parties.[13] The existing literature on the PSI's history is, in this regard, a case in point. With its obsessive insistence on the so-called 'anomaly' which Italian socialism is said to display before 1976 (when after the advent of Craxi to the leadership of the party, its transformation into a non-Marxist social-democratic party is widely accepted), it fails to see the numerous comparisons that could be drawn between the Italian socialists and their European sister-parties.

Before concluding, I need to mention some methodological issues. The sources used to study the two Lefts are similar: party or sympathetic press, party documents, electoral material, oral interviews, and so forth. As far as the 1950s and 1960s are concerned, archival sources have also been looked at, although the reader will note discrepancies in relation to their use. This is due to the disarray of the PSI's Archive at the time this research was carried out: in contrast with the impressive organisation of Labour's archive, most of the Italian Socialist Party's papers had not yet been catalogued and were not accessible to scholars. In this regard, I am afraid stereotypes about Italian inefficiency are neither misplaced nor exaggerated.

Part I

The 'Golden Years' of Capitalism and the Foundations of Revisionism

1
Rethinking Socialism

'Croslandism' and the rise of Keynesian socialism

The years from 1950 to 1973 were years of unparalleled growth for the whole Western world. The labels which scholars have attached to them are indeed telling: 'the golden years',[1] 'the glorious decades',[2] 'the golden age'.[3] As Eric Hobsbawm put it, what is striking about them is not their occurrence but their extraordinary scale and depth.[4] This sound trend cycle was, in fact, marked by unprecedentedly high rates of growth and productivity; the output per man hour turned out to be twice as much as the average in the previous period from 1913 to 1950.[5] World output of manufactured goods quadrupled between the early 1950s and the early 1970s.[6]

Especially for those who had lived through the 1930s, the rapid and seemingly irreversible resurgence of capitalism appeared almost incredible.[7] Capitalism now displayed an unexpected renewed vitality and, most significantly, the capacity to solve the bogy of the earlier generation, namely unemployment. By the early 1960s, although in a few countries like Italy the percentage remained slightly higher, the average of the labour force out of work in Western Europe was only 1.5 per cent.

The economic achievements of those years were, indeed, accompanied by dramatic qualitative advances.[8] The establishment of full employment meant the expansion of the trade unions' bargaining power; far beyond simply obtaining the full legitimisation which in many countries like Italy had been long denied, workers' organisations acquired an increasingly large role in the policy-making of their individual countries. Wages and salaries increased substantially. Private consumption grew significantly and earned the mid-1960s the label of 'age of consumption'.

It is, however, indubitable that the 'really striking aspect' of this reformed capitalism was its welfarism.[9] The share of government spending devoted to collective social services (health, education, pensions, and so on) greatly increased after the war and rose from 15 per cent in 1952 to 24 per cent in 1973.[10] This significant expansion was by no means solely the construct of left-wing governments. In fact, the reverse was the case. Spending on welfare rose under Macmillan, Adenauer, de Gaulle and, in Italy, under the Christian Democrat-dominated coalitions.[11]

A broad political consensus developed in all Western countries from the late 1950s. Whatever the party in office, the mixed economy, the principle of welfare state provision and full employment were no longer questioned. Social-democratic 'incursions' were now increasingly accepted by capital.[12] The memory of the inter-war Great Slump was still vivid. Keynesian policies had long emerged as a better recipe than *laissez-faire* doctrine not only to keep capitalism alive but also to make it function more effectively. As a result of the thriving stage capitalism had reached in those years, it now became, to a degree unknown in the past, of what Adam Przeworski refers to as the 'reproduction of consent'.[13] The improved living conditions of vast sections of the population were to constitute the premises for an enduring wide social settlement which would come to an end only in the 1980s. What Hobsbawm defines as the 'marriage between economic liberalism and social-democracy' in fact became the crucial feature of all Western European advanced capitalist countries' political systems.[14]

The alliance between capital and working-class parties was by no means new. Western European governments had appreciated since early in the century the need to come to terms with working-class organisations. Nevertheless, this time the premises were fairly different. Capital did not now necessitate, in order to survive, simply 'social peace', but, paradoxically, a socialist tinged management based on Keynesianism, a high degree of planning, incomes policy, public investment in education and research. The rapid technological change, the pace of which accelerated in these years as never before, the large investments required by monopoly industries and the long-term emergence of their effects, the eternal inherent incapability of capitalism to match consumption and production which the modern capitalist large-scale economies further accentuated, called for state intervention well beyond the welfare area. Planning and state economic management gradually emerged as a formula which all Western countries sooner or later accepted and adopted even if in different forms and degrees.[15]

Social-democratic solutions ended up dominating parties' programmes whatever their political affiliations. This came after an overall reappraisal of their doctrine and means, which socialist and social-democratic parties all went through during the 1950s.

Revisionism was not something new to socialists. Since their birth in the late nineteenth century, they had been confronted with the need to constantly adapt their policies and theory to altered socio-economic circumstances. The implementation of universal suffrage challenged the belief in revolution as the unique way to socialism. Long waves of capitalism's expansion, such as the one which occurred at the turn of the century, called for a reconsideration, like the one Bernstein attempted, of the idea of the inevitable collapse of the system. The response of capitalism to the Great Slump of the late 1920s and the transformed role of the state which followed laid the foundations for further reinterpretations of Marxism in the 1930s such as Austro-Marxism and neo-socialism.

However, the new wave of revisionism which spread in the 1950s had no equals in any preceding attempt. To start with, it represented a veritable and unprecedented ideological overhaul. The nationalisation of the means of production, which had been central to European socialists' policies since the inter-war years, came now to lose relevance to socialist objectives. The existence of forms of private ownership was no longer seen as an obstacle to the establishment of socialism. Secondly, it had a broad impact which the precursors of the 1950s revisionists were denied. The theses elaborated by Anthony Crosland in his *The Future of Socialism* (1956)[16] are very similar to those put forward by Bernstein. The 'collapse theory' and the 'pauperisation theory' were denounced by the German thinker without any success more than fifty years before Crosland made them the core of his attack against the Old Left. All the same, it is indisputable that only the 'golden years' and the prosperity which Western countries experienced in the decade following the end of the war provided the conditions for revisionism to make a real breakthrough in socialist thinking.[17]

Many Western European socialist parties had adopted Keynesianism in the late 1930s. Keynes equipped them with short-term policies which allowed them to make some further steps towards socialism once in office, in other words to reconcile their long-term commitment to a socialist society with their participation in government. The revolutionary novelty of this new phase of revisionism was the claim that Keynesianism had to be regarded no longer as a temporary set of policies, but rather as itself conducive to socialism and needing to be adopted as the new ideology which socialist parties should rely on.[18] Keynesianism turned out to be the third way between communism and capitalism that socialist parties had long been in search of. It assured a good and apparently permanent functioning of the system; it produced full employment; of greatest importance, it provided the theoretical basis for greater equality and a fairer redistribution, since it related economic expansion to widespread consumption.[19] The case of British Labour in the 1950s is, in this respect, quite exemplary.

The Great Slump in 1929 had marked the defeat of MacDonald's evolutionism and paved the way for the growing influence of a technocratic *'dirigiste'* kind of socialism. The economy was then in a state of overall disarray. *Labour's Immediate Programme* (1937) placed an almost exclusive emphasis on the takeover of the 'commanding heights' of the economy, with ameliorative measures and redistribution being relegated to secondary importance. The first priority of the party at that stage seemed to be a state-led reconstruction of the economy. Planning and the nationalisation of basic industries and services were to remain the pillars of future Labour policies and documents, a tendency which was further strengthened by the outbreak of war and the extension of state controls which it called for.[20]

However, things had changed substantially by the early 1950s. The socio-economic circumstances Labour was confronted with were now, in fact, considerably altered. Due to the stability and strength displayed by contemporary capitalism, the technocratic socialists' theoretical influence lost more and more ground. Most of the assumptions from which they originated collapsed one after the other: principally, the unreliability of the mixed economy and privately owned companies in terms of economic efficiency, and the incompatibility of a greater social equality with the capitalist market economy. The order of priorities established in the 1930s was thus reversed. Ameliorative measures ended up gaining increasing importance in the party's policies. Increasingly more emphasis was put on fiscal and budgetary management; the belief that full employment and greater social equality were a matter of budgetary manipulation and fiscal management irrespective of the size of the nationalised sector made a real breakthrough in the party's thinking, and Keynesian economists like Hugh Gaitskell and Douglas Jay came to play an increasingly large part, first in the government's policies and later, after the end of the Attlee government, in the party policy-making.[21]

After the turmoil of the 1930s and the dismissal of most of the Fabian assumptions which those years had witnessed, the *New Fabian Essays*, published in 1952,[22] opened a new era in which full confidence was again to be placed in the gradual and, most of all, inevitable, advance of socialism. The two preconditions, from which the late nineteenth century belief in the historical necessity of socialism had emerged, had returned; that is, a sound economy and a ruling class carrying out pro-socialist policies. Full employment and widespread affluence were by 1955 an incontrovertible fact. Living standards had risen considerably and this was reflected in the growth of private consumption which occurred simultaneously: refrigerators, televisions, washing machines were no longer the privilege of a lucky few.[23] Furthermore, to the dismay of those Labour exponents who were strongly convinced that the Conservatives' return to office would entail the disruption of Labour's major achievements, public spending in the social budget had grown, even if only slightly. Over the whole decade the percentage of total government expenditure invested in social services went from 42.9 per cent in 1951 to 43.5 per cent in 1963.[24]

Thus a strongly deterministic approach again appeared in the Labour Party's thinking. Temporarily challenged by the inter-war Great Slump, it was now provided with new powerful arguments. The process of self-transformation of capitalism into socialism was seen to be irreversible.[25] The present system had, according to authors like Crosland, already given way to a new system in between capitalism and socialism. Capitalism had not simply changed its clothes, but had rather modified its inherent essence to the extent that a new 'thing'[26] had replaced it and a further step towards a socialist society had been taken. In a few years the full establishment of a socialist society would be accomplished.

The 1950s socio-economic circumstances were to lead to the hegemony of centre–right revisionist thinking for the entire decade. No major intellectual challenge managed to threaten their theoretical dominance. Revisionist ideas and the reconsideration of common ownership as an ideal in itself made their way gradually into official party statements throughout the 1950s. The Labour document *Industry and Society* (1957), the first real revisionist document Labour produced, signalled, in this regard, a real turning point. The role that public ownership could play in achieving socialists' aims emerged considerably reduced in importance; the success of the mixed economy was fully recognised; of greater significance, for the first time, was a much more flexible approach to the whole question of nationalisation. The new forms that common ownership could take, such as competitive public enterprise or state shareholding, were systematically dealt with. The centre–right revisionists' emphasis on the phenomenon of 'managerialism'[27] was also apparent. An entire section of *Industry and Society* addressed the changes which had occurred in the structure of industry in line with 'Separation of Ownership from Control' (as one of its sections reads) theories and the idea of an increasingly pronounced separation between 'managerial/directorial interest'.[28]

The revisionists' theoretical dominance over Labour Party's policies also explains the scarce weight accorded throughout the 1950s to planning. Keynesian socialism relied on the market mechanism and replaced the idea of direct state control of the economy with fiscal or budgetary intervention.[29] As Crosland argued in his *The Future of Socialism*, the 'pre-war argument (for planning) based as it was on the combination of manifest inefficiency and glaring inequality displayed by the capitalism of the 1930s' had lost much of 'its force in the expansionist full employment economy and the Welfare State of the 1950s'.[30] As a result, economic planning tended to be conceived throughout the decade in a very minimalist way; that is, solely in terms of Keynesian management of broad macro-economics aggregates: 'a skilful and determined fiscal policy',[31] it was argued, would be able to get the right balance between consumption, investment and government expenditure.

The loss of centrality of planning in Labour's discourse is well reflected in the Labour declarations up the late 1950s. Labour election manifestos in 1951 and 1955 made hardly any reference to planning whose meaning, when it is mentioned, does not go beyond taxation policies aimed at helping productive investments.[32] *Industry and Society* (1957) and specifically the publication of *Planning for Progress* (1958),[33] both produced in the climate of the growing debate on stop–go policies and the first signs of awareness of British economic difficulties, undoubtedly reflected a greater attention paid to planning. However, both documents were far from attaching to it the centrality which the Labour Party would do during the Wilson years.[34] Most important, while recognising the need for some degree of control and planning, they both suffered from considerable ambiguity and vagueness on the sort of machinery which planning would require, and were evidently affected by the principled reluctance to make exaggerated concessions to policies which would necessarily entail some limitations on individual liberty. The great emphasis they put on persuasive methods[35] contrasted sharply with the far more resolute commitment displayed by the centre–left technocratic group shortly afterwards in its detailed design of a planning machinery with 'bite', including incentives as well as disincentives.

In sum, centre–right revisionists' optimism over economic expansion led to an almost exclusive concern with a fair and equal redistribution of resources whose incessant growth and expansion was hardly questioned. The focus, it was argued, had to be directed, from then onwards, to a different and more subtle set of measures. Labour's future aspirations were no longer to be primarily economic in character. In spite of the broad social equality obtained through the redistribution of income in the past few years, Britain still displayed the paradox of a persistently class-ridden society. However, remaining class inequalities, it was stated, were more related to psychological differences than material ones. Class consciousness and social discontent seemed to rest on other factors besides income differences, and sociological rather than economic explanations better accounted for them. A future Labour government would need to show greater concern for questions of status, like patterns of consumption, non-wage privileges within industry, forms of elite education and social hierarchy.[36]

The vision of British society which the Bevanite group held was certainly far less optimistic and enthusiastic than the centre–right revisionists. The Bevanites challenged the idea that the changes which occurred under the Attlee government were significant enough to suggest a revision of Labour's traditional objectives and means. The deficiencies of the already established nationalised sector, its lack of any accountability and provision for workers' participation or control were openly conceded. Nevertheless, the common ownership principle still remained valid. Any talk of managerialism or attempt to demonstrate that capital had been humanised[37] were dismissed. The revisionist argument whereby revolutionary changes in terms of power relationships had occurred was thoroughly rejected. Equality was still regarded as inseparable from state ownership and planning. Though it was admitted that a fairer redistribution of income had been achieved, the concentration of capital and economic privilege, it was said, still remained untouched.[38] Equal power arguments apart, other reasons, such as the concentration of power which characterised the modern oligopoly or the risk of inflation, still made a strong case for the enlargement of public control.[39]

The Bevanites' critique of the revisionist argument was not limited to the question of public ownership. Two more issues (which will be fully investigated in the next chapter) were the object of intense debate. First, there was the question of the future nature of the party and the electorally oriented strategy the Right wanted to enforce at the expense of strong ideological and principle commitments. Second, there was the question of the so-called 'artificial wants' – mass consumerism, advertising, 'affluent society' values and private prosperity – which, while being something to accept and welcome if Labour wanted to outlive the transformed society for the revisionists, still remained for the Left not only morally reproachable but a long-term threat to the whole of society. The Tories' policies, by fulfilling consumption demand, had certainly deluded British people into thinking they were an affluent society like America; yet it had also proved irresponsible and did not take into account any serious evaluation of the long-term economic consequences of the growing gap between private and public spending.[40] *The Affluent Society* (1958), by the Harvard economist John Galbraith,[41] certainly provided some support for Crossman and his group's arguments about capitalism's weaknesses and inherent contradictions. Galbraith questioned part of the optimism which had pervaded his previous publications. Affluent societies were said to sacrifice communal welfare, the requirements of future growth and a balanced allocation of resources. The gap already existing between private prosperity and public squalor, he argued, would get larger in the long run and productivity rates were destined to decline further.[42]

However, in the 'You've never had it so good' Britain of the 1950s there was little room for pessimistic scenarios to gain ground. In the climate of general complacency and optimism prompted by an apparently efficient welfare capitalism, the hegemony which centre–right revisionists managed to exert over the party's thinking was to remain unchallenged until the late 1950s. The cake to be shared was believed to be constantly growing. The revisionists' case and their almost exclusive concern with redistribution seemed to rest on solid arguments. As Bogdanor and Skidelsky put it, the re-opening of the debate on the larger questions of Britain's future, both domestic and international, was to belong to the story of the 1960s.[43]

1956: the rediscovery of an 'Italian' road to socialism

Between 1958 and 1963 Italy went through what is usually referred to as an 'economic miracle', which, without any doubt, represented a unique and exceptional phase of Italian economic history. Italy transformed its economy in those years from a rural into an industrialised one, closing the gap which had existed since its birth as a nation, with other European countries like France, Germany or Great Britain. The scale of expansion was dramatic, especially if compared with previous rates of expansion and subsequent performances. The GDP grew by an average of 5.8 per cent per year with peaks of 7.5 per cent between 1958–61. If we consider that in the years from 1897 to 1913, which are commonly regarded as another period of thriving expansion and growth in Italian economic history, the GDP was 2.7 per cent, the relevance of the above percentages becomes clear.[44] Italy joined Germany, Japan, and Austria as one of the countries with the highest productivity rates in the years from 1950 to 1973, almost double those achieved by the UK and the USA.[45]

Even if there were some profound differences between sectors, Italian industry rapidly expanded and became increasingly stronger. The Italian socio-economic structure came to be, after almost 15 years since the end of the war, similar in many respects to that of more economically mature countries, such as Britain. The rural sector declined dramatically. The general domestic product originating from agriculture fell from 52.9 per cent (1945) to 13.9 per cent (1963). Industry's contribution to the national product increased from 20.5 per cent in 1945 to 38.9 per cent in 1963, approaching the other advanced capitalist countries' rates: UK (1963: 45.8 per cent); France (1963: 47.6 per cent); Sweden (1963: 43.0 per cent); Germany (1963: 52.7 per cent).[46] Similarly, the distribution of the labour force by sector went through substantial changes: the percentage of those employed in agriculture fell from 40 per cent in 1951 to 28.2 per cent in 1961. The labour force occupied in industry and services expanded considerably, passing respectively to 39.4 per cent and 29.5 per cent in 1961; 42.2 per cent and 36.6 per cent in 1972.[47] Unemployment rates got closer to the Western European average: after the peaks of 8.8 per cent in 1954 and 9.4 per cent in 1956, from 1961 onwards they stabilised at only one point above the average of the other advanced capitalist states (ranging from 3.5 per cent to 2.5 per cent).[48] Lastly, living standards improved markedly for large sections of the population. The national net income *per head* almost doubled, increasing from $557 in 1952 to $970 in 1963.[49]

The profound transformations which the Italian socio-economic landscape underwent during these years exerted far-reaching effects on the Italian political scenario. Italy's partial conforming to neo-capitalist patterns[50] led to the emergence of new problems similar to those other advanced capitalist states had long been dealing with; the need for greater control and predetermination of certain economic variables began to be felt with increasing urgency. Salaries, for example, increasingly became a matter of public concern. Italian workers' wages were so low in 1951 that half of the 'productive' population employed 93–95 per cent of its income exclusively in 'survival spending' with nothing remaining for other spending.[51] From the late 1950s wages began to rise substantially, especially in the more dynamic and highly profitable sectors which not only could afford it, but for which any strike and loss of working days represented a severe problem. The extended bargaining power and strength of the trade unions, following full employment, now, even in Italy, made a strong case for negotiation.

State intervention was, in fact, increasingly regarded as essential to the inherent needs of the system at that time. In the wake of the economic miracle came a series of major problems which demanded an immediate political response in terms of reforms. The unregulated framework in which Italian economic expansion had been developing in fact resulted in severe imbalances; the increasingly large discrepancy between Northern and Southern regions, the backward state in which a substantial proportion of Italian industry remained, and the explosion of private consumption at the expense of public spending, all posed a real threat for further growth if not immediately addressed. Planning and 'corrective' reforms would soon make significant inroads in the national political agenda. The premises for the alliance between neo-capitalism and social-democracy made their appearance in the late 1950s, as it did in the rest of Western Europe at that time. The need for a reliable, genuinely democratic, left-wing party now became particularly urgent.

The end of the Italian 'anomaly'

The election in 1953 marked an important date for Italian politics; while in fact the left-wing vote emerged considerably increased, the majority gained by the centrist coalition (Christian Democrats, Liberals, Republicans and Social Democrats) was extremely narrow. This opened new possibilities for the PSI, whose candidature in government now seemed to be the only way to reinforce the existing coalition government. The centre–left formula came to be the core of any political discussion and this had far-reaching effects on the PSI. From the mid-1950s, socialists embarked upon what is conventionally referred to as a process of 'social-democratisation'.

Italian socialism's process of differentiation from other European socialist and social-democratic parties, which had been under way since early in the century, reached its apex in the years immediately after the end of the war. By 1948 the PSI had lost its earlier hegemony over the working class and the trade unions to the communists; its electoral support, after the departure of the group led by Saragat in 1947, was rather limited (10 per cent) compared with its European equivalents, which, with the exception of Italy, France and Finland, after the war could count on at least one third of the vote.[52] What is most relevant is that, in line with the strategy of unity with the communists pursued by the party since 1943, Italian socialists fully adhered to Third International theoretical assumptions with the well-known twin pillars: the idea of an imminent and final crisis of capitalism leading to a new fascist wave, and the Leninist notion of the bourgeois state as a mere instrument of monopoly capitalism.[53] The search for an intermediate way between the socialism of redistribution and communism was abandoned. Any 'third way' and gradualist strategy were ruled out and dismissed as foolish.

However, 1956 was to signal a veritable turning point for the PSI; the revisionist phase which Italian socialists embarked on was in fact to bring Nenni's party into line with the rest of Western European socialist parties. As Antonio Giolitti argued in an interview in September 1957 in *Mondo Operaio*, Italy was now faced with problems common to the other advanced capitalist countries such as the full utilisation of the potential of technical progress, monopoly concentration or the discrepancy between private consumption and public squalor. The issues which Italian socialism had to address were those related to contemporary capitalism: incomes policy, the new function of public enterprise, the effects of automation, and so on – questions about which the Soviet model had little to say.[54]

The new political circumstances combined with the post-war socio-economic scenario which confronted the Italian socialists called for an overall reassessment of the party's policies and strategies. This occurred within a rigorously Marxist framework. The PSI never renounced its Marxist past, as, for example, the German SPD did with Bad Godesberg; it had no alternative but to move towards the centre while retaining its Marxist labels. Many factors contributed to this: first of all, the electoral threat posed by the strongest communist party in Western Europe standing on their left. The threat represented by Togliatti's party greatly influenced the consistency of the socialists' revisionism, which always had to be tinged with a good deal of verbal radicalism.[55] The electoral problems the PSI faced were, to some extent, the opposite of those facing British Labour in the same period. In contrast to the UK, electorally speaking, the Left in Italy was far from being in crisis and discredited in the 1950s. The PSI found itself in the awkward position of moving towards the centre in order to enter a coalition government, while its 'natural' electorate was still clinging to traditional left symbols and values. The electoral trends in the years from 1956 to 1976 demonstrated the foolishness of such an aspiration. Nenni's dream of giving birth, together with other progressive forces such as the Republican Party, to a 'third force' which would fit between the DC and the PCI and constitute a valid political alternative soon turned out to be a failure. Togliatti's party, instead of declining, as was the case with other strong European communist parties (for example the French), grew unremittingly until 1976. The 1958 elections could be taken as the first real test of the new route embarked on by the PSI. The socialists got 14.2 per cent, 1.5 per cent more than in 1953. However, although such a gain was widely hailed as an electoral success, it should be regarded as a considerable setback. The socialists' increase was not, in fact, at the expense of the communists. The new votes came from the moderate socialist electorate, as a result of groups like UP (*Unione Popolare* – Popular Union) or USI (*Unione Socialista Indipendente* – Independent Socialist Union) joining the PSI.[56]

In spite of Hungary and Khrushchev's revelations at the CPSU Congress in 1956, the PCI's electoral score remained fairly stable (22.6 per cent in 1953 and 22.7 per cent in 1958) which was a serious blow to the new strategy the socialists offered the electorate. The following election destroyed any misplaced optimism: in 1963 the PSI's score decreased to 13.8 per cent, in contrast to the PCI's growth to 25.3 per cent.[57] However, it was in 1968 that the final disaster took place: the PSU (*Partito Socialista Unificato* – Unified Socialist Party, the party which was formed after the merger of the PSI with the PSDI in 1966) gained only 14.5 per cent, not only almost the same percentage gained by the PSI alone ten years before, but one quarter less than the total of the votes that the two parties (PSI and PSDI) had obtained separately at the previous election. By contrast, the PCI's growth proceeded unabated: the communists won 26.9 per cent which, combined with the 4.5 per cent of the PSIUP (*Partito Socialista Italiano di Unità Proletaria* – Italian Socialist Party of Proletarian Unity, the new party which had broken away in 1964 from the PSI dissenting from its newly adopted reformist line), signalled the definitive relegation of the socialists to a minor role in the DC-led government coalitions.[58] In the final analysis, Italian socialists had to deal with a radical electorate and deeply entrenched anti-systemic and antagonistic cultures that had always punished any shift towards the centre attempted by left-wing parties. The flourishing of extremist and revolutionary groups in the late 1960s and 1970s in response to the 'institutionalisation' of the PCI could be taken as further confirmation of the difficulties persistently encountered by the Italian Left in abandoning a radical character.

Furthermore, the new course encountered strong resistance within the party that in fact had historically, always proven to be more radical than its European counterparts. Change in terminology and thinking were resisted to the bitter end by the left-wing factions, which explains the numerous ambiguities that remained in the socialists' proposals and which neither the autonomist current nor the Left had any interest in clarifying for the sake of the party's unity.

In spite of the difficulties encountered in the PSI's revisionist course, the Italian socialists came to acquire many features in common with their European equivalents in the 1956–64 period. From 1959 onwards the PSI identification with the democratic European Left was more and more emphasised within the PSI itself. Being an important element of the new identity that the autonomists were trying to enforce in the party, no opportunities were missed to reiterate the similarities that were said to exist with their Western European counterparts. As Giolitti wrote in *Mondo Operaio*, after the congress of Naples (1959), the PSI now fully belonged to the European democratic Left. The 'affinities in terms of traditions, ideals, socio-economic environment, with the other European socialist and social-democratic parties were incontrovertible'.[59] The congress at Venice in 1957 signalled the rupture of the long subjection of the PSI to the PCI and the rediscovery of its own autonomous identity. The Italian Socialist Party was now something separate from the communist world. It declared itself an opposition party, a political alternative. It operated in a country where, in spite of some remaining elements of backwardness and the so-called *capitalismo straccione* (beggars' capitalism), all the major European socio-economic patterns were now present. The questions facing the Italian socialists were quantitatively but not qualitatively different from those confronting their European counterparts.[60]

The cultural reawakening of the PSI

From 1953 a new phase opened for the Italian socialists. Their political and cultural dependence on the PCI began to be weakened. This culminated in 1956 and signalled the definitive end of the so-called frontist phase. The CPSU congress in 1956 performed a crucial function in bringing to the surface the underlying crisis which had long affected the Italian Left.[61] New cultural developments now found the right circumstances to grow and gain ground. 'The big absentee', as Alberto Asor Rosa defined socialist culture in the decade following the end of the war, regained strength and momentum.[62] This was to signal the end of what Franco Fortini, referring to the years from 1947 to 1957, not unfairly defined as the 'ten winters'.[63] A new 'Copernican Revolution' was opening up.[64]

Both the socialists and the communists questioned their previous dogmas and assumptions and embarked upon an overall revision of their strategies and tactics. Many of the issues which the two parties addressed were similar: the relationship between the party and the working class; the re-interpretation of the Marxist notion of the state as a bourgeois instrument; structural reforms; the question of capitalist growth and technical progress; the relationship with religion and Catholic masses. However, it is indisputable that the socialists displayed greater agility and speed in taking the first steps on the revisionist path which, in fact, won them an undisputed temporary leadership in the Italian cultural debate. The socialists were far less saddled with symbols and elements of identification with the Soviet Union than the communists and it was easier for them to break away from the earlier phase. The cultural ferment in socialist circles in those years was unique in the history of the party; it included significant and far-reaching journals such as *Tempi Moderni, Passato e Presente*; works such as *Socialismo e Verità* by Roberto Guiducci, *Riforme Rivoluzione* by Antonio Giolitti,[65] and the studies produced on the question of workers' control by Renato Panzieri and Lucio Libertini;[66] last but not least, a revitalised *Mondo Operaio*, which after 1956 became a fertile laboratory for new ideas, debates, themes such as neo-capitalism and its features, went well beyond the lack of imagination which had characterised the party's press before then.[67]

The attitude of the Communist Party towards the crisis of Stalinism is a controversial matter. While some contemporary commentators tended to deny that communists showed any sign of change,[68] some scholars have argued that, in fact, 1956 represented a watershed both for Togliatti's party and for Nenni's.[69] The death of Stalin and the Khrushchev revelations also had considerable impact on the PCI. This was made even more so by important events challenging the party's strategy and which could not be ignored. These included economic expansion; the defeat of FIOM (*Federazione Italiana Operai Metallurgici*) – the CGIL's organisation for metal-workers – in 1955 at the elections for the renewal of internal commissions in the car company Fiat which reflected a discrepancy between the newly formed working class and the CGIL, as well as the failure of Togliatti's party to grasp the new changes in work organisation and finally, a rapidly changing society: massive waves of migration from the South and the depopulation of rural areas called for an overall reconsideration of the PCI's major concern with rural policies which had so far marked its post-war conduct.[70]

The adaptation to the era of de-Stalinisation was relatively easy, thanks to the availability of the ideological baggage elaborated by Togliatti in the years 1944–7, in turn extracted from Gramsci's theoretical formulations of the inter-war years of the 'Italian road to Socialism'. Gramsci's gradualist road to socialism, after being abruptly discarded with the outbreak of the Cold War, was, in fact, gradually revamped from the VIII congress (1957) onwards.[71] Togliatti's famous interview in *Nuovi Argomenti* in 1956, the debate raised in *Il Contemporaneo* in the same year on the growing inadequacy of Leninist ideological traditions in interpreting present circumstances, the conference on Gramsci held in 1958, all signalled important steps in a process of revision which culminated in the early 1960s.

Nevertheless, communists' conduct in what went down in history as the years of the so-called *disgelo* (thaw) was marked by a great deal of slowness and awkwardness. The communists' rediscovery of the 'Italian road to socialism' was affected, as far as the 1950s were concerned, by severe limitations and was hardly comparable with the rethinking which characterised the socialists' cultural debate in the same years. A comparison between the scripts of Renato Panzieri and Mario Alicata, in charge respectively of the cultural department of the PSI and the PCI after 1955, indeed mirrors the delay of the PCI in opening up towards revisionist change and questioning Stalinism and Zdanovism's main tenets.[72] The departure of intellectuals which the PCI suffered in 1956 tells us, after all, a good deal about the resistance encountered by those who tried to challenge the party's orthodoxy.[73] Similarly telling are the attitudes adopted by the PCI towards the Hungarian events as well as the critical pamphlet *Revisionismo Nuovo e Antico*[74] which Luigi Longo, a prominent communist, published in response to Giolitti's *Riforme e Rivoluzione*, one of the most important revisionist texts produced in those years. Only in 1962, following the transformation of *Rinascita* into a weekly magazine and the birth of *Critica Marxista*, would the PCI appear seriously engaged in the analysis of the new society. In particular, the conference on the 'New Tendencies of Italian Capitalism' (*Le Nuove Tendenze del Capitalismo Italiano*)[75] held in 1962 at the Gramsci Institute has to be regarded as a real turning point. Post-war capitalism and all its new trends were, for the first time, fully investigated: state capitalism, the great economic expansion which the Italian economy was undergoing, the system's greater stability, the technological revolution,[76] and the new role of the state.[77]

The abandonment of the frontist policy by the PSI entailed the rediscovery of all those peculiar socialist elements which had been put aside during the Cold War years. Those minority currents, whose theoretical references were more Hendrik de Man's neo-socialism and the liberal socialism of Carlo Rosselli than of Marx, and which had played a marginal role only a few years before (thinking in particular of intellectuals like Franco Fortini, Franco Momigliano, Alessandro Pizzorno, Roberto Guiducci), came to represent a primary ideological reference;[78] they in fact ended up constituting the platform for a political and cultural reappraisal by the party in search of a new and, most of all, autonomous identity. Roberto Guiducci in particular, although largely ignored by most of the literature existing on the socialists' new autonomist course, played a major role in furnishing the party with substantial analysis and new ideas. His *Socialismo e Verità*, published in 1956, was a considerable asset for those involved in rethinking the party's doctrine at that time. All later works referred to it as the starting point of any revisionist discourse. Although the content of the two books differs substantially, and *Socialismo e Verità* was more in tune with neo-Marxist than New Fabian studies, in terms of theoretical weight, it would not be inappropriate to compare it to Crosland's *The Future of Socialism*.

An overall revision of the party's assumptions and doctrine was urgently needed. As Guiducci wrote, left-wing parties had so far been committed to a defensive battle: in the climate of the Cold War, any questioning of the deeply rooted dogmas of the socialist tradition was criticised as an attack on the working class and a deliberate attempt to weaken its struggle against capital. However, the arms had now been laid down; the Left had to take off its 'military uniform' and put on 'civilian clothes'.[79] All those areas of culture so far neglected such as economy, sociology, scientific methodology, modern historiography, had to be approached and systematically investigated.[80]

Left-wing parties' denial of the dramatic transformations Italy had been undergoing meant leaving the cultural leadership to neo-capitalist reformism, Giolitti argued, in *Riforme e Rivoluzione*: recognition of the changes undergone by capitalism did not mean making 'any concessions to an unprincipled revisionism; it rather entailed the relinquishment of old and outlived interpretations on the crisis of capitalism, which recent events had been challenging, and that Marxist theory not only could, but had to, change'.[81]

As we saw earlier, the Italian socialists' adherence to Third International theoretical assumptions meant the unquestioned adoption of the creed of the imminent end of capitalism. Capitalism was, in fact, seen to be in a profound crisis in the early 1950s: unemployment; the violent repression of any workers' and peasants' agitation; the laws passed in that period restricting the right of protest and giving vast powers to the police; the censorship imposed on the press; all these factors were regarded as incontrovertible proof of a faltering and doomed system which, on the verge of collapse, was prepared to try anything to survive.[82]

As a result of this negative vision, socialists failed to recognise the first signs of what was to culminate in the economic miracle, namely the far-reaching migratory movements towards the big cities, growing economic and commercial exchanges with the most industrialised countries, the dramatic development of manufacturing industry in the industrial triangle in the North, and the gradual decrease in unemployment.

From 1957 onwards an awareness of the socialists' inability to study neo-capitalism's transformations and its new features became particularly sharp.[83] As Vasetti lamented in *Mondo Operaio*, an increasingly wide discrepancy between Italy's socio-economic reality and the interpretation given to it had occurred. The Left's enduring commitment to the dogma of the inevitability of the crisis of capitalism, and its unquestioned retention of an abstract model which had long failed to match reality, was preventing working-class parties from seriously analysing existing developments and, in particular, the significance of the economic expansion Italy had been experiencing since the early 1950s.[84]

Only a few months later a series of articles focusing on neo-capitalism appeared in *Mondo Operaio*. The time had come for a serious reappraisal of the socio-economic trends at work. The question of neo-capitalism and the investigation of its principal features dominated the issues of the PSI's monthly journal from 1957 to 1958. As Panzieri put it, the study of the new forms assumed by capitalism came to acquire an indisputable centrality; it was, in other words, of crucial importance for the 'what is to be done?' of the working-class movement.[85]

The debate on contemporary capitalism that was taking place at a European level did not pass unnoticed. In 1957 John Strachey's *Contemporary Capitalism* was translated and published in Italy.[86] It provoked a debate within neo-Marxist circles[87] which is reflected in *Mondo Operaio*.

Competition with the communist bloc, it was argued, had forced capitalism to adopt several stabilising measures.[88] Three macroeconomic features were said to characterise post-war capitalism: the lack of deep cyclical crises, its uninterrupted expansion since the end of the war, and the extraordinarily fast pace of technological progress.[89] Another deeply entrenched dogma which was dismissed, along with that of the imminent crisis of capitalism, was the belief in the gradual impoverishment of the majority of the population. The increased prosperity of certain sections of the working class was now an incontrovertible fact. In large industries where full employment had nearly been achieved, salaries were rising in proportion to productivity rates. Even if a large gap among sectors of society still remained, it had not been further enlarged.[90]

Another sign of change in post-war capitalism, which did not go unnoticed was democratisation: capitalism had seemingly accepted the democratic rules. The danger of a fascist counterrevolution was now seen as highly unlikely. The increasingly great involvement of the working-class movement in policy-making and the successful forms of integration of the masses carried out by the ruling class had in fact paved the way for a peaceful way to counter the working class's advance.[91]

As mentioned earlier, New Fabians' studies on post-war capitalism all concluded that capitalism was irrevocably transforming itself into socialism. The neo-Marxist approach, which the Italian socialists' analyses drew from, indeed recognised the profound modifications capitalism had been going through; however, they were a long way from being accepted as evidence that a socialist society was about to take the place of the existing system.[92] Although considerably modified, capitalism was still said to remain an unjust and irrational system. Not only did the inherent contradictions of capitalism persist unchanged but so did its main guiding principles, principally its profit-led nature. Italian socialists recognised that profound changes in the form of ownership had occurred: the tendency towards managerialism. However, they did not give it the same weight as the New Fabian scholars did and, even before them, the 'institutionalist school' did. Managers' actions were certainly seen as more functional than entrepreneurs' in relation to the long-term interests of the company, but, it was still argued, they were strongly influenced by private profit considerations.[93]

The analyses of the socialists had to distance themselves from the 'utopian' view which assumed that the contradictions of capitalism could be eliminated gradually until it would be spontaneously transformed into socialism. This is what the New Fabian studies contended was taking place by virtue of technological progress and the extension of political democracy.[94] As opposed to the determinist New Fabian approach, socialist society was seen as something which was not going to take place naturally, but had to be the result of voluntaristic action. The strict link between economy and politics remained a cornerstone of Marxist thinking in parties like the PSI.

A socialist revolution, in the final analysis, was still regarded by Nenni's group as indispensable to the construction of a socialist society, though they did not think it would be violent. In fact, the overall reappraisal of socio-economic trends at work led the Italian socialists to formulate a new political strategy for achieving socialism. The considerable stability gained by capitalism; the increased political strength of the labour movement; the new relevance attached to democracy after the CPSU congress; the profoundly transformed functions of the state; all made a strong case for a gradual and democratic road to socialism. Structural reformism was, in fact, to become the key idea of the new PSI autonomist course.

The notion of structural reforms was not new in socialist thinking. It was, in fact, first advanced by the Austro-Marxists (who listed among their most prominent exponents Otto Bauer, Max Adler, Karl Renner and Rudolf Hilferding) who, in an attempt to get around the rigid dichotomy of 'reforms or revolution' which had followed the Soviet revolution, had developed the concept of 'slow revolution'. In some respects this was a strategic concept for those parties like the PSI which, while still committed to a socialist revolution, were confronted by different socio-economic conditions to those which characterised Russia in 1917. The 'slow revolution' which Austro-Marxists advocated recognised the profoundly modified role of the capitalist state, which had come as the result of the 1929–31 crisis, and the extent to which the *laissez-faire* economy had now been replaced with a fairly complicated system of constraints and regulations. Given these new circumstances, the extent to which incursions into the system were possible for any socialist party which achieved power, they claimed, had considerably enlarged and a socialist society could be built from within capitalism itself.

Structural reformism was more a rediscovery than a discovery for the PSI. Not only had it already exerted a strong appeal on Italian socialists in exile during the 1930s but it had also been further elaborated and adapted to the Italian scenario by Gramsci. Gramsci's rejection of the notion of violent revolution and his idea of 'revolution as a process' would constitute a major pillar of both the PSI and the PCI's process of ideological revision in the post-war years.[95]

A new road to socialism: the autonomist group's ascendancy

The CPSU congress in 1956 is rightly regarded as a watershed for the Italian socialists.[96] In contrast to the degeneration of the Soviet system, the commitment to democracy was reinstated. The article by Nenni, 'Luci ed ombre del congresso di Mosca' (trans.: bright and dark points of the Moscow congress), published first in *Avanti!* and later in *Mondo Operaio*,[97] began a process of reassessment of the relationship between socialism and democracy which was to culminate in the full acceptance of the democratic parliamentary road at the congress of February 1957.[98]

The route to socialism for Western European socialist parties had to be unequivocally by parliamentary methods. After all, Marx himself had contended that in circumstances where working-class parties were allowed to exert their voice, violent revolution would not be strictly necessary.[99] Gramsci, socialist autonomists argued, clearly distinguished between 'modern' and 'backward' countries, namely Western and Eastern countries. While the former possessed a balanced relationship between the state and civil society and stable institutions, the latter were far more fragile.[100] It was an incontrovertible fact that violent revolution and the dictatorship of the proletariat had so far occurred only in economically backward countries where productive forces had scarcely developed and democracy was almost non-existent. Socialist parties operating in economically advanced and democratic countries had to renounce any kind of 'war of movement' and undertake instead a 'war of position'. The notion of the dictatorship of the proletariat had to be put aside and replaced with the notion of hegemony. Hegemony, as Giolitti argued, was the peaceful road to socialism. It meant the political organisation and formation of working class-consciousness, so that workers could take full advantage of the democratic and parliamentary system in which they operated.[101]

In a speech at the PSI congress in 1963, Lombardi contended that Italian socialists had to accept as an accomplished fact the demise of the 'revolutionary myth' within the European labour movements. The belief that a socialist society could emerge only from the destruction of the bourgeois state had to be dismissed. The socialist revolution would be a democratic revolution by parliamentary means.[102] It was now conceived as a gradual revolutionary process carried out through the implementation of revolutionary reforms; that is, 'structural reforms'.[103]

The conquest of the state was now possible from within. As Lombardi argued at the central committee of the party held in April 1956, the experience of the SFIO and of the British Labour Party provided considerable evidence of the adequacy of bourgeois institutions for the socialist conquest of power.[104] The state could now no longer be regarded as part of the 'superstructure' but was itself the 'structure'.[105] The fact was it was no longer a super-structural body exclusively in charge of administrative activities, but was now containing and managing a substantial sector of the economy.[106] The increased power of the working-class parties and universal suffrage had both resulted in the first incursions by the state into the economic sphere; it was, however, years of disillusionment with the self-regulatory capability of the system during the interwar period which had signalled the considerable extension of state intervention in the economy and the definitive assertion of what was now referred to as 'state capitalism'.[107] The state was now the guarantor not only of social order but also of economic stability in terms of price controls, surplus consumption and demand creation, credit management and direction, public services provision, manpower training and scientific and cultural development.[108]

There was no doubt that public intervention had always been manipulated by capitalist forces; however, the preconditions for exerting increased control over the economy had been laid. By capturing the heights of the state machine, socialists would be in a position to replace capitalist management with their own. State intervention in the economic sphere would then be directed to its more obvious end, namely the public interest.[109]

Of course, socialists were taking a considerable risk: that their reforms would bring about the conservation of capitalism rather than its replacement;[110] as Guiducci argued, socialist reforms, far from disrupting the capitalist enemy, could act instead as measures which could make it even stronger.[111] The capitulation of the PSI to neo-capitalist forces was a certainty nourished among those sections in the party which increasingly distanced themselves from what they regarded as a dangerous process of 'social-democratisation'.

The 'Appeal to Socialists', presented by some intellectuals to the 32nd congress in 1957, signalled the peak of the autonomists' ideological reappraisal but also the end of their apparently uncontested ascendancy within the party. In fact, it signalled the emergence of an irreconcilable disagreement with left-wing revisionists, among whom the more prominent members included: Renato Panzieri, Vittorio Foa, Luciano della Mea and Lucio Libertini.[112] The latter represented in Italy the 'New Left' which arose in 1956 in almost every Western European country. The alliance between this group and other elements on the left of the party, like Vecchietti, Valori, Basso, to mention only a few, was to mount a strong resistance before the autonomists could obtain full control of the party.

Nenni was accused of bringing the party into line with the European revisionist tradition. A 'different party', which was not the right wing of the labour movement but rather the left wing of a bourgeois front, was seen as gradually making its way into the PSI's ranks.[113] As Lelio Basso put it, socialists were now faced with the paradox of being taught socialism in its 'modern' reformulation by those who had never been socialists. More and more genuine socialist traditions, ideals and jargon were disappearing. There was a strong fear that the PSI already had 'one foot outside of the working class movement'.[114] An 'ideological demobilisation' was said to be under way. Autonomists employed Marxism exclusively as a useful label with which to conceal their accommodation to capitalism.[115]

In fact, in spite of the accusations of 'social-democratisation', autonomists regarded themselves as profoundly different from the tainted European social-democratic parties: the route to socialism they envisaged, it was said, was a third way between maximalism and the socialism of redistribution. As an article in *Mondo Operaio* in 1956 argued, the acceptance of a parliamentary road did not entail any concession to reformism. Reformists accepted a 'compromise' with capitalism; they believed in the possibility of reforming and cohabitating with it. Although it was true that socialists were prepared to ally themselves with the progressive sections of the Italian bourgeoisie, this would never entail the end of their antagonism to capitalism and their long-term commitment to its replacement with a more equal and just system.[116] As it was reinstated in the 1961 congress, autonomists stood between the sterile maximalism of those who refused to accept the need for an overall revision of the socialist strategies and still clung to old-fashioned analyses of capitalism, and those who had surrendered to social-democratic reformist practices.[117]

After all, it was the 'third way' which better matched capitalism's requirements in the late 1950s. At the same time as the first signs of a slackening in Western European economies was emerging, planning and state management of the economy came to be seen as crucial for further expansion. The proponents of a socialism of redistribution would soon give way to technocratic socialists, as the dominance that Harold Wilson and the centre–left technocratic group around him established in the British Labour Party from the early 1960s well shows.

Wilsonism and the revival of technocratic socialism

If, in the boom of the affluent society in the 1950s, the Left's arguments sounded old-fashioned and detached from reality, by the early 1960s the reverse had become the case.

As Kenneth Morgan put it, Britain indulged throughout the 1950s in a state of complacent hedonism. Real setbacks such as the Suez crisis, the threat to sterling in mid-1957 or the crisis in defence policy which followed the end of Blue Streak in 1960, were not accorded great importance and were regarded instead as temporary difficulties. The confidence of the British people was left untouched.[118] The vision of a nation which belonged to the past persisted and the tradition of greatness was tenaciously adhered to. Conservatives' success relied on a solidly rooted picture of Britain as an increasingly healthy, better housed, better educated and more prosperous country. At the beginning of 1960 a Gallup poll revealed that two-thirds of those surveyed regarded their nation as the country with the most to offer ordinary people in terms of happiness and contentment.[119] However, over the next three years such confidence was to be eroded. From 1961 the perception of internal decay could no longer be avoided. As Arthur Koestler wrote in *Suicide of a Nation?* the average Englishman had kept his head 'buried in the sand with the tranquil conviction that Reality was a nasty word invented by foreigners'. Time had now come to abandon the 'ostrich attitude'.[120] The slow pace of economic growth, the increasingly evident external weaknesses and the crisis of Britain's world role were eventually admitted; this opened an era of self-examination for the whole country.[121]

The 1960s, the stagnant society and the rise of the centre–left technocratic group

It was during these years that the so-called 'State of England' literature flourished, a genre which is still alive and well today. Among the most influential works produced in the early 1960s were Michael Shanks' *The Stagnant Society* (1961), Anthony Sampson's *Anatomy of Britain* (1962), Anthony Hartley's *A State of England* (1963) and Arthur Koestler's *Suicide of a Nation?* (1963). All these works devoted very little attention to purely economic matters. They all carried the unmistakable revisionist bias towards sociological and psychological, rather than structural, explanations. Both Shanks' *The Stagnant Society* and Koestler's *Suicide of a Nation?* open with the typical revisionist argument whereby it was the 'psychological apartheid between the bourgeoisie and the proletariat' and not material inequalities which must constitute a matter of concern for Britain.[122] Although he was the industrial editor of the *Financial Times* and an economist, Michael Shanks came to argue that the country had now reached a point where it would be more useful to 'call in sociology and psychology to help solve Britain's current economic problems'.[123]

Indeed, sociological and psychological factors were crucial to understanding the country's lack of dynamism; nevertheless, it was soon to become clear that Britain's diminished economic competitiveness compared with its European partners had much more to do with economic questions such as the absence of any serious planning on the French model, and the lack of state intervention in key sectors such as scientific research and technological progress.

The British economy at the end of the 1950s was in a rather sluggish state. Most important, in contrast with the lack of awareness in previous years, was that economic decline was now fully recognised and became the focus of concern of the national quality press and political circles. Abundant statistical evidence drawn from various sources such as OEEC figures confirmed Britain's comparative failure and the dismal record of the first industrial nation. Britain's annual rates of growth at 2.6 per cent per year was less than all other developed countries in the Western world, except Ireland. The country's share of world exports had fallen from 26.2 per cent in 1953 to 20.6 per cent in 1961, and its share of manufacturing exports from the eleven major manufacturing countries fell from 20 per cent of the total in 1954 to well under 14 per cent in 1964.[124]

Contemporary research did not confine itself to slow economic growth. For the first time, the limits of Britain's affluent society were accepted. It was clear that large sections of the population did not share the much hailed prosperity of the 1950s. For the first time the idea of 'Two Englands', one in the North the other in the South, emerged.[125] Talk of 'the casualties of the welfare State'[126] made its way into the political debate. Some immediate action had to be taken; most of all, a new sense of economic direction had to be regained.

Once the alleged limits of the present system and some of its fallacies became increasingly difficult to deny, the technocratic case for increased state intervention both in terms of planning and common ownership gained strength in the party's inner debate. Crosland's assumptions fell by the wayside one by one in those years: irreversible economic growth, the efficient working of capitalism, the inevitable disappearance of inequalities and social injustice. Keynesianism was showing limitations in coping with the problems which the British economy faced. The disastrous consequences of the well-known 'stop and go' economic policy Conservatives had been pursuing since their return to power were becoming increasingly clear. Recurrent deficits of the balance of payments and soaring inflation not only represented an undeniable obstacle to progress in the redistribution of the existing cake, but made the precondition for any extension of the taxation system, namely the enlargement of the cake, rather improbable.

The time had come for the Left to replace the revisionists in terms of the party's theoretical leadership. As Crossman wrote in 1964 in an article shortly before Labour returned to power: 'history made the Revisionists look pretty silly'.[127] Crosland's *The Conservative Enemy*,[128] published in 1962, tried to update his previous contentions: the contrast between private and public squalor was admitted; however, social distortions continued to be regarded as a question of still too limited taxation. Economic growth remained a marginal issue, almost untouched, leaving aside the notion of planning which Crosland's strong attachment to the values of individual freedom and consumer choice made acceptable only in its weakest form; as Thomas Balogh put it, even with less conviction and commitment than the Conservatives themselves.[129]

Indeed, the successful counterattack of the Left is not only explained by the new economic circumstances which Britain was faced with. The intellectual ability displayed now by the Left was, in fact, considerably greater than in previous years. The mid-1950s were marked by an increasingly pronounced divergence between the doctrinal attachment to public ownership and the apparent persistence of the 'equal power' arguments of Left personalities such as Michael Foot, Barbara Castle, Jennie Lee and the more pragmatic approach displayed by Wilson's centre–left group (Richard Crossman, Thomas Balogh, Harold Wilson) who championed a more instrumental notion of planning and state ownership strictly connected with economic efficiency arguments. The split which followed led to the emergence of a less doctrinaire and 'modern' Left able to pose a serious threat to the established theoretical dominance of the Right.[130] Balogh, Crossman and Wilson were not an organised faction such as the Gaitskellites or the Bevanites; however, the production-oriented aspects of their socialism would soon earn them a distinctiveness as a group apart. The priority attributed to economic efficiency rather than equality discourses; the emphasis placed on planning; the abandonment of any Bevanite moral condemnation of consumerist society,[131] constituted the foundations of their soon-to-come success both within the party and at the polls.

Wilson had for a long time been an isolated voice among the Bevanites in connecting planning and common ownership with Britain's economic record. One of the first and most significant appearances of the notion of common ownership as strictly linked with a planned economic expansion is in *In Place of Dollars* (1953);[132] it was later further developed in the Fabian Pamphlet by Harold Wilson in 1957 entitled *Post-War Economic Policies in Britain*. All the themes which would dominate Labour's electoral campaign in 1964 were addressed: the stagnation of capital investment and industrial re-equipment; the misplaced priorities in consumption; the case for a sufficiently purposeful direction of the economy and increased public control to ensure that the main requirements of the nation could be met, namely exports and a high investment economy.[133] Planning and common ownership were regarded not only as the precondition for a more equal redistribution of wealth but were also strongly connected with Britain's economic survival.

The so-called centre–left technocratic group which emerged from the Bevanite faction produced in this period a substantial number of well-articulated theoretical works, devoid of the naiveté which had marked the Bevanites' ideas. The arguments which Keynesian centre–right revisionists were now confronted with were far more solid and substantiated than had been the case only a few years earlier.

The centre–right revisionists' hegemony on the wane

The dominance of centre–right revisionism within the party reached its peak in 1957: this was the year in which *Industry and Society*, a genuine revisionist party's document, was published; unilateralism was overwhelmingly rejected; Bevan gave up his challenge to Gaitskell's leadership.[134] The power structure of the party was then inherently anti-Left; Bevanites were confined to the margins of the party and were unable to offer any resistance. No serious threat to the Right's political supremacy was posed until 1959.

The defeat of Gaitskell's attempt to amend Clause Four in 1959 and the victory of unilateralism at the Labour conference in 1960 came as a considerable shock and prompted immediate action among revisionists in order to re-establish their political control over the party machine. The Campaign for Democratic Socialism (CDS) was launched in 1960 by Bill Rodgers and Anthony Crosland with the purpose of compensating for the loss of the trade unions' vital support and remedying the scarce and inadequate organisation of moderate sections in favour of Gaitskell's policies in the party constituencies. In contrast with the decline of influence in the trade unions which had occurred in the years 1945–51, the Left managed during that time to make a veritable breakthrough in the constituency realm. When the Labour government fell in 1951, the constituency parties had become the backbone of the Labour Left and methods of communication were developed in order to maximise their impact on Labour's annual conferences. The rationale behind the CDS's concerted mobilisation was the belief that the Right had until then underestimated its own strength in the constituencies and needed to be more integrated in order to prevent a 'well organised minority' from establishing its control over the party.[135] A monthly magazine, *Campaign*, was set up and thanks to hard work in propaganda and organisation, considerable inroads were made in the constituency parties.

The campaign produced immediate results. The Right managed to regain the lost terrain which was reflected in Gaitskell's inner-party victory over the hydrogen-bomb issue in 1961. Dropping the pursuit of constitutional revision and the adoption of a new conciliatory mood opened a new more peaceful era for the party and put an end to the heated climate which had characterised the party's last two years. The Right now seemed to be very much in control. However, in spite of the successful re-establishment of their political hold on the party, it is a fact that during this time it is possible to observe their gradual decline in terms of theoretical hegemony.

Many scholars regard the series of party policy documents and resolutions which followed 1959 as the result of a compromise between revisionism and traditionalism.[136] Their argument is that revisionists appreciated the need for a more compromising approach towards the Left, and this resulted in the production of policy proposals in which their objectives were diluted in some socialist rhetoric. As discussed in the introduction, this author does not agree with such a view. Two factors are actually omitted: first, the prior existence of two different Lefts (Old Left and the technocratic centre–left) and the substantial distinctions which existed between them; second, the extent to which these documents, far from being simply a mixture of old leftism and revisionism, instead signalled the ascendancy of a new set of policies; that is, those championed by the centre–left group, which were quite distinct from Gaitskellites' and Bevanites'. Documents like *Labour in the Sixties* (1960) and *Signposts for the Sixties* (1961) cannot be regarded as the victory of Croslandism behind a facade of traditionalism; instead, they should be considered as the beginning of the contamination of pure revisionist arguments with centre–left technocratic issues. For a start, the Old Left's principled commitment to common ownership completely disappeared, which rules out the persistence of any traditionalism. Further, the impact of the revival of more 'structural measures' such as planning and, even if in different and more pragmatic terms, common ownership and the decline of the centre–right revisionists' almost exclusive concern with redistribution are evident. A great deal of attention is devoted to economic expansion, which as we saw above, revisionists had claimed was no longer a matter of concern for socialists. The argument was made that socialism was more than relevant in an era of prosperity because of the challenge posed by automation and technological revolution if the state did not intervene. Education is for the first time overtly connected with economic needs and not just with status and classless society discourses. The limits of the affluent society are accepted as opposed to the deeply-held revisionist belief in the emancipatory role of private consumption and in the individual freedom of determining personal needs. Wilson's triumph as the new leader after Gaitskell's unexpected death in 1963, only confirmed the definitive hold on the party of the centre–left by adding political leadership to their already established theoretical hegemony.

It was at this stage of the Labour Party's history that the Italian socialists and their British counterparts began to display considerable similarities. After Nenni's autonomist course prevailed in the PSI and the technocratic soul in the Labour Party, both parties came to champion quite a similar 'third way' between the Keynesian mixed economy and communism. The next chapter will explore in detail what their alleged third way stood for.

2
Structural Reforms and the 'Socialist' Management of Capitalism

The revival of the 'Third Way'

Both the PSI and the British Labour Party came to champion, at this stage of their histories, a quite similar 'third way' between a Keynesian mixed economy and communism. In contrast to the attempt by centre–right revisionists such as Crosland to pass off Keynesianism as socialism, 'real' socialism, as the following paragraphs will show, was reasserted as still valid and relevant.

The totalitarian nature of the communist bloc was fiercely rejected. From 1956 onwards, although democracy had always been the distinctive element of European social-democratic parties after their breakaway from the Third International, an even greater concern with individual freedom and liberty became manifested. Even the Labour Party, whose credentials concerning the party's attitude towards democratic methods and the parliamentary way were beyond dispute, felt the need to reassert its position in this regard. In 1956 an official NEC policy document entitled *Personal Freedom: Labour's Policy for the Individual and Society*[1] addressed issues such as the relationship between the state and the individual citizen and warned of the threat posed by the former, even in democratic states, to the latter.[2] In particular, the PSI, because of its previous frontist policies and close identification with the Soviet Union, came to put great emphasis on the issues of democracy and individual liberty. Soon after Khrushchev's revelations in 1956, talk of the party's commitment to democracy dominated the party's press and internal debate, and this culminated in fully accepting the democratic parliamentary road at the Venice congress in 1957.[3]

However, the rejection of Stalinism did not entail full accommodation with Keynesianism: both political forces distanced themselves from the 'redistributive socialism' epitomised in Italy by the PSDI led by Saragat and in Great Britain by centre–right revisionists. The evolutionary approach adopted by centre–right revisionists, according to which capitalism was gradually evolving into a socialist society, was rejected. No matter how much more stable, better functioning and more equal capitalism might be – and assertions to the contrary would have been untenable in the prosperous 1950s and 1960s – it was still regarded as a system which was a long way from representing a further step towards a socialist society.

The case for socialism was, therefore, restated in renewed terms. Structural reforms were to be the key idea of both the Italian socialists and the Labour Party's policies: capitalism, although accepted in the short and medium term, was, in the long term, to be replaced. A systematic intervention in the very structure of the economy, which the enlarged role of the state in the economy now allowed, would put a socialist society in its place.

The word 'socialism', which during the 1950s had fallen into disuse and become a tainted label to shun, once more acquired an unexpected centrality in both political forces' discourse. Indeed, its revival could be partially explained by the need of both political forces for internal peace. As we saw in the previous chapter, there was strong resistance in both the PSI and the Labour Party to any change in the party's doctrine and strategy. Maintaining a facade of traditional symbols came to be seen as crucial for both parties' survival. However, the rediscovery of socialism reflected the attempt to emphasise the rupture with Keynesian socialism and the new 'third way' which both claimed to embody.

Automation and the new case for socialism

In Crossman's Fabian pamphlet *Socialism and the New Despotism* of 1955, which was mainly concerned with the presumed conflict between socialism, liberty and freedom, he wondered whether there could be a third way between communism and the Keynesian mixed economy: 'Are the only alternatives left to the socialists in the 1950s either to watch Mr Macmillan bring the British mixed economy into line with the American system or else to join the communist party?'[4] According to Crossman, the conviction, reinforced by years of Cold War propaganda, that complete transformation to socialism, as in the Soviet Union, would necessarily degenerate into a totalitarian state had led to the socialists' retreat in adopting views that would have been dismissed only a few years earlier as 'black reaction'.[5] To withstand the revisionists' attempts to deprive the party of its socialist character, Crossman wrote that what the party needed was 'first a new, creative socialist idea and secondly a situation to which it was demonstrably relevant'. Both these requirements were met in the early 1960s.[6]

A hundred years after Marx, the pace of technological change had speeded up so much that, in Crossman's words, dangerous forces were exploding in societies that dragged along behind science and technology, unable to adapt themselves to them. The question facing Labour, as well as the other European socialist parties, was how to 'become the masters not the slaves of technological change'.[7]

The socialist principle that power had to be made accountable had been strengthened, not weakened, by the increasing rate of technological change and the concentration of economic power which it entailed. As Wilson declared in his famous Scarborough speech of 1963, 'if there had never been a case for Socialism before, automation would have created it'. Only if technological progress became part of national planning could that progress be directed to national ends.[8]

Wilsonism and the close connection it entailed between 'scientific revolution' and socialism represented, without any doubt, an important source of inspiration for European socialism in the early 1960s. The oft-quoted speech he delivered at the Scarborough conference acted as a veritable guideline for the future strategies of all socialist parties in Western Europe. Italian socialists themselves relied heavily on Wilson's concepts in formulating their new way forward to socialism: a technological and scientific revolution, whose economic and social effects were to be far greater than the ones caused by the first industrial revolution in Britain one hundred and fifty years earlier, was under way. Only greater public control over the economy would assure full employment of the resources which the scientific revolution could offer and at the same time 'neutralise' disruptive and harmful effects such as technological unemployment which would undoubtedly result. As an article in *Mondo Operaio* stated:

> Harold Wilson has the merit of having liberated the Left from old and out of date ideologies and demonstrated the validity of Socialism in the new socio-economic reality brought about by what he defines as the 'scientific revolution' ... Socialism is not a more or less desirable political option, but it represents instead the political and social form historically corresponding to the scientific revolution under way.[9]

Talk of automation and its economic and social effects came to be very much the subject of debate among professional economists, politicians and trade unions in all Western European countries and the USA from the mid-1950s onwards. Automation was clearly making rapid headway in an increasing number of economic sectors, not only in industry, as was initially thought to be the case; partial automation was becoming the defining feature of the whole economy from the car industry and trades and services to public administration.[10]

The effects of automation were, indeed, extremely controversial. 'Optimists' and 'Pessimists'[11] looked at the future developments of the process with both enthusiasm and fear. Many issues were at stake: to start with, there was much concern with the effects which automation might have on employment. Automation was, in fact, argued by many to be conducive to so-called 'technological unemployment'; it would entail, in other words, an expulsion of workers from the productive process at a greater speed than had been the case with 'mechanisation'.[12] Other burning questions related to automation included the presumed downgrading effects that introduction of automated machines was said to entail, the effects of automation on the size of industries and companies, and the extent to which automation might bring about a greater stability in the economy as optimists claimed or, as pessimists claimed, greater uncertainty and instability.[13]

A far more in-depth investigation is needed than can be given here to fully address all the implications and the real effects of automation in those years. However, what we are concerned with is not the strengths and weaknesses of the arguments employed by optimists and pessimists, but rather how automation, regardless of whether it was well or ill founded, was perceived by pessimists, mainly from the Left. On the whole, the key argument advanced by the latter was that automation should be welcomed on the condition that it was regulated; if it were introduced in an unregulated manner in a 'free economy', it was argued, serious dangers to the stability of both the economic and social structure were likely.

This, in many respects, challenged both the notion of technological progress advanced by evolutionary socialists in the mould of British centre–right revisionists and American liberal theorists like Peter Drucker or John Diebold as being something good in itself for the collectivity, and their faith in the progressive nature of automation.[14] Technological progress, it was argued, was something which had to be directed. In the hands of capitalism, it would certainly not give way to an equal and fair society, let alone to a socialist society, but would instead strengthen the power of monopolies and further enlarge social inequalities.[15] Technological revolution, in other words, did not contain any inherent law conducive to social progress and would only turn out to be a positive factor if managed by progressive forces.[16]

As Roberto Guiducci stated, capitalism had long displayed an inherent inability to achieve technical progress together with social advance. The 'myth of Industry', in C. Wright Mills' formulation,[17] had long shown its weakness: the positivist and scientific nineteenth century belief that industry would provide humanity with the solution to any problem was no longer acceptable.[18] The explosion of private consumerism and the subordination of people's needs to production clearly demonstrated the extent to which industry and greater productivity, if left to themselves, did not automatically produce social progress.[19]

Nenni's speech at the Venice Congress in 1957 echoed Guiducci's arguments: If the development of the second industrial revolution was left to itself, restricted only by useless *a posteriori* palliatives, it would produce destructive tendencies which no free society would be able to resist.[20]

There were many areas detected by European left-wing parties where, if only the state had intervened consistently, automation could have resulted in a real advance for the many and not only for the few. First, if technological unemployment was to be contained, the educational system as a whole had to be radically reformed in order to give children a training suited to an automated age. Second, far-reaching forward planning would be required to assure full employment and a readjustment of employment opportunities through retraining policies. Third, the increased leisure time and greater purchasing power that automation entailed called for some form of state intervention for it to be of real benefit to the workers and not just to the so-called private leisure industries. Fourth, greater industrial democracy had to be established in the factories so as to counterbalance the alienation produced by automation. Finally, consistent controls and intervention in the economy by the state had to take place so as to reduce the degree of economic instability which automation was said to produce in terms of unemployment or underconsumption. The prior condition for the survival of an automated economy was the creation of a stable, large and easily predictable market. As an article which appeared in *Mondo Operaio* in 1956 put it, 'Only by enforcing fully comprehensive planning policies can a steady development of the various variables of economics (production, demand, employment, incomes, etc.) be secured.'[21]

Socialists and modernisation

Technological revolution not only had to be mastered. It also undeniably needed to be speeded up. In both the British and the Italian cases, socialism was reaffirmed using new modern terms which connected it closely with the modernisation process that both countries' economies and societies needed at the turn of the decade.

'Third way' claims apart, the policies of these renewed socialist parties actually happened to suit capitalism, whose further development in terms of growth and productivity rates seemed, at that stage, increasingly dependent on a major degree of economic management and the implementation of a number of rationalising reforms. This was something both Labour and the PSI were aware of. The modernisation of both countries, according to the two parties and the electorate which would soon give them its support, was now in Labour and the Italian socialists' hands. The modernisation which Labour and the PSI promised in their election manifestos, however, differed substantially: while, as far as Great Britain was concerned, it meant the revitalisation of the economy and the provision of the country with the infrastructures needed to survive in an increasingly competitive international economy; as far as Italy was concerned, modernisation was, first and foremost, the accomplishment of a liberal revolution which had never been completed; it meant, in other words, catching up with the model of modern capitalist society which countries like Great Britain had long established.

In fact, modernity came to be the *leitmotif* of the whole European Left in the 1960s. European socialist parties claimed that they possessed a better and more effective recipe than their opponents to run capitalism and to modernise the country. Especially in those countries where the image of the Right was associated with a traditional and anachronistic ruling class, unable to make the most of the technological revolution under way, the Left met few obstacles in taking over the issue of modernity and electorally capitalising on it.[22] This was not, however, the case with the French Left. Undoubtedly de Gaulle, by performing the role of a technocratic political force in France which elsewhere was played by the Left, deprived the French socialists and communists of the flag of modernity.[23] The opposite was very much the case with the British Labour Party and also, in some respects, the Italian socialists.

Talk of modernisation pervaded both British Labour Party and PSI discourse throughout the decade and was closely linked to a reappraisal of socialism by both political forces. Modernisation was the distinctive theme that would characterise Wilson's leadership. Wilson's policies were presented as nothing other than the 'reaffirmation of socialism's traditional moral and political arguments in ultra-modern terms'.[24] British socialism meant 'an attack on the complacency, on the stagnation, on the Edwardian nostalgia which seemed to underlie the attitudes and postures of the Macmillan government'.[25] Labour based its electoral campaign in 1964 on the powerful slogan of 'thirteen wasted years': the conservative administration, it was argued, had been one of missed opportunity; only by replacing it with a Labour one, would a New Britain have any chance of developing.[26] Unlike de Gaulle in France, the Conservatives in Great Britain were an easy target for Labour accusations of massive incompetence, lack of foresight and decrepitude. The Edwardian style which most of its prominent members were said to exhibit turned out to be a serious liability in years when modernity was the key word in any political discourse which was to be successful and electorally profitable.[27] Relative national decline was increasingly linked to the failure of the aristocratic Conservatives to fully employ the talents of new social groups.[28]

In quite similar terms, the Italian socialists claimed to be the 'holder of the card of modernity'.[29] As Guiducci wrote to Nenni, the country seemed suffocated and unsatisfied, people expected some degree of dynamism after many years of the 'status quo'. The growth of new modern managerial strata, the shift of manual workers and peasants towards more complex and advanced occupations, the expansion of new and freer forms of consumption and newly emerging attitudes, the pressures exerted by the young towards a more technological advanced and modern society, all reflected a dynamic society. To fully recognise the growing tensions which pervaded society, was to 'take sides with the majority of the country'. The Right, as Guiducci argued, had given life to a fictitious image of dynamism with the so-called economic miracle. The socialists' response should be a distinct and accelerated development inspired by socialists' ideas and programmes, a socialist New Deal.[30] The neo-capitalist solution was incapable of solving the problems of democratic participation which modern society posed. Socialism was the only solution capable of providing the whole of civil society, which still remained subordinated and exploited, and all workers from manual workers to technicians, 'with a global alternative which would efficiently and democratically solve the problems inherent in a *modern*,[31] free and egalitarian world'.[32]

The socio-economic problems which affected Italy and Britain at the turn of the decade and which will be addressed in more depth later had elements in common. To start with, by the end of the 1950s both countries suffered from an imbalance between public and private expenditure; private prosperity flourished during the entire 1950s at the expense of public structures and resulted in totally inadequate hospitals, schools, housing and public transport. In Italy, in particular, the imbalance between private and public consumption came to constitute an issue of major concern which no political party could ignore. Secondly, in both countries economically depressed areas existed, in the South in Italy and the North in Britain, two areas which needed a substantial intervention by the state in the form of state-assisted industrialisation in the former case and measures of revitalisation in the latter. Lastly, both British and Italian economic structures urgently needed modernisation. The declining productivity rates of British industry and the patchy and 'distorted' development of the Italian industrial infrastructure made a new and firmer managing of the economy in terms of central planning, the adoption of newly developed technologies, and the creation of the preconditions for a modern economy to develop – an improved educational system and expanded investments in scientific research – an urgent necessity. Both Labour and the Italian socialists presented themselves in these years as the only parties capable of carrying out the scientific revolution their individual countries needed.

The 'white heat of scientific revolution' and Labour's commitment to Britain's transformation through science and technology were, in fact, the main themes of Wilson's campaign in 1964. Socialism had to be harnessed to science and science to socialism, as Wilson said in his famous 1963 speech in Scarborough. Britain was living through a period of rapid scientific change and only by mobilising all the resources of science available to the country could the most be made of the scientific revolution already under way.[33]

The link between socialism and science was also a distinctive theme of the Italian socialists. Their call for the modernisation of the country in fact went hand in hand with a set of policies designed to promote scientific research and technological advancement in Italy. The degree of emphasis attached to science contrasted with Labour's policies; although the problems the two countries faced were essentially similar, the parties certainly had different priorities. What should not be forgotten is that while Italy was in the middle of the 'economic miracle' years, these were the years when the first signs of Britain's decline were perceived. This meant that while Labour's major concern was with the revitalisation of the economy, the Italian socialists took it for granted that expansion, even though undirected, would continue and, consequently, concentrated on social objectives. While for Labour modernisation would be technology-led, for the PSI it would occur primarily by establishing educational and economic infrastructures and a welfare state.

Given some differences in tone, it is nonetheless the case that the link between science and socialism – in so far as science was seen as an agent of social transformation – was present in the Italian socialists' discourse. In the mid-1950s the state of scientific research in Italy was rather bleak. Applied research was seriously underdeveloped: if the technological level of Italian industry was not severely backward it was only due to the importing of technology, both in terms of equipment and know-how, which had taken place since the end of the war. As Carlo Arnaudi, a scientist who performed a vital role in sensitising the PSI on the question of science and who was, in fact, to become the minister in charge of scientific research after the formation of the first centre–left government,[34] put it, it is clear that a country which wanted to assure itself a 'dignified place' among the other nations, and long-term prosperity for its population, could not rely for ever on importing from abroad new techniques and scientific research but instead had to make some effort itself in order to develop independent scientific research and the study of new technologies.[35]

Research could not be left to private initiative: the private sector tended to adopt a short-term perspective and was much more likely to invest money in advertising than in scientific research.[36] The promotion of scientific research was an area where the state should play a determinant role.[37]

The first months of the Wilson administration and the first steps taken by the centre–left government in Italy were to confirm the great importance which both Labour and the PSI attached to science. Immediately after the establishment of the Labour government, the Ministry of Science set up by Conservatives in 1959 was restructured and called the Ministry of State for the Support and Encouragement of Science; of even greater symbolic significance was that C. P. Snow, the author of the famous *The Two Cultures*,[38] was appointed to it. A greater number of scientists were given a wider role as scientific advisers to the government and the various ministries, while a new Ministry of Technology was also created.[39] Similarly in Italy, Carlo Arnaudi was appointed minister without portfolio for scientific research[40] of the newly established centre–left Moro government of December 1963, a recognition of the concern that socialists had long displayed over science.[41] A new Ministry for Scientific and Technological Research, with the objective of stimulating research activities and having a function of co-ordination both among domestic and international centres of scientific research, was eventually set up in February 1964.[42]

Towards a government-oriented, pragmatic, 'technocratic' Left

The previous discussion aimed at illustrating the extent to which automation furnished the Italian Socialist Party and Labour with a new rationale for the reassertion of a genuine third way towards socialism which differed from centre-right Keynesian Socialism. Yet, third way claims apart, we also saw how both the British Labour Party and the Italian socialists aimed at presenting themselves in their respective countries as newly reformed political parties in a position to put forward a credible candidature as authentic modernisers. In spite of their 'socialist' rhetoric and long-term commitment to the goal of a socialist society, they both assumed in those years increasingly pronounced features of a government-oriented, pragmatic, technocratic Left: the concern with competence and efficiency, combined with a pronounced electoral orientation, were to characterise both parties' development up to their return to power.

The recognition of the greater complexity of the socio-economic infrastructure meant an unprecedented concern with competence within political parties, a trend which applied both to Labour and the Italian socialists. From early in the 1950s much emphasis was put on providing the party with centres for socio-economic studies or groups of sympathetic technicians and specialists whom it could rely on for advice.

One of the main criticisms which had followed the Attlee government in 1945 was the lack of preparation of his ministries and of their staff. This had not only meant the inability of the Labour cabinet to make any headway against 'private oligopolists'[43] but had also considerably diminished its potential effectiveness: 'The last Labour government', Crossman wrote, 'was unable to plan largely because it did not know what was going on in the economy.'[44] Crucial to the success of a future Labour Cabinet would be to provide itself with 'eyes and ears' and expand the number of economists and statisticians available to the government in the form of a central fact-finding bureau responsible directly to the prime minister.[45] Labour's years in opposition up to 1964 were, in fact, characterised by increasing co-operation with reliable and sympathetic experts as well as according much importance to research, which the Labour Research Department itself produced.[46]

A similar concern with technical preparation was also displayed by the Italian socialists. The closer the party got to power, the more emphasis was put on the urgent need for the party to insure adequate means for their political action to be not 'the result of improvisation' but of reflection.[47] It was in these years that groups like the Turati circle were founded on the model of the British Fabian society or the French Jean Moulin centre. The function of the Turati circle was to gather together specialists and experts from different fields; this was regarded by intellectuals like Guiducci as an essential prerequisite for the success of the 'New Deal' course undertaken by the PSI and its involvement in government.

In line with the new emphasis placed on competency, great importance came to be accorded to efficiency. Equality, a concept which had always played a key role in left-wing parties' policies, gave way to efficiency-related considerations. This was, for example, reflected in the two parties' positions in relation to nationalisation which will be further discussed later: public ownership ceased to be an 'at-all-costs-moral-principle' to cling to as a dogma, but was linked instead to efficiency arguments.[48] Two other areas should be mentioned where the new concern with efficiency was evident. First, affluence and private consumerism: initially morally condemned as corrupting the most genuine values of society, consumerism now came under attack due to its disruptive effects on balanced economic growth. Second, education: this is, indeed, the field where the shift in perspective which took place at the turn of the 1950s from 'equality of opportunity' discourses to 'economic efficiency' and national competitiveness justifications was most apparent.

Since the very early post-war years education had been an issue of major concern for both the Labour Party and the Italian Socialist Party. The elitist, class-ridden school system that both Great Britain and Italy possessed in the early 1950s came under severe attack: educational opportunities needed to be expanded as a matter of civil rights and greater social justice.[49] There was a need in both countries for higher public spending in school building and staff recruitment. Furthermore, it was claimed, if real equality of opportunity was to be achieved, a thoroughgoing transformation of the system itself had to be carried out to take on its inherent hierarchical and class character in both Britain and Italy. Comprehensive schooling was endorsed generally by every Western European socialist party in those years as a precondition for working-class advancement through education.[50] The end of the tripartite system and the establishment of the comprehensive school, compulsory until 16, in Great Britain, and the merging of the various existing secondary schools into one compulsory junior comprehensive school (*scuola media unica*) for all until 14 in Italy, were the measures advanced respectively by Labour and the Italian Socialist Party in their aim to create a fairer school system and secure real social mobility.

The demand for the replacement of the tripartite system with a comprehensive system was one of the priorities of the centre–right revisionists' political agenda, and hence one of the most prominent concerns of the Labour Party itself throughout the 1950s. As we saw previously, in the prosperous and generous 'Welfarism' of the mid-1950s, centre–right revisionists claimed that capitalism had changed out of recognition, a new system, 'something in between, having taken its place'.[51] Confronted with the new scenario of 'social capitalism',[52] it was argued that those inequalities still existing were far more a matter of redistribution of resources than the result of inherent contradictions of the system which might be solved by structural changes. The final attainment of a socialist society was to be achieved, in other words, by a set of redistributive measures, hence the label of 'redistributive socialists'. Taxation was certainly the major redistributive tool Labour would rely on. Second in importance came the reform of an educational system widely regarded as a source of major inequalities. Education was, in fact, an area where the typical revisionist discourse that class consciousness and social discontent derived from factors other than income differences, such as differences in status, was quite relevant.[53]

A similar notion of education, namely the idea that pupils should not be segregated at an early age in educational institutions which only perpetuated their class conditions, was at the root of the battle engaged by the Italian socialists for the abolition of the 'three-stream' system of secondary education inherited from fascism and the establishment of a junior comprehensive school compulsory for all until 14.[54]

However, 'equality of opportunity' discourses were not to remain the only rationale behind education reform. In contrast, from the late 1950s onwards a new concept of education emerged, more in tune with the kind of technocratic efficiency-minded parties both Labour and the PSI would become under the lead respectively of the centre–left technocratic group and the socialists' autonomists. Beyond its traditional perception as a liberalising process or 'social service', and following the growing awareness of the scientific revolution which marked those years, education came to be perceived as a form of 'investment'.[55] As stated in *Learning to Live* (1958), the desire for widespread education had always been one of the great impulses in the minds of socialists. Now, to other compelling arguments for educational progress, there was added the 'challenge of a scientific age'.[56]

The challenge that the scale of technological development in the post-war years posed to any country resulted, in other words, in a far-reaching change of perspective in addressing educational matters. Labour education reform (secondary education to be comprehensive and tertiary education to be expanded), although still justified on the basis of the greater educational opportunities it would produce, from the late 1950s onwards came to be conceived as the prior condition for, as Gregory Elliot put it, a 'skilled workforce for employment in a modern economy' rather than a 'mannered elite for the administration of an Empire'.[57] The condemnation of public schools was no longer based on the perpetuation of British 'stratification and class-consciousness'[58] which it entailed, but rather to the inadequate selection of elites which these schools produced. The 'amateurism' that the 'British decline' literature mentioned in the previous chapter denounced as one of the determining factors of diminished British competitiveness in relation to its European counterparts was mainly identified with public school pupils. Public schools, as Crosland puts it, with their emphasis on 'manners and "character"', on the all-rounder and the amateur, on the insular, the orthodox and the traditional' failed to generate the 'right type of leadership for a democratic, scientific, welfare world' open to innovations and professionally and technically prepared.[59]

Thus a revolution in the attitude to education at all levels was needed. In the first place it was seen as most urgent to overcome the grave shortage of engineers and technicians. Labour documents such as *Twelve Wasted Years, Signposts for the Sixties* or the election manifestos themselves of 1959 and 1964 all advocated a greater vocational orientation at secondary school level as well as higher expenditure on universities. British investment in people, the election manifesto of 1964 argued, was still 'tragically inadequate'.[60] Particularly in the area of science, a greater number of scholarships and improved financial support were needed. In spite of the growing proportion of science students, the increasingly high demand for trained scientists and engineers remained at 'an insatiable level' during these years.[61] Comparisons with other countries were indeed alarming. In proportion to population, the United States produced two-and-a-half times, and the USSR five times, as many scientists as Great Britain.[62]

Similarly in Italy, the battle for the abolition of Latin from the junior secondary school (*scuola media*) was no longer justified exclusively on the basis of its discriminatory nature and inconsistency with equality of opportunity, but rather on the basis of the need for a more modern and scientific education as opposed to the humanistic tradition which had long prevailed in Italian culture.[63] Opposition to the private sector was no longer based solely on the breach it represented with the essential principles of a secular state but, once the school system was recognised as the key element of any planned economy, on the basis of the need for the state to exert full control over it.[64] Access to university from technical college, a measure which became law in 1961, was now no longer seen just as a major step to fight class discrimination and segregation and help social mobility, but instead as a measure crucial to the necessary expansion of the university population, which was well below that of other nations.[65]

Public ownership gets reinvented

Since their acceptance of parliamentary gradualist means, socialist parties have been caught in this paradox whereby their success is strictly related to the prosperity of capitalism, which, in theory, they are committed to replace. As Donald Sassoon put it, 'socialists faced an unavoidable paradox: in order to pay for social welfare, it was imperative that the market be made as efficient as possible; to follow socialists' policies, it was essential to be pro-capitalist'.[66] This was certainly the case of Labour and the Italian Socialist Party. While they held on to the vision of a socialist society, the economic policies they developed to return to power were policies which were, above all, aimed at a sustained and balanced growth.

The concern with expansion and productivity rates is well reflected in the economic policies that the two parties advanced at this stage. In spite of the centrality attached to traditional instruments of the Left and an apparent continuity with the past, public ownership and planning were now both conceived in a very different way, both in the form they would take and the justifications given.

Labour and the PSI did remain committed to common ownership as a question of principle, a 'totem of party ritual'.[67] As Harold Wilson argued in commenting on the attempt by Gaitskell in 1959 to ditch Clause Four from the constitution of the party, tampering with Clause Four was like denying the authority of Genesis: 'we were being asked to take the Genesis out of the Bible. You don't have to be a fundamentalist to say that the Genesis is part of the Bible'.[68] After Gaitskell's defeat, no other attempt was made until the successful one by Tony Blair in 1995. The theoretical commitment of the party to nationalise all means of production remained in place for more than thirty years and would continue to disturb the sleep of moderate members of the party in the mould of Crosland; similarly, the acceptance of the Italian Socialist Party of the mixed economy was tempered by numerous statements which stressed the long-term goal of a fully planned economy.[69]

In practice, however, both parties accepted the mixed economy and adopted, in their documents or election manifestos, a far more pragmatic approach. As we saw in the previous chapter, in late 1956 Italian socialists abandoned a catastrophist vision of capitalism and the Third International thesis stating the inevitability of its collapse. From the mid-1950s onwards a serious reappraisal of the socio-economic trends at work and of neo-capitalism was carried out. This challenged the strategy and the means which the party had so far relied upon for its 'way to socialism'. The instrument of common ownership itself was thoroughly reconsidered. Similar to the recognition made in Labour circles of the limitations of state capitalism, which followed the end of the Attlee government in 1951, Italian socialists began to ask themselves to what extent the property of industrial assets by the state, in the form it had taken place so far, represented a step towards socialism. As Vittorio Foa wrote in 1956 after the establishment of the Ministry of State Shareholding (*Ministero delle Partecipazioni Statali* – a ministry in charge of the co-ordination of giant state enterprises such as IRI and ENI), the history of public intervention in Italy, from IRI onwards, had long been a history of support and subsidy to private interests.[70] The minimal change that nationalisation had meant in terms of workers' participation and power relationships was also fully accepted.[71]

A reconsideration of nationalisation was a distinctive feature of both the revisionist Left, alias the group around Panzieri, Libertini and Foa, and of the autonomists. Nevertheless, while the former never questioned the validity of the instrument itself and confined themselves to elaborating a new formula for nationalisation which entailed a real shift in terms of power relationships and a greater extent of control by the workers (the issue of workers' democracy will be dealt with later), the autonomists pursued a revisionist course similar to others in Europe which meant a gradual distancing from it.

The arguments which lay behind the autonomist-led PSI's reappraisal of nationalisation bear a considerable resemblance to the considerations which prompted Labour and other social-democratic parties like the SPD or the SFIO's reconsideration of nationalisation. To start with, it was a question of image. Widespread hostility to nationalisation was a problem which particularly affected the Labour Party. The numerous surveys which Labour commissioned following the three electoral defeats in succession of the 1950s made a strong case for watering down the issue of common ownership.[72] It was argued, specifically in the centre–right revisionist circles, the association of the party with large-scale increases in public ownership was extremely unpopular with the majority of the electorate.[73] Nationalisation, in other words, had become an 'unfavourable issue' which the party had better get rid of. Hence Gaitskell's ineffectual attempt to revise Clause Four, a symbolic gesture whose rationale had much more to do with image-related considerations than any real constraint it ever represented in the formulation of pragmatic and moderate policies – as the history of the party since its origins well demonstrates. Similarly, Italian socialists, it was argued, could not ignore the lack of appeal that nationalisation now had among ordinary people. As Venerio Cattani wrote in *Mondo Operaio*, nationalisations had lost much of the popularity which they had enjoyed after the end of the war. Common ownership was associated in the popular imagination with the deprivation of liberty of the USSR and the Eastern bloc or with the bureaucracy and the inefficiency of the industries nationalised under fascism. Discrediting nationalisation was reflected, Cattani went on, by the few references to it in party programmes, including those of the Left, compared with the years immediately after the end of the war (the years of the Committees of National Liberation – *Comitati di Liberazione Nazionale*).[74]

Popularity apart, however, it was the new socio-economic conditions which Italian socialists, as well as their European counterparts, were confronted with in the post-war years which required an overall reappraisal of nationalisation. The profound changes that the social structure had undergone could no longer be ignored; the schematic dichotomy of bourgeoisie/proletariat allegedly produced by the industrial revolution was giving way to a far more complex social structure. As Giolitti wrote, this made the case for public ownership weaker and called for some reconsideration, if the shifting of property from private to public hands was to make some sense.[75] The organisational structure, the function and role of individual public enterprises could not be 'ideologically' determined but had to be strictly related to the nature of the economic activities they were required to carry out (for example, a distinction was made between public utilities and public enterprises operating in strategic sectors).[76]

An equally pragmatic approach was demonstrated by the Labour Party. Centre–left technocratic socialists placed a greater emphasis on the instrument of public ownership compared with intellectuals like Crosland; yet, the time for an ethical or moral approach had gone for good. The increased importance attached to public ownership by this group compared with centre–right revisionists was only due to the fact that the economic circumstances which lay behind centre–right revisionist arguments had partly disappeared (for example sustained economic growth) and there was now a stronger case than before for greater structural state intervention in terms of planning and public control in the British economy. Public ownership remained something to be approached in a flexible and pragmatic way. As Wilson wrote in 1963, nationalisation was not a question to be 'dogmatic and doctrinaire' about.[77]

The endorsement by both parties of a more flexible attitude towards public ownership resulted in a gradual reduction of the number of candidates for outright nationalisation. In 1962 the only industry, for which the PSI urged nationalisation was the electricity industry and after this was carried out later in the same year, no further proposals were put forward.[78]

Like the Italian socialists, the list of industries which Labour policy documents indicated in those years for nationalisation got smaller and smaller. While *Challenge to Britain* (1953) had listed mining-machinery, aircraft and land as candidates for some form of public ownership, *Industry and Society* made no reference to these industries at all and apart from steel and road haulage advocated nothing specific. Even after the gradual ascendancy of the centre–left group to the theoretical leadership of the party, the list of candidates for outright nationalisation remained confined to steel and road haulage with the sole addition in 1961 of building land.[79]

The more pragmatic approach which both parties adopted and the *de facto* acceptance of the mixed economy they demonstrated not only resulted in the shrinking of the list of industries for which nationalisation was advocated, but it was also recognised that nationalisation was not the only means by which the state could exert strong control over the economy.

New forms which public ownership could take, as opposed to outright nationalisation, were formulated. Competitive public enterprise and state shareholding were the two most significant proposals which Labour put forward in these years and which were to be given increasingly great importance as the years went by. The principle of competitive public enterprise made its first appearance in the Labour policy document *Labour Believes in Britain* (1949). This was the system whereby the state would acquire direct control of individual firms within given industries rather than nationalising the whole industry. While in 1949 the idea was to be applied only to the chemical industry, it was later considered also for key machine-tool firms (*Challenge to Britain* [1953]).[80] Although a little understated in the election manifesto of 1959,[81] from 1961 onwards competitive public enterprise, with functions to revitalise and modernise existing industries which were in decline or backward (such as machine tools)[82] or promote the establishment of as many new industries as possible (such as electronics, atomic energy, aeronautics), became a key issue in any Labour economic policy document.[83]

The second form of public ownership other than nationalisation which was given primary importance was state shareholding. While *Challenge to Britain* already contained a general reference to the idea of the state taking a 'controlling interest in existing enterprises'[84] to be applied to vital firms in the mining machinery industry, the party document which made a real breakthrough in this regard was *Industry and Society* (1957).[85]

The community-shareholding principle was an idea which was particularly popular with centre–right revisionists. Both Gaitskell and Crosland paid considerable attention to it in, respectively, *Socialism and Nationalisation*[86] and *The Future of Socialism*.[87] This largely explains the great importance which was initially attached to state shareholding as a means of redistribution as opposed to its use as an instrument for revitalising the economy and planning.[88]

It was only under the theoretical hegemony of centre–left technocratic socialists that, in line with the greater emphasis attached to planning measures, the function of state shareholding shifted from that of redistribution to that of a means of controlling the economy. The purchase of equity shares, which would result from the concession of financing, would allow the state not only to rescue key industries but also to establish some influence over some specific industries and their economic policies.[89] It is in those years that the Ministry of State Shareholding in Italy (*Ministero delle Partecipazioni Statali*), which will be discussed later, began to be regarded as a model in Great Britain.[90]

State shareholding and competitive public enterprise were also issues of great debate within the Italian Socialist Party in the same period. Far from being new ideas, they were forms of state intervention which Italy had long known.

In the years considered here Italy possessed one of the largest public sectors in Western Europe. However, with the exception of a few fully nationalised industries (railways and airline), the Italian public sector was mainly constituted by state shareholdings organised in public holdings such as IRI and ENI.[91] The question Italian socialists were confronted with was not whether the institution of state shareholding and mixed enterprises could be a valid alternative for the future, but how to improve an already long-established system.[92] Socialists, in the final analysis, accepted the idea of state shareholding as a form of state control; nevertheless, a reorganisation of the whole system of state shareholding was advocated. To start with, some rationalisation was urged. State shareholding was extremely heterogeneous and had little coherence. A considerable number of state shareholdings had been the result of rescues of loss-making industries, rather than *a priori* determined economic policy, and needed to be reconsidered.[93] The state, it was argued, should get rid of minority shareholding, as well as shareholding in those sectors which were not regarded as crucial areas of intervention. It should, moreover, attempt to reorganise, as any private industry would do in the same situation, its shareholding so as to create homogenous and vertically-organised holdings. Only the formation of holdings of this type, that is a holding gathering together all the state shareholding in the cement, building and motorways industries, would provide the state with a powerful means of intervention and direction of the economy, and would put it in a position to stand up to the strength of monopolies.[94]

Thus both parties began to display at this stage a far more flexible approach to public ownership for which alternatives to outright nationalisation were devised. A greater pragmatism is also apparent when looking at the cases in which the instrument of public ownership was still considered valid and necessary: all the criteria outlined were, in fact, related to economic and efficiency considerations with no hint of equal power or redistribution arguments.

Common ownership was regarded as essential to modernisation: this meant revitalisation of the economy, higher production and greater efficiency in the case of Labour, and balanced economic growth – the end of a dual economy and industrialising the South – in the case of the PSI. If we look at the six reasons listed in *Twelve Wasted Years* supporting the case for re-nationalisation of the steel industry, they are all justifications related to the economy: it argued, 'public control without public ownership had failed'. The Board had demonstrated its inability to enforce its recommendations, such as an increase in extra sheet steel capacity, and the industry had had a 'dismal performance' and 'patchwork growth'.[95] No other option but re-nationalisation was left. The technical and technological failings of the industry could only be remedied if there was a 'change in ownership and a change in management'.[96] A similar connection between nationalisation and economic justifications also characterised the programmes of the Italian socialists. The arguments for nationalisation of the energy industry had very little to do with ideology: state control of the industry would enable it to fix prices, programme power resources on a national scale and make investments where they were most needed, such as the developing areas in the South. Last but not least, the efficiency factor was advocated. The existence of a monopoly held by a few groups in the industry had meant lack of investment, low productivity and excessive profits, and uneconomic policies which only management by a united national industry could avoid.[97]

Public enterprise and an extension of direct control on the economy by the state were of crucial importance as an essential tool for effective planning. As Italian socialists argued at the *Convegno delle Partecipazioni Statali* (Conference on State Shareholding) in 1959, 'Public enterprise has to be regarded as a functional means for the effective co-ordination *ex ante* of investments, without which a market economy would suffer and private initiative would stagnate'.[98] Similarly, the Labour Manifesto of 1964 declared that 'the public sector will make a vital contribution to the national plan'. In contrast to France (the only Western European country which, in the years immediately after the war, made some use of its large public sector for planning purposes) very little use had been made of the public sector by the Attlee government for any serious planning of the economy. Scholars have frequently questioned the point of such an extension of public control in those years, given that Labour at the time seemed not to know what to do with it.[99] This was mainly due to the great autonomy which nationalised industries, organised according to the Morrisonian public corporation model, were given. However, after the mid-1950s, when planning began to assert itself in the Labour Party political agenda, an increasingly great emphasis was attached to public enterprise as an instrument of planning.[100]

The revival of planning

Planning, together with public ownership, was another key instrument central to Labour and the Italian socialists' economic policies over these years. Labour won the elections of 1964 with planning as the crucial element of any future economic policy. In fact, it is possible to talk of a sort of, if not conversion, at least re-conversion as far as the Labour Party was concerned. As we saw in the previous chapter, the centre–right revisionists' theoretical hegemony which marked Labour history during the 1950s meant that little importance was attached to planning until the end of the decade. As with public ownership, planning, the other central feature of technocratic socialism, was regarded as no longer relevant to socialist objectives. It was only after 1960 that, as a result of the assertion of the centre–left technocratic socialists' theoretical hegemony, the arguments of those who had long advocated the insufficiency of market mechanisms in allocating resources and, above all, the inability of macroeconomic management to reverse the economic decline under way and deal with the structural weaknesses of the British economy, made real ground in Labour policies.[101] In contrast to the optimism displayed by centre–right revisionists, talk of 'deficiencies and inadequacies'[102] and 'failures'[103] of private enterprise now dominated Labour statements. As documents like *Labour in the Sixties* read, socialist beliefs had been vindicated in the 1960s, since it was increasingly clear that the new post-war capitalism, if not directed, was creating 'its own insuperable problems'. If democracy was to survive, it 'must plan its resources for the common good'.[104] Planning was to become the linchpin idea of the party and was increasingly regarded as the 'magic' recipe, far more than public ownership, for the structural problems from which Britain's economy suffered.

Planning measures and a greater degree of state regulation would aim, to start with, at achieving 'a sustained and purposive economic expansion'.[105] This meant 'mobilising the resources of technology under a National Plan',[106] industrial policies securing enough investments in new equipment, training and research in those sectors of the British economy crucial to the nation's competitiveness; a greater rationalisation of the industrial sector through state assisted mergers (Industrial Reorganisation Corporation [IRC]) and larger investments in higher and technical education.[107] Last but not least, policies for retraining and resettlement to catch up with technological change and to meet the urgent need for development of new skills and new techniques were needed.[108]

The 'Tories mismanagement of economy', let alone their 'doctrinaire objection to direct controls', as *Twelve Wasted Years* put it, had not only entailed slow economic growth but also *lopsided* growth.[109] The aim of planning would, therefore, also be to put an end to a set of 'imbalances' which would seriously challenge future growth if not immediately addressed. First, the so-called contrast between 'public squalor and private affluence', in Galbraith's well-known expression, rephrased in *Signposts for the Sixties* as the contrast 'between starved community services and extravagant consumption', had to be tackled.[110] Secondly, there was the question of the 'Two Nations': the increasingly large gap between a prosperous South and a declining North.[111]

The theme of planning re-emerged as central in the ranks of the PSI in 1955 in the wake of the launch of the Vanoni Plan. This represented a completely new approach to the question of Italian economic development and its notorious 'imbalances': intended to cover the decade 1955–64, its aim was to encourage growth while ensuring government control on economic priorities and its intervention to correct distortions. As Roggi puts it, 'the Vanoni Plan remains one of the most quoted and at the same time least realised documents in the post-war years'. Nevertheless, the cultural impact it had was considerable,[112] particularly for the PSI. From the late 1950s onwards, similarly to Labour, Italian socialists came to attach an increasingly great importance to planning, as opposed to their previous almost sole concern with nationalisation. This was reflected in the emphasis put on it in the PSI congresses in Naples (1959), Milan (1961) and Rome (1963).[113] Planning was to be the key element for nationalisation or any other form of state intervention in the economy to be effective.[114]

In January 1962 the economic department of the PSI, chaired by Lombardi and Giolitti, presented an economic programme to the party's executive and the Central Committee which was unanimously accepted. This programme stated as the major objective of the party 'a planning policy for a balanced economic development' which, in turn, included 'structural reforms in some key sectors of the present capitalist system'.[115] Of greater significance, given the importance of alliances in a political system like the Italian one, planning not only furnished Italian socialists with new policies for the new post-1956 course undertaken, but it also represented a terrain of convergence with the political parties which, in a few years time, were to take part in the first centre–left government. These were the Christian Democrats and the Republican Party which came around to the question of planning at almost the same time and recognised the need for greater direct control of the economy by the state.

The economic miracle that Italy experienced in the late 1950s, together with a new prosperity, also produced a number of dramatic imbalances. To start with, there was the problem of relatively disadvantaged areas; the spurt which the advanced Northern sector experienced further enlarged the historical gap between North and South.[116] Italy's economic structure not only suffered from so-called 'territorial dualism' but also from profound sectorial imbalances: in contrast to extremely dynamic and advanced industries like those in the so-called industrial triangle, other sectors like agriculture and retailing persisted in their backwardness and low productivity rates. Finally, there was the gap between private prosperity and social consumption. State intervention had been grossly inadequate in the most essential social services: while there had been a growth in demand for consumer products typical of high income levels such as luxurious flats, cars and household electric appliances, other consumer products far more essential to guarantee minimum standards of living remained below the per capita level of most West European advanced countries.[117]

Both in Great Britain and Italy, by means of planning and some extension of the public sector, the state was called on to restore the primacy of the community's interests over the private ones; yet if the areas where the state was urged to intervene were the same (deprived areas, imbalance between private and public consumption, and so on), the order of priorities was different. While the British economy was plunged into a phase of decline, Italy was still going through the 'economic miracle years' with its economy still expanding. This meant that while the key aim of Labour planning was economic revival, Italian socialists, even if wrongly, assumed that the expansion of the economy would continue, and thus concentrated on social objectives. In other words, while in Great Britain the rediscovery of planning was closely related to faltering economic growth, as far as Italy was concerned it was more a question of redirecting growth towards certain sectors rather than others.

Three documents can be considered the theoretical and empirical bases of Italian planning: La Malfa's '*Nota aggiuntiva*' – additional note – to the 'General Report on the Economic Situation of the Country in 1961' (1962),[118] the Giolitti Plan (1965) and the Pieraccini Plan (1966–70). The statement of what were to be the main objectives of planning remained virtually unchanged in all of them: the achievement of full employment, the elimination of both sectorial imbalances between industry and agriculture and regional differences, a greater balance between private and public consumption.[119] In Giolitti's words, Italian planning was to be aimed at 'an increase in civilisation' far more than an increase in production and national income.[120]

In line with the lack of either an ideological or ethical approach from the Italian socialists or Labour concerning nationalisation, planning measures were justified solely on the basis of efficiency-related considerations. When first included in European socialist parties' policies in the 1930s, planning entailed both a technocratic and an ethical dimension. Planning would ensure a more efficient use of resources while at the same time it would be a means of attaining socialist objectives of a non-economic kind. By diminishing or replacing the market system, planning was, in fact, thought to promote a sense of common purpose and solidarity within society as opposed to competitive individualism and selfishness. The Labour Bevanite Left's advocacy of planning was, for example, pervaded with ethical considerations. Planning was regarded as a valuable means of converting society to socialist attitudes and transforming it into a 'more civilised and less acquisitive' one.[121]

Under the dominance of centre–left technocratic socialists within Labour and the autonomists in the PSI all ethical justifications were to disappear, giving way instead to a sole concern with efficiency. In this regard the two parties' attitudes towards consumption was very emblematic.

Both Great Britain and Italy respectively, in the climate of Macmillan's 'you've never had it so good' and on the wave of the 'economic miracle', came to enjoy a prosperity unknown before. Durable goods, previously the monopoly of the middle classes, were increasingly within the reach of everyone. Famous films like *Il sorpasso* (1962 – Dino Risi) or *Boom* (1963 – Vittorio De Sica) well reflected the new climate which even countries like Italy experienced, even though it ranked low compared to more 'affluent' ones such as Britain.[122] As soon as signs of prosperity appeared, the attitude of many sections of the European Left was of moral reproach. The so-called 'artificial wants', mass consumerism and private prosperity, while accepted and welcomed by British Labour centre–right revisionists, if not only for electoral considerations,[123] were throughout the 1950s the object of severe criticism and moral condemnation by the Labour Left, both the Bevanites and the then emerging centre–left group. The American model of the affluent society, to which Conservative-led Britain seemed to aspire, was, as Thomas Balogh put it, 'a very unattractive prospect' with its 'spiritual insecurity, its lack of fulfilment, its neuroses and fears, its increasingly strident mass conditioning'; consumerism and the artificial stimulation of new needs would lead, in the long term, to 'growing spiritual poverty ... dissatisfaction ... guilt ... impatience and aggression'.[124] 'Get rich quick' values were regarded as an obstacle to 'the establishment of a real community'.[125] 'Selfish materialism' was something Labour should never conform to.[126]

Italian socialist intellectuals' position on the new consumerism was similar. Consumerism was regarded as a new and subtle form of alienation. An article which appeared in *Mondo Operaio* in 1958 argued that alienation, as described by Marx, had given way, in neo-capitalist societies, to far more subtle forms of alienation such as 'the alienation of consumption'; that is, the subjection of the collectivity to the hegemony of big businesses in determining what were to be their needs: 'it is no longer the needs which determine supply but *vice versa*'.[127] The cultural expression of the uneasiness of some sections of the Left with the affluent working class, a working class which seemed ambitious, devoid of values, corrupted by materialist sirens – like the one depicted in films such as *Room at the Top* or novels such as *Saturday Night and Sunday Morning* – was the rise of the angry cultural movements that began with John Osborne's famous *Look Back in Anger*.[128] The 'angry' generation expressed in films, theatrical pieces and books their contempt for such an embourgeoised working class. In this way the works of John Osborne, Alan Sillitoe or Arnold Wesker correspond to those by Italian authors such as Volponi, Mastronardi, Arbasino, and so on, or the 'angry one' (*arrabbiato*) *par excellence*, Luciano Bianciardi, with his famous *L'Integrazione* and *La Vita Agra*[129] (the title, 'the bitter life', was deliberately opposed to Fellini's *La Dolce Vita*). In all of them the common theme was anger against any form of 'integration', embourgeoisement and the lack of 'great causes' left to fight for.

As argued earlier, from the late 1950s in both Britain and Italy a marked contrast had emerged between private prosperity and 'public squalor'. British 'public squalor' was not comparable in scale to the appalling conditions in which some areas in Italy, specifically the South, were plunged. Yet, given some differences in scale, the debate on the affluent society became, by the end of the decade, very vivid and heated in both countries. By the time private versus social consumption became a central issue in the political debate, following the lead of the centre–left technocratic group and the autonomists, Labour and the Italian socialists were talking a different language. Any moral approach faded away to make way for economic arguments. Moral criticism apart, private consumption was criticised because of its pernicious effects on the economy. As Wilson wrote in *A Four Year Plan*, the 'frivolous and unproductive' investments of affluent society meant an ever-diminishing share of national income going to fixed investments and a lack of expenditure in those areas crucial to competitiveness and future expansion.[130]

It is indisputable that the publication of the much-quoted *The Affluent Society* (1958)[131] by John Galbraith provided European left-wing parties with new and far more powerful arguments against private consumption than those previously used. As is well known, the main argument advanced by the American economist was that Western affluent mixed economies had not only long displayed their inability to achieve a balanced allocation of resources but were also doomed to sacrifice communal welfare and the requirements of future growth. In spite of the increasingly apparent affluence and prosperity their citizens had experienced in the last ten years, capitalist countries were, in fact, jeopardising their long-term expansion and productivity rates.

It should not be forgotten that these were also the years in which the 'Soviet challenge' argument made its appearance: the Cold War, it was argued, had moved from the military to the economic sphere. In the face of a thriving Soviet economy, whose strength and ability to keep pace with technological change could only be explained by its adoption of planning and common ownership, it would not take long for the capitalist world to capitulate under the weight of its own contradictions.[132] 'In terms of military power, of industrial development, of technological advance, of mass literacy, and, eventually, mass consumption too', Crossman wrote in *Labour in the Affluent Society* (1960), 'the planned Socialist economy, as exemplified in the Communist states', was proving 'its capacity to outpace and overtake the wealthy and comfortable Western economies'.[133] Two factors in particular explained the success of socialist economies: to start with, the capacity of planned economies to bring inflation under control by planned income distribution; secondly, 'the economic use of resources' which planned economies were capable of, as opposed to 'the wastefulness of the artificially induced obsolescence which is the motive force' of affluent societies in the West.[134] Planned economies were able to allocate national resources according to a system of priorities, allotting so much to producer goods, so much to consumer goods, so much to health, education, defence so as to secure constantly increasing growth.

Galbraith's thesis, otherwise referred to in Italy as 'Galbraith's paradox'[135] also made considerable headway in the Italian socialists' debate; as was the case with Labour, it helped to shift the party's condemnation of consumerism from moral and ideological criteria to far more pragmatic terms, as becomes evident from considering the party's press in the years from 1960 up to the PSI's return to power.[136] The hidden persuasion of advertising came, for example, from the early 1960s onwards to be no longer criticised for its corrupting effects on working-class minds, but rather as a 'waste of money'[137] and irrational use of resources. As Fuà and Sylos Labini stated in *Idee per la Programmazione Economica*, the money spent in advertising in the struggle by individual companies to attract as many consumers as possible meant an increase in production costs which, in turn, pushed up the costs of distribution.[138] A similar argument was also developed in Labour documents such as *Twelve Wasted Years*: 'Competitive advertising often simply cancels itself out with no possible advantage to either business or the community' with the only result a waste of money which could be invested in far more social expenses.[139] Indeed, the concern with some degree of consumer protection and regulation, which put advertising under some control and guaranteed an improvement in consumers' information,[140] remained an issue of increasing importance. However, crusading tones disappeared and arguments related to the economic rather than moral costs came decisively to the forefront.

Economics apart, electoral considerations also played an important role in toning down the condemnation of consumerism. As Giolitti wrote in 1968, 'criticism of the affluent society is not an adequate answer; on the contrary it is a wrong answer since it takes for granted what still has to be verified, namely that the working class agrees on the criticism of affluence and is prepared to renounce it'.[141] An intellectual 'luddite attitude' towards fridges, TVs and vacuum cleaners[142] was hence rather inadvisable: not only was it apt to alienate traditional working-class constituencies but it would also conflict with the efforts which parties like Labour or the Italian socialists were making in those years to expand their consensus among the middle classes and transform themselves, in the words of the famous German political scientist Otto Kircheimer, into 'catch-all' parties.

Towards a 'catch-all' party

Both the British Labour Party and the Italian socialists, simultaneously with other European counterparts, came to acquire from the mid-1950s a pronounced electoral orientation. Two characteristics which had long constituted their distinctiveness from bourgeois parties, namely a mass party nature and a working-class appeal, then began to weaken.

Western European socialist parties' membership consistently declined throughout the whole post-war period. Individual membership of the Labour Party increased to 1013022 in 1952. It then declined steadily until it reached 277000 in 1981.[143] As for the PSI, after a period (1949–53) in which party membership consistently recovered from the crisis of 1948, it started declining again after 1956: membership fell from 780000 in 1953 to 480000 in 1957, and after the split of the PSIUP in 1964, further declined to 446000; on the eve of unification with the PSDI in 1966 the party did not count more than 435000 members.[144]

Losses in membership, attendance at party meetings and reading of party newspapers were nothing other than various facets of the process which French intellectuals described as *dépolitisation*.[145] Greater and broader leisure possibilities were now available to a greater proportion of the population. The growing ownership of cars and TV sets entailed a considerable atomisation and privatisation of leisure time which significantly affected party membership rates. Workers, as the large body of studies on political behaviour which flourished in those years argued, although still tending to display a considerable loyalty to parties of their class on election day, showed much less commitment to these parties for the rest of the year.

However, it was also the attitude of the parties themselves and their clear intent to expand their electoral appeal at the expense of the long cultivated 'organic relation' with the working class which determined the gradual shift in the member/voter ratio.[146] In the 'end of ideology'[147] climate – a phenomenon which, although overestimated by contemporary commentators, entailed *de facto* a relatively more volatile electorate – flexibility and adaptability became crucial to any party.

While lightening their mass party nature, Western European socialist parties also divested themselves of a clear-cut working-class image. Far-reaching transformations in the social environment, namely the expansion of the middle class and the so-called 'embourgeoisement' of the working class, suggested a broadening of the electoral appeal, if the new economic and social circumstances produced by the 'golden years' of capitalism were to be withstood.

Changes in class composition which were already occurring in the inter-war years intensified in the post-war years. As Ralf Dahrendorf wrote in his groundbreaking *Class and Class Conflict in Industrial Society* (1959), by the time Marx died, about one out of every twenty members of the labour force was in what might roughly be described as a clerical occupation; by the late 1950s it was one out of every five and, in tertiary industries, one out of every three.[148] Increasing automation of the industrial sector, the parallel increase in the tertiary sector, expansion of the state sector in areas such as education and health, all trends which accelerated from the mid-1950s onwards, meant a further growth of the 'new middle classes' (salaried employees in industry, technical experts, middle management, clerks, trade and commerce workers, salesmen, civil servants), a trend which could not but concern socialist parties. The fact that in countries like Italy, France, Holland and Finland the working class in the 1950s did not exceed a percentage between 40 and 50 per cent of the total of the socialist parties' electorate[149] shows that, in the last analysis, their incursions into the middle-class vote were already quite significant. Nevertheless, the more the middle class grew, the greater and more relevant was the challenge posed.

To capture the middle-class vote became a veritable obsession for the Labour Party from the mid-1950s onwards. The failure to exert an effective appeal to middle strata was, without any doubt, regarded as one of the major factors accounting for the three successive election defeats the party suffered in the 1950s (1951, 1955, 1959).[150] While the Conservatives had long managed to make considerable inroads into the working-class electorate, retaining one-third of their votes, Labour had so far not been successful in making a similar breakthrough into the middle strata. For elections to be won, Labour, it was argued, needed at least one-quarter of middle-class votes. In 1945 and 1950 this had been the case. But by 1955 the ratio had gone down to 20 per cent and, according to surveys on voting intentions, it seemed it would fall even further.[151] There was a growing fear that Labour could be wiped out as a major party, as had been the case with the Liberals early in the century following the growth of the working class. Urgent action had to be taken, as revisionists in Crosland's mould claimed, in order to create a new image which would secure the enlargement of the appeal of the party to broader sectors of the population.

Even after the replacement of centre–right revisionists by the centre–left technocratic group, the concern with the middle-class vote did not decrease in importance. The rhetoric of science which Labour employed in the 1964 campaign was indeed fully in tune with a 'new middle class' minded electoral strategy. Labour tried to present itself in a dynamic light in the attempt to exert a greater appeal towards those social groups who hoped to prosper most within a thriving economy.[152] The replacement of the old division based on class with a new one based on progress–conservatism, was clearly designed to break the enduring special relationship between the 'middle majority' and the Conservative Party.

Talk of modernity was at the heart of a similar 'new middle class' oriented strategy that the Italian socialists pursued after their candidature to government in 1959. As Nenni stated at the 1963 congress, the notion of class and class struggle now applied to the whole world of labour and its various categories. The gap between workers and middle classes had now been bridged.[153] The old dichotomy between bourgeois capitalists–working class had to be replaced with a new one based on the division between those in favour of planning and structural reforms and those opposing reforms and defending the status quo.[154]

The concern with the middle-class vote was not new to Italian socialists. Late industrialisation had produced a social structure in Italy which was far from being as dichotomous as it was in Britain, where the peasants disappeared at a pace unknown elsewhere from the 1850s leading to a clear contraposition between workers and industrialists. Since very early in its formation, the Italian Socialist Party had had to adjust its initial single-class appeal to the presence of a considerable rural sector. Moving to the post-war years, the need for a 'trans-class' appeal remained unchanged: in 1958 33 per cent of the socialist vote came from share-croppers and salaried agricultural workers, two-thirds of which had traditionally voted for either the PCI or the PSI.[155] However, the Italian socialists scored fairly poor results among the petite and middle bourgeoisie which, in fact, represented only 12 per cent of the socialist electorate at the 1963 elections.[156] In the light of the rapid expansion under way of public administration and the tertiary sector, greater inroads in these occupational strata were to be crucial for the future expansion of the party.

The need to divest themselves of a working-class party image was not only dictated by the real enlargement of the middle class. Socialist parties also had to cope with a new development usually referred to as the 'embourgeoisement' of the working class. As Dahrendorf put it in *Class and Class Conflict in Industrial Society* (1959), the working class, far from being 'a homogeneous group of equally unskilled and impoverished people', was, by the end of the 1950s, 'a stratum differentiated by numerous subtle and not-so-subtle distinctions'.[157] Contrary to Marx's predictions of the growing homogeneity of labour from the assumption that the technical development of industry would tend to abolish all differences of skill and qualification, labour had been going through a process of real 'decomposition'. The labour force of advanced industry could now be divided into at least three distinct groups: a growing stratum of highly skilled workmen who increasingly merged with both engineers and white-collar employees; a relatively stable stratum of semiskilled workers with a high degree of diffuse as well as specific industrial experience; a stratum of totally unskilled labourers, usually newcomers to industry (beginners, former agricultural labourers, immigrants). These three groups differed not only in their level of skill, but also in other attributes and determinants of social status. The prolonged training and the salaried condition of skilled workers gave, for example, a proportion of workers the possibility of 'white-collar' status. The 'worker' as a single entity was no longer a tenable idea. In his place, a plurality of status and skill groups, whose interests often diverged, had emerged.[158]

Social mobility represented one of the most studied areas of sociological inquiry in those years. In this regard the work by Seymour Lipset and Reinhard Bendix, *Social Mobility in Industrial Society* (1959) was a real landmark: as opposed to Marx's belief in class closure, a great intergenerational mobility, they argued, had appeared since the beginning of industrialisation and had accelerated in the post-war years with the extraordinary expansion at work of the tertiary sector and white-collar work.[159] Greater educational opportunities had turned out to be a powerful instrument of social change. Individuals who stayed at their place of birth and in the occupation of their father throughout their life had become a rare exception.[160] All this had far-reaching implications for class solidarity: as the instability of classes grew, it was said, the intensity of class conflict was bound to diminish. As Dahrendorf put it, 'instead of advancing their claims as members of homogeneous groups, people were more likely to compete with each other as individuals for a place in the sun'.[161]

The decline of class consciousness which social mobility entailed, combined with the self-assignment of a considerable number of manual workers to the middle class due to the greater prosperity they enjoyed, constituted a real electoral challenge to socialist parties and called for an overall reconsideration of their image and appeal. The 'embourgeoisement of the working class' was, for example, a long-enduring obsession of the British Labour Party. Labour's three successive electoral defeats of 1951,[162] 1955 and 1959 were not only explicable through the party's failure to capture the middle-class vote, but were also a result of the defection from the parts of an increasingly large number of manual workers which had been occurring since 1951. Labour's vote had fallen from 48.8 per cent in 1951 to 44 per cent in 1959 and the steady erosion of its electoral record in the new towns and affluent working-class areas was largely responsible for it.[163]

'Deviant' working-class voters were not a new problem and much has been written about 'deferential voters', where by deference is meant the 'abnegation by the working class of political leadership in favour of the socially superior, traditional and hereditary elites' and by 'belief in the intrinsic personal qualities of the elite; perception of the elite's good will or indulgence as necessary for working-class well being; preference for the symbolic and institutional status quo over change; and an evaluation of the Conservative party as distinctively national'.[164] However, what worried Labour was that this long-enduring pattern of deferential voting was now combined with an even more far-reaching one, that of the tendency for the newly prosperous skilled workers to assign themselves subjectively to the middle class and vote for the party which the British middle class traditionally identified with: the Conservative Party.[165]

A considerable number of studies were produced in these years to investigate the 'affluent worker': the core idea common to all of them was that the growing prosperity of the 'affluent' working class was turning many of Labour's natural supporters into Conservative voters.[166] As centre–right revisionists argued, the image of the Labour Party had become steadily less appropriate to changing social conditions. Labour, according to numerous surveys which were produced in those years, notably Mark Abrams and Richard Rose's *Must Labour Lose?* was associated with austerity, controls, nationalisation and trade unions; this undoubtedly contributed to the desertion of the newly affluent workers fearful of being deprived of the new prosperity that the Conservatives had granted them. Most significant was the close identification of Labour with the working class, 'the underdog', which, given the strong correlation between political attitudes and social class composition which characterised British electoral behaviour, turned out to be a liability.[167]

The party, it was argued, had to adapt to new circumstances and to adjust to the new reality. The British party system, according to the theory of the 'swing of the pendulum' worked well only with a recurrent alternation of the two main parties; the electorate usually behaved as if it was aware of it; it followed that, if Labour had not alienated itself with its radical messages and backward image, it would have been brought back to power in the election of 1959. There was no point, it was argued, in keeping 'doctrinal purity' and remaining in opposition for 'thirty years'. Labour had to accept 'the limitations of political action', 'grapple with pragmatic questions of choice and priorities and perceive the need for reconciliation and compromise'.[168] Furthermore, a radical livening up of the party's image had to be carried out: Labour had to rid itself of the image of being a working-class, pro-austerity party and present itself instead as a broadly based, national, people's party.[169]

Crucial to a successful adaptation to the new environment was a greater reliance on studies on voting behaviour and political attitudes of the electorate.[170] Labour, it was said, was twenty years behind the Tories in the volume and quality of party research, publicity, propaganda, servicing MPs and so on.[171] Labour's commissioning of social surveys and concern with voting behaviour studies intensified in these years. In the process of livening up the party's image, as the revisionists advocated, the existence of guidelines to 'bring the party, the voters and trends in society into harmony'[172] was of the greatest urgency. *Learning to Live*, the document on education which Labour published in 1958 was, for example, itself the product of such a new approach to politics: the study group which produced it relied heavily on a survey commissioned by Mark Abrams on educational themes; the survey was conducted among men and women between 39 and 49 years of age who had at least one child between 5 and 16 years of age, and covered such matters as opinions on comprehensive schools, school-leaving age, part-time further education, the 11-plus examination, school grants and public schools.[173]

The 'marketisation of politics', a course which Labour seemed to have embarked upon, was an issue of major confrontation with the Left of the party. What was at stake was the very essence of the party itself. The revisionists' approach departed from the assumption that old allegiances and convictions had been weakened; voters were regarded as consumers of politics, just as they were consumers of mass-marketed commodities. The notion of the party which resulted was of a party whose task was to work out the existing demand and try to meet it. Parties had to comply with the public mood, adjust themselves to 'what people want'.[174] Needless to say, such a concept of the party strongly conflicted with the notion of the party 'as agenda-setting vanguards'[175] underlying the birth of socialist political organisations. Indeed, both the Marxist emphasis on the role of working-class political organisations in the formation of class consciousness and the Fabian paternalistic approach whereby the masses had to be guided by enlightened guides constituted a powerful source of theoretical resistance to the new course advocated by revisionists.

According to the Left, Labour's defeat in the 1959 elections was not a symptom of wrong policies but of bad propaganda. The problem was one of 'education not of surrender' as Bevan claimed.[176] The revisionists' claims that Labour had to adapt to the new environment were thoroughly rejected. As Crossman argued in *Labour in the Affluent Society*, published only one month after Crosland's *Can Labour Win?* the Labour Party should remain a 'Socialist challenge to the established order'; it would have been a very short-sighted mistake to turn the party's back on unorthodox and anti-Establishment policies while complacently coming to terms with the 'affluent society' and transforming itself into a 'humane, decent and business-like alternative'[177] as the revisionists urged. Labour had to adopt a long-term vision, irrespective of its unpopularity, and remain committed to radical change ready for the time when history would prove the liability of the present system.[178] The same theme, in almost the same terms, was raised by Richard Titmuss. The 'welfare state myth' and the assumption that most of the profound inequalities had already been solved posed a real danger for the future of Labour; these misconceived beliefs, which seemed to have made considerable headway among Labour circles, strengthened the trend towards conformity and political consensus creating a fertile terrain for what he called the danger of 'political atheism'.[179] Discussions of image and the need for advertising were attacked as immoral and a waste of money. Better organisation, rather than the methods used to sell detergents, it was said, would better achieve the party's electoral recovery.[180]

Admittedly, regardless of any talk of immorality in those years, when it came to winning elections, no substantial differences seemed to exist between the centre–right and the centre–left group. The electoral campaign that Labour waged under the lead of the Wilson centre–left group was, in fact, to be very much concerned with the party's image. Labour's strategy closely adhered to the guidelines drawn up by a survey produced by Mark Abrams in 1962–3 which tailored the party's appeal to the 'centre majority' and an enormous amount of money, more than ever before, was spent on advertising.[181]

The phenomenon of 'embourgeoised' working-class defection was certainly much more limited in Italy than in Great Britain. This was for two reasons. To start with, social mobility and a better redistribution of prosperity were much less pronounced than in the UK.[182] In a study of upward mobility from the occupational categories of manual workers, farm workers, and routine non-manual employees into those of farm-ownership and high level non-manual positions, Denmark and Great Britain scored respectively 22 per cent and 20 per cent, while Italy did not exceed 8 per cent.[183] As far as private consumption was concerned, suffice it to say that only 1 per cent of workers owned a washing machine in 1957, 2 per cent owned a refrigerator and 1 per cent owned a car.[184] Secondly, it should not be forgotten that the Italian socialists were well used to seeing a considerable proportion of the working-class vote for other parties. In contrast to the firm grip that Labour had on the majority of the working-class vote, this vote was distributed in Italy among many other political forces, a pattern which also applied to other Western European countries.[185] Many reasons accounted for it: on the one hand, a proportional electoral system which meant that three left-wing parties (PCI, PSI and PSDI), not counting smaller formations, competed for the working-class vote. On the other hand, in contrast with Great Britain, where other divisive factors such as religion, language and nationalism never played a determinant role at this time, class was never the major determinant of voting behaviour in Italy: consider, for example, the DC stronghold on Catholic workers' vote in Veneto or the substantial inroads of the PCI in the affluent middle class of the Emilia Romagna.[186] While British political attitudes seemed to be primarily correlated with social class position, up to the point that the proportion of the working class which voted for the Conservatives was always seen as an anomaly worthy of investigation, different divisions cutting across classes operated in Italy; religion, for example played an important role.[187]

The Italian Left had had to compete with a Catholic party since 1919 when the Popular Party was founded. As for the post-war years, deeply rooted religious traditions and the organisational machine of Catholic Action meant that the DC and the Catholic trade unions managed to make even greater inroads into the working-class vote, especially among women.[188] It is worth noting that religion, although in the form of anti-clericalism, played a considerable role in the broad support which communists retained in the so-called 'red' regions (Emilia Romagna, Marche and Umbria) where historically resentment against the Pope had developed when they were subjected, to the exploitative Pontifical State.[189]

Nevertheless, despite the above qualifications, in the 1950s the Italian socialists were also confronted with transformations in the working class and the problem of 'working class aristocracies'. Although, as we have seen above, if calculated on a national level mass consumption was still very low, differences between the various regions were marked. Suffice it to say that at the end of 1958 in Piedmont there were 48 cars for every 1000 inhabitants, while there were only 7 in Basilicata.[190] Since the achievement of full employment in the late 1950s, manual workers of the advanced sector, mainly in the North, achieved a substantial increase in their wages with the result that a small proportion of manual workers considerably improved their living conditions. In an interview, Vittorio Foa, a leading PSI and CGIL member, recalled the revolutionary effects which TV and cars had on Italian workers' lives and deeply-rooted habits.[191] The rapid diffusion of television in individual households resulted in the end of collective television in bars and clubs and a revival of forms of family privacy.[192] In the so-called 'new quarters' like the Comasina in Milan (the biggest public housing estate in Italy, completed in 1958–60), which were built in response to the wave of immigration from the South to the industrial North in the 1950s, social isolation became a defining feature of working-class life. As opposed to the typical *case a ringhiera* (long balconies with a number of flats close together), the form of working-class housing previously prevailing and which meant an 'enforced intimacy' with neighbours,[193] the new estates entailed a far more class-mixed and atomised life for their inhabitants.

New life-style patterns were combined with considerable differentiations along the lines of skill and sector. As Silvio Leonardi put it in his *Progresso Tecnico e Rapporti di Lavoro* (1957), automation meant the growth of the so-called 'non-productive' workers, that is technical experts and administrative staff, who rose from an average of 5 per cent of the total of employees at the beginning of the century to an average, in many plants, of 25–30 per cent.[194] At the same time, new categories of manual workers had emerged, with new qualifications making them less dependent on their manual ability and relying more on a general technical education.[195]

In the 1950s skilled workers tended to vote for moderate parties. The ratio of skilled workers to unqualified workers had always been higher in parties such as the DC and, above all, the PSDI. This was also reflected in the high percentage of votes obtained by the UIL (*Unione Italiana del Lavoro* – the social-democrat/republican union) and the CISL (*Confederazione Italiana dei Sindacati dei Lavoratori* – the Catholic union) in those industries where a high proportion of skilled workers were employed. As opposed to the weakness demonstrated by the PCI among these strata, socialists did quite well, coming third after the DC and the PSDI.[196] However, in view of the losses to the communists among unqualified workers which the shift towards the centre was likely to provoke, as discussions in *Mondo Operaio* on this question in the years from 1957 shows, it appeared even more urgent to increase their appeal to this sector of the working population.

The overall reappraisal of party doctrine which the autonomists had undertaken since the mid-1950s included reconsideration of the long-held dichotomous view of class structure. The schematic contraposition between the bourgeoisie and the proletariat, Giolitti wrote, was no longer an adequate instrument for looking at social class structure. The presumed uniformity of the two groups was no longer a reality. The labels 'proletarian' or 'bourgeois' were, in fact, far from resolving the complexity of contemporary capitalist society. Of similar significance, in terms of theoretical relevance, class consciousness was now said to be only one of the several elements which determined social behaviour. Other sociological factors such as occupation, qualifications, income, consumption patterns and use of leisure time contributed, to a great extent, to shaping social stratification.[197]

The PSI, it was argued, had better relinquish the myth of a united working class and undertake instead a detailed investigation of the profound modifications which the working class was undergoing. The working class had been reduced for a long time to 'an ideological entity, an abstraction'[198] at the cost of a gap widening between the party and the class it was supposed to represent.[199] The type of industry which still witnessed a clear-cut confrontation between capitalists on one side and the working-class on the other had given way, it was argued, to an 'immense stratified organisational pyramid' made up of unqualified, qualified, skilled workers, engineers, administrative staff, up to a distant and anonymous board of directors. Together with differentiations in skills, this meant considerable differentiations in salaries and wages which could not but exert a negative effect on class solidarity.[200] Furthermore, the tendency of an increasingly large number of employers to adopt company policies inspired by the doctrine of 'human relations' – that is the whole body of American sociological literature arguing that there was an identity of interests between workers and their corporations – also worked in favour of a steady integration of the worker into society. Many factors which now characterised the modern industrial economy such as full employment, high qualifications and a skilled labour force, the high cost provoked by any industrial conflict, induced the companies' managerial groups to adopt a different attitude towards employees from 'old capitalist proprietors': crucial to the interest of the company itself was the establishment of relations with the employees which were as tight and permanent as possible. Hence the conversion to 'human relations' and the adoption of integrationist techniques whose major aim was the total identification of the worker's interests with the company's.[201]

Many other factors were said to be at work in the weakening of class consciousness: the increasing spread of durable goods and leisure pastimes such as TV, radio, cinema and sport created a fertile ground for the 'integration' of the worker now no longer segregated from bourgeois society and opposed to it as an 'enemy in land to be conquered'. The workers now aspired to the comforts which had hitherto been the monopoly of the bourgeoisie – the car, the scooter, TV, cinema, radio and holidays – and ended up mingling with it.[202] The increasing weakening of 'organic links with the masses' which was denounced after the electoral setback of the 1963 elections was not regarded as an organisational problem but rather as a result of the party's detachment from the reality of the working class and its failure to fully understand the new dynamics in society. Action had to be taken immediately to catch up with the far-reaching social changes described above. As a matter of fact, from 1957 onwards the PSI adopted a clear electoralist direction attaching increasingly great importance to the construction of a 'moderate' image.[203] If, admittedly, this was more due to the need to earn the necessary legitimacy to sit in a coalition government with the Christian Democrats, it was, undoubtedly, also due to the need to adapt the party to the new social developments under way.

In spite of the strong resistance which the process of diluting the two parties' class connotations and their transformation into 'people's' parties met, it did have a considerable impact. It is no coincidence that in both Great Britain and Italy at some point in the 1950s there was talk of giving life to a new 'radical' political pole which would transcend old political formations. Talk of a 'Lib–Lab' alliance, an alliance between the right-wing of the Labour Party and the Liberals in Great Britain[204] had its Italian counterpart in the revival of the idea of a 'liberal democratic' cultural and political front: this would take place by means of a stronger and closer co-operation between the 'renewed' Socialist Party, the Republican Party and all those minor liberal and radical groups gathered around journals like *Il Mulino, Nuovi Argomenti, Comunità, Il Ponte, Nord e Sud* which in the highly ideological climate of the years immediately after the end of the war had been totally overshadowed.[205]

In the 'post-politics' phase new issues outside the field of economic policy had acquired significant importance which crossed old divides. The new attention that centre–right revisionists claimed Labour should pay to individual liberties[206] made obsolete, for example, the existing division between Left and Right and called instead for the 'highly salutary influence'[207] which the Liberals could exert on Labour in this regard. As far as the Italian socialists were concerned, the battle for a more secular society did not represent the only terrain where a convergence with lay parties took place, and a greater co-operation was advocated. Planning and reforms were, in fact, the key elements of the 'special relationship' which existed between La Malfa, the leader of the Republican Party, and Nenni. Progress and modernity were now the new division around which socialist parties would locate themselves in the political spectrum.

Part II

The End of Social Capitalism: From Old to New Revisionism

3
The Crisis of Social-Democratic Politics

Back in power: the 'socialist' management of crisis

In December 1963, the first centre–left government was formed. Less than a year later, in October 1964, the Labour Party was returned to office on a great wave of expectations. After ten years of reassessing theory and making profound revisions of their main policies, the Italian socialists and their British counterparts were finally in a position to implement their 'socialist' management of capitalism. Nevertheless, the experience in government was soon to become a source of disappointment and frustration for both parties.

The programme put forward by the Christian Democratic Prime Minister (*presidente del consiglio*) Aldo Moro in January 1964 during his presentation to parliament of the new centre–left coalition almost overlapped with the platform presented by the PSI during its 1963 congress, and offered some grounds for optimism. Moro's speech made reference to the many reforms that centre–left reformists had been discussing over the last five years, including planning, the elimination of geographical disparities, agrarian reform, municipal reform, educational reform, fiscal reform, a package of anti-monopoly laws, and so on. Not without good reason was it dubbed by the liberal leader Malagodi 'short observations on the Universe'.[1]

However, by the time the socialists were able to enter a coalition government, the centre–left formula had already lost its momentum. What are usually regarded as the two major reforms implemented in the 1960s – namely, the nationalisation of the electricity industry and the establishment of a single compulsory school system for students aged 11 to 14 (*scuola media unica*) – had already been implemented by the 1962 Fanfani government, a sort of hybrid centre–left from which the PSI simply abstained. By the end of 1962 the so-called 'reflux' had already begun.

The local elections held in June 1962 provided a clear warning to the Christian Democrats: the alliance with the socialists led to a loss of almost 2 per cent, mainly to parties to their right on the political spectrum, with respect to the previous local elections (the DC's share fell from 33.3 per cent to 31.5 per cent). However, gains were not achieved among the moderate left-wing electorate, which tended to favour the PSDI (Saragat's party grew by almost 2 per cent).[2] If the DC's electoral base was to be preserved, no further concessions could be made to the PSI.[3]

The deterioration of the Italian economy also militated against implementing a far-reaching programme of reforms. By early 1963, the increasingly large balance of payments deficit and growing inflation, both partly the outcome of the wage increases that resulted from 1962 labour demands, became matters of concern and alarm. As with the case of their British counterparts, by the time the Italian socialists were invited into the cabinet, short-termism and pressures to implement deflationary measures had already made great inroads in economic and political circles. In a document produced by the PSI a few months after the Moro government was created, entitled *Nota sull'attuale congiuntura economica in Italia e sulle politiche per fronteggiarla* (Note on the present economic conjuncture and policies to deal with it),[4] the Italian socialists themselves showed their awareness of the need to complement long-term reforms with short-term measures. Structural reforms, it was argued, should go hand in hand with immediate anti-inflationary measures, ranging from state control of rents (*equo canone*) to a partial revision of the public sector investment plans. Nevertheless, what supposedly was meant to be the integration of short-term devices with long-term reforms soon resulted in the notorious formula coined by Moro of the 'two stages-policy – *politica dei due tempi* – that amounted to prioritising the former policy and postponing *ad aeternum* the latter.

Some important pieces of social legislation were implemented throughout the 1960s. During the 1966–8 period, a reform of the health system, which was the precursor to the 1978 legislation creating the USL (*Unità Sanitaria Locale*, the National Health Service), was passed. Other reforms, notably the reform of mental institutions in July 1967, the establishment of state nursery schools in 1968, and the pension reform of 1968 were carried out before the end of the legislature.[5] It is beyond doubt that these reforms contributed to Italy's catching up, if only partially, with other advanced countries in terms of its welfare state. However, the reforms carried out by the various centre–left governments that succeeded one another in the 1960s were not 'structural' in a way conducive to creating a socialist society, nor did they lead to a greater rationalisation of Italian capitalism.

At the end of the 1963–8 legislature, some of the most significant items of the 1964 Moro programme, such as the reform of the public administration, were put in abeyance. The short-lived Ministry of Scientific Research, established in 1964, was sacrificed by the socialists during negotiations over the third Moro government of February 1966. Those reforms that were eventually implemented were greatly watered down. These included agrarian reform (the Green Plan of 1964–5), and the urban reform (1967). As for planning, it was left unimplemented. While the Giolitti Plan was voted on in January 1965, and the Planning and Budget Ministry, the CIPE (*Comitato Intergovernativo per la Programmazione Economica*, Intergovernmental Committee for Economic Planning), the ISPE (*Istituto per la Programmazione Economica*, Institute for Economic Planning) were established a few months later, no provisions were made to ensure these institutions were effective. No concessions were made to any 'disincentives' or coercive powers as socialists had urged in the past years in order for the plan to have real 'bite': planning guidelines instead remained 'indicative' and non-binding. No reform of joint-stock companies was, for example, carried out, depriving planning authorities of a means by which they could have exerted real control over the private sector.[6]

Wilson's 1964–6 and 1966–70 governments resulted in similar disappointments. On taking office, Labour found itself grappling with an overheated economy and a balance of payments crisis. It soon became clear that adherence to the Plan's original targets and the achievement of a healthy balance of payments would have been possible only if there was a change in the exchange rate of sterling.[7] Yet, the previous two devaluations had also been carried out by Labour prime ministers and chancellors (Prime Minister MacDonald and Chancellor Snowden in 1931, and Prime Minister Attlee and Chancellor Cripps in 1949). Thus, in an effort to earn credibility as 'economically trustworthy',[8] Prime Minister Wilson and Chancellor Callaghan resisted devaluation until the very last in order to avoid tainting Labour again with a third attack on sterling.

Labour's insistence on keeping the pound at the exchange rate set in 1949, together with the failure of the government's incomes policy, was to produce 'a series of missed opportunities'.[9] When devaluation was finally carried out in November 1967, it was too late; devaluation was followed by a harsh set of deflationary policies that, while re-establishing a positive balance of payments, gave a final blow to Labour's industrial policy. The Department of Economic Affairs had been established with a view to creating a 'pressure group for economic growth' within Whitehall and oppose the Treasury's policy of giving primacy to finance and the international parity of the pound. Economists such as Samuel Brittan, who was to play an active role in Labour planning, had warned Labour of the need to design DEA in such a way as to break the Treasury stronghold on economic policy-making.[10] Yet throughout the era of Labour governments the Treasury's concerns over sterling continued to predominate. The DEA and its long-term growth plans were completely subordinated to the Treasury's 'draconian measures' and traditional short-term deflationary polices.[11] By giving primacy to maintaining the value of the pound, domestic production could not but become a secondary concern. Labour's experience in government was marked from the very beginning by a steady retreat from its initial planning targets.

During the 1964 elections, Labour had claimed that the NEDC's growth target of 4 per cent was not high enough. The implementation of Labour's social programme would require a growth rate of between 5 per cent and 6 per cent. Once they had taken office and their grasp of the situation of the British economy became stronger, their economic targets were scaled down. The growth rate outlined in the National Plan of September 1965 was 3.8 per cent, 0.2 per cent less than projected in the NEDC's plan.[12]

The DEA's role became more circumscribed after Brown's departure in August 1966. After this, many DEA responsibilities were lost to other departments: in August 1967, external economic policy passed to the Board of Trade, in March 1968, responsibility for prices and incomes policy was handed over to the Department of Employment and Productivity, led by Barbara Castle.

Only on the micro-economic level were some measures aimed at promoting modernisation successfully carried out. The IRC (Industrial Reorganisation Corporation) is one example. This was a public body that was modelled along the lines of the Italian public holdings company IRI to promote mergers and greater rationalisation of the industrial sector by means of financial assistance, or by way of advice and recommendations. Its main task was to intervene where wasteful duplication existed, or economies of scale in production needed to be improved so that, as Wilson put it, companies 'were dragged, kicking and screaming if necessary, into the twentieth century'.[13] A few important takeovers took place under pressure from the IRC: these included the merger of GEC and English Electric in 1968, which was to produce one of the world's major industrial corporations; it also included the reorganisation of the nuclear industry.[14] Furthermore, the Ministry of Technology was formed in October 1964 out of the rationalisation of a range of committees, institutes and foundations responsible for encouraging technical innovation and scientific research. The Industrial Expansion Act of 1968 further enlarged the ministry's powers; according to the Act, the introduction of new industrial methods that might not otherwise be profitable in the short term could be promoted by means of direct loans, or else by the state taking a stake in the company.[15]

The rate of growth of Britain's industrial productivity, although low by international standards (Britain's 4.0 per cent growth rate lagged behind the 6.0 per cent growth rate of other countries such as West Germany, France or Italy)[16] was positively affected by these measures. Nevertheless, in spite of the many microeconomic adjustments that were made in order to achieve the modernisation that Labour had promised in the 1963 elections, Labour's inability to foster a favourable economic climate militated against far-reaching results.

As was the case in Italy, Labour had a stronger record in other areas such as social and civil rights. While failing to stick to its contended 'structural reformism', it was still successful in carrying out a Keynesian socialist agenda. The Wilson administration, to its credit, implemented a number of 'progressive' statutes, including the Race Relations Act (1965) which made racial discrimination illegal; Penal Reform and the abolition of capital punishment in 1965, the Abortion Act 1967, the Family Planning Act 1967, the Divorce Act 1968, the Matrimonial Property Act 1970. The government also reformed the laws governing homosexuality, allowing private homosexual acts between consenting adults. The Wilson years were also years of large-scale infrastructure investments in the public sector and conspicuously high social spending. A rapid increase in cash benefits such as pensions, supplementary benefits, family allowances and health benefits (specifically, NHS prescription charges were abolished) occurred. Education expenditure also grew considerably. Although some of Labour's electoral promises did not materialise – the school leaving age was not raised and non-comprehensive schools were left untouched and independent – thanks to the position of then Minister of Education, Crosland, the Labour government was very active in education.[17] The number of comprehensive schools expanded from 265 schools in 1964 to over 1000 by 1970. Higher education also grew. By 1970 there were twice as many students in higher education as in the previous decade. Seven new universities were built and others were expanded. The Open University, a remarkable instrument of social mobility, was founded. The problem was that the substantial increase in social expenditure was not paid for by economic growth, but was largely financed by means of foreign borrowing. Social reforms rested, in fact, on very weak foundations. The economic growth which should have made them possible was not there.

One crucial area impacting economic growth where both parties failed to achieve successes was incomes policy. Since the end of the 1950s, with full employment almost achieved in Western Europe, incomes policy became a major issue of debate. Especially in those countries heavily dependent on exports, such as Britain and Italy, controlling inflation by means of wage restraints was of the greatest urgency for the sake of international competitiveness.

The idea that wages should be held in check was not palatable to parties traditionally committed to raising working-class living standards and, to a greater or lesser extent, possessing strong links with the trade union movement. However, the question of wage levels was inescapable. Belgium, Austria, Holland, Norway, Denmark and Sweden were all countries which experienced some degree of anti-inflationary incomes policy under the guidance of socialist parties.[18] British Labour and the Italian socialists also committed themselves in the years preceding their return to power to some kind of incomes policy.

The debate over wage restraint dominated British politics from 1955 onwards. In that year, with unemployment falling to 1 per cent and the trade unions in a position of unprecedented bargaining strength, wage-driven inflation started accelerating and became an issue of real concern. Rising consumer prices were seriously jeopardising British competitiveness, the country's balance of payments, and Britain's future economic growth. The 1950s witnessed a succession of failed attempts by Conservative governments to achieve any sort of agreement with trade unions similar to the one Stafford Cripps had successfully accompanied in the years 1948–50. Under the leadership of trade unionists such as the left-wing Frank Cousins, who was general secretary of the Transport and General Workers Union, from 1956 onwards, any talk of wage restraint was rebuffed. The only option left to Conservatives was a traditional deflationary policy which led to the notorious 'stop–go' measures.[19] Even in the early 1960s, when the new planning body, NEDC, was formed, there was no real progress in the area of incomes policy. Doubts about government sincerity over planning were combined with a general lack of enthusiasm for the idea of the trade union movement going into partnership with a Tory government.[20]

In the light of a likely return to power in 1964 of the Labour Party, trade unions preferred to leave any experiment with incomes policy to a 'friendly' government.

The heated debate that went on throughout the decade over growth and wages gave rise to a growing concern in Labour ranks over incomes policy from 1957. In fact, the issue of incomes policy had made its way on to the Labour platform in 1958 with the publication of *Planning for Progress*.[21] It would later be reiterated in the 1959 election manifesto and became a key issue in the 1964 election.[22] The recognition of the need for some form of incomes policy was one of the few issues, if not the only one, that won unanimous consent within the party. Although opinion differed on the form that it should take, essays by centre–right and centre–left Labour personalities such as Gaitskell, Bevan and Crossman were replete with statements in favour of a national wages policy.[23] Both electoral and economic considerations counted. Labour needed to convince the electorate that a Labour government could work with the trade unions;[24] successful co-operation with trade unions was one of the 'strongest cards' the Labour Party had, one which the Conservatives lacked.[25]

Even the New Left did not mount any resistance to the idea of an incomes policy. On the contrary, provided it was carried out in a framework of a planned and expansionary economy, and included all incomes and profits, the New Left was among its loudest advocates (if not pioneers, if we consider that Ken Alexander and John Hughes' pamphlet *A Socialist Wages Plan* was published in 1959).[26] By making some concessions concerning increases in cash wage terms, workers would be guaranteed a sustained advance in real wages and conditions. A co-ordinated incomes policy would aim at increasing real earned incomes, while stabilising prices, and creating 'the conditions for some improvements in the real social wage by improved collective provision (family allowances and so on), and improvements in security of income (via higher unemployment pay, less unemployment, better redundancy and training provision)'.[27]

The caution with which Labour acted on this issue was due more to the trade unions' uneasiness at any talk of wage determination than to internal party resistance. British trade unions, in contrast to their Italian counterparts, long regarded any attempt to turn their economic claims into more political ones with suspicion. Their reluctance to look beyond demands for wage increases became an object of some debate even within the Labour Left from the mid-1950s onwards. The abandonment by the trade unions of narrow and short-term goals, and the adoption instead of a wider political perspective, came to be seen as crucial to successful planning.[28] The way ahead towards further advances for the working class, it was argued, was not in pressing for wage increases. Such claims, if pushed too far, might help destroy the full employment on which trade union power so largely depended. Trade unions should take into consideration political as well as industrial action.[29]

The delicacy of the question of voluntary wage restraint had appeared clear since the first steps were made by Labour towards a more specific commitment to incomes policy. In the process of drafting *Planning for Progress* (1958), strong pressures from the TUC were exerted,[30] so that any specific commitment was toned down and turned into a much broader and vaguer statement declaring the future Labour government's 'right to rely on the goodwill and co-operation of the trade union movement'.[31] It was in recognition of the trade unions' unwillingness to make any precise commitment on incomes policy that, in spite of the increasing centrality of this issue within British politics, incomes policy was, surprisingly, toned down and not given the emphasis that might have been expected. No reference to it can be found in *Signposts for the Sixties* (1961). Despite the importance attached to it at the 1963 conference, no policy documents or statements were produced in 1962 or 1963 on the issue.[32]

The veiled hostility demonstrated by the trade unions to any excessively advanced and specific commitment regarding incomes policy resulted in incomes policy proposals that emphasised voluntary trade unions' participation. One of the last acts of the Conservative government in the area of incomes policy had been the 'Pay Pause', a complete freeze on wages announced on 25 July 1961, which had been launched without first attempting to consult with unions and employers to secure their support. Needless to say, it turned out to be a complete failure and was rescinded within a few months (April 1962). The 'way ahead' advocated by Labour would be toward union co-operation and the right of full consultation[33] within a framework of trade union autonomy.[34] As Thomas Balogh wrote in 1958, 'one-sided regimentation of labour' was 'impracticable';[35] the precondition of any successful incomes policy was the whole-hearted support of the workers. Co-operation had to be secured by giving some assurances in advance concerning the 'equity in sacrifice and greater social justice'. Workers should receive assurances that 'the sacrifice will not be in vain, that the restraint on wages on which the restoration of British prosperity depends would in due and not too distant future yield positive results in increasing living standards.'[36] Hence, the party commitment to comprehensive planning and the reiterated claims that restraints would be imposed on all incomes, profits, dividends and rents as well as wages and salaries.[37]

A similarly voluntary attitude permeated Italian socialists' attitude towards the question of incomes policy. In contrast to Britain and other European countries, incomes policy was not a real issue of concern in Italy until quite late. Italy suffered from persistently high unemployment throughout the 1950s. Consequently, trade unions remained weak and divided and were not in a position to cause cost–push inflation. In contrast, while in Great Britain many attributed the responsibility for most of the economic difficulties that the country was experiencing to trade unions, it was largely recognised that the economic miracle in Italy had occurred at the expense of workers' wages. Although these improved during the 1950s, they did so at a rate slower than the productivity rate, and at a rate slower that the European average over the entire decade.[38]

Within the context of a fairly sound balance of payments situation and with little public debt, the Italian government could successfully control inflation almost exclusively through monetary policy up to the early 1960s. What is more, full employment, rather than incomes policy, remained the issue at the fore, and was to become the major concern of Italian economic planning in all its configurations, from the Vanoni Plan to discussions preceding the formulation of the Giolitti Plan in 1964.[39]

Incomes policy made its way into Italian political debate after 1962. Against a backdrop of almost full employment within the advanced industrial sector, Italy experienced a great wave of strikes in 1962. That year the number of hours of strikes was 181 million, as opposed to 79 million the previous year. This was equalled only in 1969, during the so-called 'Hot Autumn'.[40] The result was exceptionally large wage increases, which grew far more quickly than productivity levels. Between 1958 and 1964, wages increased faster than anywhere else in Europe. In the years 1962–3, Italy confronted for the first time a situation of rising prices and balance of payments difficulties: by 1962 the economic miracle had almost run its course; inflation rose from 1–2 per cent to 4–5 per cent during this period. Calls for wage determination began to gain ground in various industrial sectors. Of greater significance was that incomes policy began to be regarded as a crucial element in planning policies discussed in those years. Ugo La Malfa, one of the most vociferous advocates of incomes policy, sought a policy aimed at re-establishing some connection between productivity rates and wages.

However, not all the political forces in favour of planning were in support of incomes policy. On the contrary, incomes policy was an extremely divisive issue in the pro-planning front; in particular the socialists were initially strongly critical of any attempt to contain wages.[41] There were many reasons for this position. To start with, there were social justice concerns. Although Italian wages had recently increased considerably they still remained, as Giolitti argued in 1962, below the European average. Compared to British hourly wages (UK = 100), in Germany wages stood at 94, France at 93, Belgium at 93, and Italy at 81. Economic reasons were also put forward: as Lombardi argued in 1959, the theory of imperfect competition had long demonstrated that wage claims, far from damaging the economy, contributed to its proper functioning. In economies dominated by oligopolies, wage control would lead, in a situation where technological progress allowed for lower and lower costs and in which competition was limited, to even greater profit margins and the risk of an overproduction crisis.[42]

Socialists also questioned the argument, often put forward in those years, that inflation was caused by cost-push factors. Rising prices were not due to increases in wages, but to the rising cost of living which was, in turn, provoked by a number of 'deformations and imbalances' that the Italian economy suffered from. These included high food prices and high living costs resulting from an inefficient retailing system, and expensive housing which was in turn the result of years of real estate speculation. The solution to inflation was not to impose wage restraint on the workers, but rather structural reforms were needed to sort out the problem at its very origin.[43] The report on planning produced in 1962 by Fuà and Sylos Labini therefore rejected an incomes policy. They argued that the increase in wages underway established a fairer balance with profits, whose margins had grown over the past decade at a great pace. Further future increases could be expected and were fully justified. The growth of the wages–profits ratio was to remain one of the socialists' major objectives.[44]

One year later, however, the approaching prospect of government, combined with a deteriorating balance of payments situation, was to produce some second thoughts. By 1963 the PSI came round to the idea that wage rises needed to be linked to productivity. As with Labour's proposals, a considerable ambiguity surrounded the policies elaborated in this area, and a great emphasis was put on the voluntary nature that any wage moderation should have. As the 1963 PSI programmatic document reads, 'incomes policy will not be and cannot be the result of something imposed by the state, an unacceptable limitation from outside of trade unions freedom and action'; it should instead be the result of 'the autonomous and responsible attitude which the working class will adopt in the light of its crucial role in economy and concern with the general interest'.[45] Trade unions' action, it was argued, had to remain free and autonomous. Trade unions should participate on a consultative level in the formulation of the Plan. This would allow them to delineate and carry out their policies in line with planning policies and the objectives set out by the government.[46]

Autonomy and responsibility were thus the two principles that should inspire trade unions' claims, it was argued.[47] As in the case of Great Britain, trade unions' co-operation and 'responsibility' were expected to be gained by giving some assurances not only that an incomes policy would include profits, private incomes from capital, as well as self-employment, but also that through a broadly planned economy, wage moderation would be compensated by other gains in terms of costs of living, real incomes, cheaper housing, transport, schools, hospitals – the end, in other words, of those structural imbalances mentioned above.[48]

Italian socialists had to be far more cautious than their British counterparts in trying to impose upon the CGIL, the most powerful socialist–communist trade union federation in Italy, any specific commitments on the question of incomes policy. To start with, socialists did not hold the sort of organic relationship with CGIL that is crucial to a successful incomes policy. Not only was the CGIL politically dominated by the Communist Party, but its minority socialist faction was mainly drawn from the Left of the party. Hence the union was closer to the communists and hardly supportive of the autonomist group's centre–left policies. It might be worth remembering that a large proportion of socialist trade unionists joined the PSIUP when the PSI split in 1964. What is more, the PSI was confronted with a trade union which, in spite of some reappraisal of its policies, was not prepared to give up the confrontational approach which had long inspired its action, and was unlikely to fit in with the model of a supportive and co-operative partner expected by the pro-planning forces.

The process of reconsideration which the PSI and, to a lesser extent, the PCI, embarked upon in those years did not leave CGIL untouched. Neo-capitalism, the economic miracle and technological progress represented a challenge to Italian trade unions as much as it did to left-wing political parties. The notorious defeat of CGIL in the internal commission ballots of March 1955 had clearly shown the need for some reappraisal of the union's strategies and policies. From the mid-1950s onwards the CGIL embarked upon a more in-depth attempt to understand the changes under way in the productive process, which meant a greater comprehension of the transformations occurring in the labour market, in the social structure, and in the strategies now elaborated. The transmission-belt theory (the idea that it was the party, the PCI, which developed economic and social policy, and the union which simply applied it within its own sphere of action) was questioned. Greater autonomy from political parties, namely the PCI and PSI, was sought. In turn, greater co-operation with the other two trade unions, CISL and UIL, was pursued. In contrast to the high level of politicisation that marked the post-war years, a 'return to the factory' (*ritorno alla fabbrica*) was advocated, with efforts made towards greater internal democratisation.[49]

Yet the decrease of what has been described as an 'excess of militancy', or 'leftist deviations', was not enough for the CGIL to become, by the time the first planning proposals were advanced, the 'modern' trade union which planning called for.[50] As the left-leaning sociologist Franco Momigliano put it, the CGIL still demonstrated little awareness of the need to elaborate medium and long-term planned strategies. In contrast it still tended to regard abstention from strikes and social unrest as the workers' surrender and acceptance of their weakness in power relationships with capital, rather than as the indispensable element of an active and carefully planned strategy.[51]

The CGIL seemed at first to adhere to the voluntary incomes policy proposed by the PSI. It ruled out any *a priori* subordination of wages and salaries to productivity;[52] it nevertheless accepted that 'in the light of what was going to be a planned economy aimed at transferring key economic decisions into the hands of public powers, trade unions might look at such a new economic and political context as a new terrain for co-ordinating their claims'.[53] However, by the time the centre–left government produced the Pieraccini Plan, the CGIL, as opposed to the far more supportive CISL, decided to abstain in the vote on whether to support the government's plan. Their criticism focused on the absence of the necessary guarantees for a successful implementation: sufficient public investment, adequate credit selectivity, targeting of monetary resources allocations, and finally, incentives for private capital to invest in areas requiring development.[54] The suspicions, nourished by the CGIL over whether a government where socialists held a subordinate position could deliver the sort of reforms which had been promised, were not ill-founded. Yet, in the last analysis what was rejected was the so-called reformist nature of the plan which, it was argued, could not obtain the CGIL's co-operation as long as it aimed to keep intact the existing model of development.[55]

In the final analysis, the adoption of a voluntary policy,[56] a strategy pursued both by the PSI and Labour, was a complete failure. Labour proved no more successful than its Italian counterpart. From the beginning of its mandate, Wilson's cabinet took efforts to establish a healthy and co-operative relationship with the trade unions. A ministerial job was created for Frank Cousins of the Transport and General Workers Union. Trade unions' legal immunities, which had been challenged during the Conservative government, were bolstered with the 1965 Trade Disputes Act.[57] Nevertheless, after a very short period, against a background of increasing unofficial strike action and growing wage-push inflation, the attitude of the Labour government began to change.

Labour had returned to office with no specific commitment by the trade unions except a vague promise that, given some assurances concerning the growth of the national economy and a fair redistribution of sacrifices, some form of voluntary wage restraint could be taken into consideration. In the light of the increasing subordination of the National Plan to the Treasury's diktat, the trade unions' already half-hearted support of the government's policies started faltering. In fact, by the time the *Joint Statement of Intent*, announcing the National Plan in December 1964, was issued, and the National Plan was launched in 1965, the trade unions' positive attitude had vanished. As many trade unions leaders saw it, the alleged joint venture between the government and unions had taken the shape of an attempt to secure economic stability at the expense of members' living standards.[58] The two government White Papers, *The Machinery of Prices and Incomes Policy* and *Prices and Incomes Policy*, which committed the trade unions to submitting wage claims to a National Board of Prices and Incomes within a limit of 3–3.5 per cent, were accepted. Yet, some moves taken by the government, such as increases in indirect taxation, gave the *coup de grâce* to what little confidence was left in the possibility of future co-operation. The following years were marked by growing distrust, escalating into an open confrontation that reached its peak during the 1966 seamen's strike, and the publication of the notorious White Paper by Barbara Castle in 1968, *In Place of Strife*. On both occasions, the government tried to impose upon the trade unions' bargaining power elements of compulsion or statutory limitations on strike action (for example the Prices and Incomes Act entailed fines for those breaking the guidelines; as far as *In Place of Strife* was concerned, a 'conciliation pause' could be imposed on unofficial disputes, and secret ballots before official strikes could be required, and fines levied, by an Industrial Board if unions breached the new legislation)[59] which were unacceptable to trade unions. Attacked by several members of the Cabinet, a majority of the NEC, and a large number of Labour MPs, *In Place of Strife* was finally dropped. It was clear that Labour's attempt to hold inflation in check by means of wage containment had failed.[60] As Noel Thompson put it, an incomes policy that had been seen as an integral element of planning ended up assuming a deflationary, crisis-management role.[61]

By the end of the 1960s, both Labour and the PSI seemed to have run out of steam. The most distinctive items of their technocratic socialist policies had been dropped with both parties sticking to a traditional Keynesian agenda that had by then already started faltering. Faced with the explosion of direct action in the form of mass protests, the revival of worker militancy, the student and feminist movements, the sexual revolution, they suddenly seemed old-fashioned and behind events, rather than the 'modernisers' they had claimed to be a decade earlier. That was soon to be the fate for most of their sister parties.

Socialism in retreat

From the mid-1960s to the late 1970s, European politics were influenced by high profile socialist leaders such as Olof Palme, Willy Brandt, Harold Wilson and Bruno Kreisky, who dominated both the national and international stage. However, there was a paradox, for what was a period of political hegemony for social democracy in government corresponded with the beginning of a crisis in social-democratic politics.

By the mid-1970s, the post-war great capitalist boom came to an end. The collapse of the fixed exchange rate system of Bretton Woods in 1971 and the oil price hikes that began in 1973 deeply affected Western European economies, which entered a long period of economic recession and monetary instability. A new phase of slow economic growth began. With just a few exceptions (Austria, Sweden and in some respects France), Western European governments – most of them dominated by socialist parties – failed to find agreements with trade unions over wage restraint policies, leading to serious balance of payment and exchange problems. Public sector deficits were also spiralling out of control, while the public sector was left unmodernised and heavily subsidised. At the same time, for all the attempts to curb welfare expenditure, social spending continued to expand much faster than the capacity of the economy to sustain it. The demand for education and social infrastructure spending had been steadily progressing since the late 1950s. The 1960s cultural and social revolution, and the erosion of traditional attitudes towards the role of the family, contributed to an inevitable additional increase in the demand for state-provided social welfare, which remained hard for Western European governments, regardless of their political inclinations, to ignore.[62]

Hit by both external and internal factors, and caught up in the vicious circle of 'stagflation', Western European economies confronted a long and irreversible phase of low economic growth that had far-reaching consequences for the model of 'social capitalism' which had been hegemonic since the end of the war.[63] The real miracle of the 1945–70 period was that governments were able to reconcile capital profitability, economic growth, full employment and welfare. For socialist parties, the convergence between social democracy and the economic orthodoxies of the day, that is growth management and macroeconomic interventionism, was a real panacea. Keynesian economics eliminated the dilemma between capitalism and socialism. For almost thirty years left-wing parties seemed to have it all. After 1973, however, against a background of growing international economic instability and interdependence, Keynesian nation-centred responses seemed increasingly impotent. Economic growth and capital profitability were increasingly irreconcilable with full employment and welfare. Tough choices loomed on the horizon that opened up a phase of deep crisis for all socialist parties, without exception.

The social-democratic commitment to full employment rested upon the assumption that individual governments would be free to raise the level of demand and use the Keynesian regulators as they wished. The 1970s saw the crumbling of that assumption altogether. Governments were no longer masters in their own houses.[64] The restrictive monetary policies which the IMF forced upon the centrist Christian Democratic Italian government in 1975, and upon the Callaghan Cabinet in 1976, made quite clear that unilateral reflation was simply no longer feasible. Co-ordinated Keynesian reflation might have provided an effective answer.[65] However, that was a time when the European Left was still stubbornly clinging to policies centred on the nation–state. The recipe for crisis management which most European socialist governments, such as the Wilson/Callaghan governments in Britain (1974–9) and the Schmidt administrations in West Germany (1974–82), resorted to was a strategy based on restrictive monetary solutions, with the post-war orthodox Keynesian commitment to full employment slowly evolving into a commitment to controlling inflation. The only social-democratic government that managed to pursue a successful expansive economic strategy in the 1980s was the Swedish SAP. That, however, was a unique case, owing to trade unions' traditional good relationships with the government, and the room for manoeuvre that the latter had to implement policies of wage restraint. The failure of Mitternand's growth-oriented 'French experiment' (1981–3) was the swan-song of Keynesian interventionism.[66] It was a further definitive illustration that the preconditions of the social-democratic hegemonic model of the earlier years had vanished for good.

The decline of Keynesian economics and the retreat from traditional socialist principles and goals such as free collective bargaining or full employment opened a period of profound disorientation for socialist parties. Of greater significance, it was to lead to a long period in opposition for most of them. Capital accumulation now required a recipe for deflation, wage discipline and welfare cuts. Much as they tried to adapt to new economic circumstances, it was hard to continue to present themselves as the 'natural parties' of government. After a decade of political dominance, some of the biggest European social-democratic parties were ousted from government. The defeat of British Labour in 1979 was to be the first in a long series of electoral setbacks which shortly after hit other socialist parties in Belgium (1981), Norway (1981), Denmark (1982), Germany (1983) and Austria (1986). Where socialist parties remained in power, mainly in Southern Europe, they pursued deflationary policies as firmly, if not more enthusiastically, than their centre or centre–right opponents. In this regard the Italian case is quite exemplary.

In the wake of the long series of unsuccessful centre–left governments, and the failure of socialist unification, which had come abruptly to an end after the disappointing results for the PSU at the 1968 elections, the Italian socialists of the early 1970s were a party which was electorally weak (in the 1972 elections the PSI took 9.6 per cent, its lowest point since the birth of the party), disorientated, and in the middle of a deep 'identity crisis'. Of greater significance, following the Eurocommunist turning point and Berlinguer's 1973 launch of the new strategy for a 'government of national unity', socialists now also suffered from political marginalisation. The DC–PCI axis, which dominated Italian politics in the 1970s, deprived the 'left-wing unity' strategy, which the PSI leader Antonio De Martino launched on the French model in 1969, of its main precondition – a Communist Party interested in it.

Craxi's takeover of the PSI's leadership in 1976 was to pave the way for a radical change in the party's image and strategy. In the years from 1976 to 1978, socialists entered a period of fertile debate which attracted the widespread endorsement of a high number of well-known intellectuals such as Norberto Bobbio, Giorgio Ruffolo, Giuliano Amato, Luciano Cafagna, Gaetano Arfè, Federico Cohen, Tristano Codignola, Paolo Flores

D'Arcais, Lucio Colletti and Ernesto Galli della Loggia. Some of them had already contributed to the rethinking of the party that had given rise to Nenni's autonomist course; after years of frustration and disillusionment, which followed the PSI's disappointing experience in government and their persistent political and electoral subordination to the PCI, many socialists saw in Craxi a second chance for a genuine renewal and rebirth.

The reassessment of the party's main ideological tenets, which had been initiated in the mid-1950s and given a new, though short-lived, boost in the years leading up to the socialist unification of the 1966–8 period,[67] was then eventually brought to its final completion. Traditions such as Proudhon libertarianism or Rosselli's Liberal Socialism, became the new 'Socialist Gospel'[68] in opposition to what *Mondo Operaio* now described as 'authoritarian Marxism'.[69] Any ambiguity concerning the party's attitude towards the capitalist mode of production was dropped. The hammer and sickle was replaced by a red carnation: there should be no more ambivalence concerning which 'family' and tradition the Italian socialists belonged to. It was social democracy which was to be symbolically sealed by the election of Craxi a few years later as vice-president of the Socialist International.

During these years Craxi carried out a veritable 'genetic mutation' of the party. By the time the PCI–DC strategy of national unity collapsed in 1979, and the Italian socialists once again became an indispensable coalition partner for the Christian Democrats, the PSI had transformed itself into a moderate, centrist, reformist, 'opinion' party whose natural electoral constituency was no longer the traditional working class – though important, this component of the socialist vote was in decline throughout the 1980s – but rather the growing tertiary sector and the emerging new entrepreneurial middle classes which post-Fordist restructuring was nourishing, particularly in Northern Italy.[70] It was to be the *onda lunga* (long wave)[71] strategy that would eventually deprive the PCI of its leadership on the Left.

Modernisation and governability became the leitmotif of the party's new political agenda. As was the case with other Southern European socialist parties then in office – Papandreou's PASOK, Gonzalez's PSOE and Soares's Portuguese socialists – 'old' ideologies and political programmes gave way to economic realism and pragmatism. In 1983, Craxi's five party coalition government's key economic policy objectives were the reduction of public sector deficit, deregulation, and privatisation. Of greater significance was the unprecedented confrontational approach towards trade unions that was adopted, which reached its peak with the 1984 reform of the wage indexation system that had been in operation since 1975. The Craxi government's neo-liberalism was, in fact, inconsistent. The clientelistic practices on which both his party and the DC rested their electoral and political power required an interventionist strategy in the South which nullified the austerity policies pursued nationally. This was reflected in the growth of Italy's public debt levels throughout the 1980s. However, his government successfully fostered a new mini-economic miracle, helped by positive international economic conditions, which, among other factors, explains the slow but steady growth in electoral fortunes of the Italian socialists throughout the decade.

The ideological overhaul carried out by Craxi was made possible by a number of factors. To start with, the more vociferous and radical fringes that had expressed fierce resistance to Nenni's earlier steps on the road towards social-democratisation had eventually left the party in 1964 following the PSIUP break. Secondly, by the time Craxi took hold of the party's leadership, 75 per cent of the socialists' apparatus was made up of new younger members, less ideologically oriented, and quite keen, after years of political marginalisation and electoral decline, on the promise of change embodied by the new leader.[72] The removal of past symbols and policies drained some of the party's traditional supporters. However, this was compensated for by the PSI's ability, thanks to its return to office and its more pivotal and influential position within the government compared with its previous participation, to consolidate its power base and electoral support by means of clientelistic practices and an effective spoils-sharing system with its DC ally. This also explains the Socialists' 'southernisation' which occurred in these years. Lastly, thanks to a strong leadership style and a number of internal reforms, such as the direct election of the party's leader from 1981 onwards, Craxi was able to exert a much greater control of the party than his predecessors. After the 1981 congress, his 'reformist faction' could count on an unprecedented 70 per cent support. As for internal opposition, it was fragmented and weak.[73]

A strong and highly personalised leadership style, combined with greater pragmatism and increasingly populist tones were the recipe for success among all Southern European socialist parties (the Spanish, Greek and Portuguese also had an advantageous political climate following the fall of dictatorial regimes). This was a route that Northern social-democratic parties, which were more saddled with past traditions, symbols and far stronger party organisations, could not take. Change for them was to be far more troubled and drawn out, resulting in a number of spectacular electoral setbacks. In 1983, for example, both British Labour and the SPD scored record low shares of the vote and this opened up a period of conservative hegemony.

The history of British Labour in the 1980s is an illustrative case in point. Faced with the failure of the Wilson and Callaghan governments, and the crisis of distributional socialism, the 1979 electoral defeat for the party led to a marked shift to the left. Earlier revisionists of any brand were increasingly isolated and on retreat. The repudiation of the earlier social-democratic approach paved the way for the growing influence of far more radical factions within the party, such as the 'unreconstructed' Trotskyite Left. The election of Michael Foot as leader in 1980 signalled the beginning of one of the most left-wing periods of Labour Party leadership, both in tone and aspiration.

The 'alternative' economic strategy (AES) of planning and protection, whose foundations had been developed throughout the 1970s, was eventually embraced in place of failed Keynesianism. The bible of those years became Stuart Holland's *The Socialist Challenge* (1975);[74] ownership and control of strategic companies within a framework of planning came to be once again regarded as the new route to socialism. Together with economic planning and nationalisation, notions such as workers' control and participatory democracy, ideas which had never previously made inroads in the party's agenda except in their softer guises, now found a place in Labour's policy documents.[75]

In point of fact, Labour's programme did not go far beyond old-fashioned and traditional ideas, having very little consideration of the profound transformations undergone since the mid-1970s by advanced economies. The commitment to unilateral disarmament and its anti-Europe stance testified to a naive political voluntarism with scant awareness of the new global dimension of international economics and its implications for nation–states' power of intervention. Similarly, the 'patriarchal productivism'[76] of the AES reflected a disregard for new social movement issues, such as feminism and ecology, which made Labour's programme out of touch with the majority of British progressive and radical elements. As pointed out earlier 'conservatism' rather than radicalism would better describe Labour's policies in the years from 1979 to 1983.[77] Not surprisingly, the expression 'radical', a word which in the English language had so far been commonly used to refer to socialists, began to be used in the 1980s to describe Margaret Thatcher's politics.

The price the party paid was quite high. In 1981 the split of the Social Democratic Party further deprived Labour of its moderate voices.

In 1983, Labour experienced its worst electoral defeat ever and almost lost its position as the main opposition party within the political landscape to the Liberal Alliance (Liberals and the SDP). The bottom had been reached, and the time had come for change.

The rise of neo-revisionism

Despite the number of Cassandras predicting the imminent death of Labourism, Labour's suicidal march ended in 1983. In the years that followed, under the new leadership of Neil Kinnock, who replaced Michael Foot in 1983 and embodied the 'soft' Left which had distanced itself from the extremist hard Left since 1981, a new phase of reconsideration of the party's identity and direction opened up. Internal constraints and resistance made overnight change impossible and suggested the need for caution. However, by the 1987 elections, important changes in the party's organisational structure had already been accomplished, and a reassertion of the leadership's authority over the party's rank and file membership resulted. Anti-Europeanism and the AES were dropped.[78] While reaffirming Labour's commitment to reverse the privatisation of public utilities (British Telecom and British Gas) carried out by the Conservative government, Labour revived a more flexible and market-oriented notion of social ownership such as state shareholding or competitive public enterprise instead of outright nationalisation.[79]

While Labour returned to its earlier position before its radical shift to the left, the problem remained of how to devise an alternative to the old Keynesianism. The SDP's platform was of limited use. As Donald Sassoon points out, for all the rhetoric of modernisation which David Owen's party successfully filtered through the media, their approach was conventionally Keynesian and, with the exception of a greater concern with 'new politics' issues and the centrality attached to Europe as the *deus ex machina* for the Left's crisis, they provided Labour with few new ideas on which a radical break from past orthodox classic social–democratic politics could be carried out.[80]

The 1987 defeat gave a new boost to the search for a post-Keynesian alternative, and a far more wide-ranging review of the party's policies and doctrines. What was needed, it was argued, was a more accurate analysis of the political and socio-economic developments under way. Think Tanks sympathetic to Labour like the IPPR – Institute of Public Policy Research – were founded. Conservative-leaning research centres had been flourishing throughout the decade and the knowledge gap had to be closed. As had been the case in the 1950s, radical intellectuals were as active as their more moderate counterparts[81] in providing Labour with a far more realistic picture of the new context within which the party should rethink and reassess its agenda. *Marxism Today* and intellectuals such as Eric Hobsbawm and Martin Jacques played a notable role in putting Labour in touch with the fundamental changes in capitalism and the post-industrial transformation that the British economy and society had been going through over the last twenty years.[82]

Meet the Challenge, Make the Change. A New Agenda for Britain, Final Report of Labour's Policy Review for the 1990s, issued in 1989, laid the foundations of the new revisionism. Labour now openly accepted the vital role that the market should play in the economy. The limits of Keynesian demand management and the constraints on public spending and borrowing were now strategically, not only tactically, accepted. State intervention, it was argued, had to focus more on the supply-side of the economy.[83]

Labour's unexpected fourth successive defeat in the 1992 elections further accelerated the party's march towards 'new post-Keynesian revisionism', which continued unabated under the leadership of John Smith and was eventually brought to completion by Tony Blair, the 'moderniser' *par excellence*. The role played by Blair in the party's modernisation had admittedly more to do with theoretical systematisation and image reshaping than with any input of new ideas which, by then, had already made progress in the party's agenda.

Up to 1994, as Tony Wright, a prominent figure of British neo-revisionist thinking, points out, there was still no 'New Idea' capable of giving coherence to assorted policy initiatives, and conferring a new identity on the Left.[84] 'The Big Idea', something media-catchy and electorally attractive, comparable in appeal to Wilson's big idea of a New Britain forged in the 'white heat of the technological revolution', was still missing. Yet it was to be of vital importance for two reasons: first, to convince the moderate electorate that Labour had changed for good; second, Labour's traditional supporters had to be persuaded that the new agenda was not, as left-wing opponents argued, simply reheated Conservative policies.

At some point it seemed that the 'stakeholder economy' could be the 'new vision framework' Labour was seeking.[85] However, it had a very short life. Stakeholder economy is a very foggy and nebulous concept that lends itself to a multitude of interpretations. Shortly after the slogan of stakeholder economy was picked up and 'spun', Blair's softer version, that is, a general restatement of rights and responsibilities within society for both employers and employees, was challenged by a more radical one which entailed statutory intervention to ensure that institutions and firms accepted responsibilities towards employees as well as substantial changes to the financial system. It was soon apparent that the corporate legislation advocated by proponents such as Will Hutton,[86] to constrain corporate behaviour and responsibilities, conflicted with the new pro-business attitude and image Labour was tirelessly trying to build up.[87] The enthusiastic support of trade unionists such as John Monks and John Emmonds (of the GMB union), who both saw a stakeholding economy as a new opportunity for trade unions to have a stake in management, proved to be fatal and the 'stakeholder economy' was shelved for good.[88]

The Big Idea eventually came from the US. The 'third way', which underlay the electoral success of the 'New' Democrats and Bill Clinton in the 1990s became, from 1994 onwards, and particularly after its European formulation by Anthony Giddens in *The Third Way* (1998),[89] the wider framework within which Labour would 'market' its renovated policies. In 1997, after eighteen years of Conservative government, and after ten years of drastically reshaping its agenda and image, Labour eventually managed to retake possession of 10 Downing Street.

Its return to office was preceded by one year by the victory of the Olive Tree centre–left alliance in Italy in 1996. The PDS, the PCI's heir, was the largest party of the coalition. The party founded by Antonio Gramsci, which had spent only two years in office since its birth in 1921, was now in power after fifty years of opposition. Very little remained of its name, past symbols or policies by that time. After almost twenty years of reassessment of the party's agenda and doctrine, the PDS had in fact transformed itself into a medium-sized social-democratic party. It now occupied the political space left vacant by the move to the right, and subsequent downfall of the old PSI under the weight of the anti-corruption *Mani Pulite* ('Clean Hands') operation.

By the mid-1980s, the PCI was a party in political, ideological and electoral disarray. After thirty years of steady growth, its electoral share was on the decline. From the 1976 election onwards, when it reached its historical peak of 34.4 per cent, it consistently lost votes. The Communists' vote shrank to 30.4 per cent in 1979, to 29.9 per cent in 1983 and 26.6 per cent in 1987.[90] At the same time, the PSI's share grew from 9.8 per cent in 1979 to 14.7 per cent in 1987. The socialists' vote, combined with the PSDI and the radicals, totalled 20 per cent in 1987. Craxi's 'long wave' strategy seemed to be working, and overtaking the PCI was becoming a possibility.

Against a background of steady electoral decline, and amidst the crisis of the Soviet Bloc and really existing socialism, an overall re-appraisal of the party's policies and strategies was urged. The party, it was lamented, had failed to understand the far-reaching transformations that international capitalism had been undergoing over the past twenty years and very little investigation had been attempted concerning the new distinctive features and fundamental changes inherent in the collapse of the Fordist model. The PCI's defeat at the 1985 *scala mobile* referendum, promoted by the communist-led CGIL, to repeal the reform of the wage indexation system carried out by the Craxi government, was regarded as a further illustration of the growing gap between the party and its rank and file on the one hand, and the electorate on the other.[91] The overwhelming majority of the 'Nos' came from the Northern industrialised regions, which meant that large sectors of the working class had voted against the PCI.

Following the death of Enrico Berlinguer in 1984, Eurocommunism began to be questioned. It was eventually discarded in 1987, since the crisis of the Soviet Union and Gorbachev's new course deprived it of any sense. The revision of the eurocommunist position paved the way to a gradual reorientation of the party towards Western European social democracy, which the PCI had been moving towards since the early 1980s. At the 1986 party XVII Congress,[92] Natta's party endorsed the 'Euroleft ideology' which Peter Glotz, the SPD leader from 1980 to 1987, had outlined in his *Manifesto for a New European Left*, published in 1985.[93] The latter was the first attempt of European social democrats to respond to the crisis of Keynesian nation-centred politics. It was in fact a new route to socialism which passed through the creation of a supranational European order to make possible the co-ordination among socialist parties of their economic and social policies, and to maintain welfare and equality goals.

The 1986 party congress resolution, while leaving untouched some of the party's distinctive features such as democratic centralism (which was discarded only in the late 1980s), was an important step toward the PCI's move towards the social-democratic family. The paradox was that this occurred at a time when welfare capitalism and social-democratic politics were going through a deep and seemingly irreversible crisis. However, once having taken up a traditional Keynesian interventionist agenda, the PCI soon realised that the journey was not over. Instead, it had to stay on the new path towards a new revisionism which its recently acquired sister parties had been marching towards – some hesitantly and others more convincingly – over the course of the last decade.

As was the case with Labour, electoral defeats acted as a very powerful stimulus to accelerate the pace of change and modernisation.

The 1987 electoral setback opened the way to the new younger generation leadership of so-called *quarantenni* ('forty somethings'), which
included people such as Massimo D'Alema, Livia Turco, Piero Fassino,
Fabio Mussi, led by Achille Occhetto, and who pushed for the PCI's social-
democratisation even further. Italian communists left the Communist
Group in the European Parliament in June 1989, and eventually joined
the ranks of the Socialist International in 1993.[94]

The fall of the Berlin Wall precipitated the renewal. Anything remotely
connected with communism was now a liability which no nostalgia
could justify. The *de facto* endorsement of a social-democratic agenda had
to be followed, it was argued, by a change of name and image if Italian
communists were to fully capitalise, electorally and politically, on the
epochal changes which both the international system and Italian politics
were undergoing. What should be noted is, that as was the case with the
Italian socialists in the mid-1950s, this move was taken by the PCI to
gain new legitimacy and put an end to the notorious *conventio ad excludendum*, a tacit agreement which ruled out communists' participation in
government during the Cold War years, in order to increase its electoral
appeal. Particularly after 1993, when the anti-corruption Clean Hands
operation swept away traditional mainstream parties such as the DC and
the PSI, and new political spaces opened up which were unthink-
able only a few years before, the heirs of Gramsci endorsed even more
resolutely the conviction that, to secure their position as a hegemoni-
cal left-wing party, within a new 'bipartisan' so-called Italian Second
Republic, a general overhaul was required.

In November 1989, Achille Occhetto, the new PCI leader elected in June
1988, announced an imminent re-branding of the party. At the Rimini
Congress in 1991, after two years of fierce and heated internal debate, less
focused on policies than on identity issues, the party was eventually re-
founded. The name was symbolically changed to the Democratic Party of
the Left and an oak adopted as its new symbol. The breakaway of the
orthodox traditionalist fringe led by Armando Cossutta and some *ingraiani*
(the old 'New Left') gave birth to the party of Communist Refoundation,
and signalled the final rupture of the PDS with the old Communist tradition. The die had been cast, and the *conventio ad excludendum* factor, eventually defused. No more constraints existed to the party's participation
within a coalition government.[95]

4
Shaping a 'Post-Fordist' Third Way

The 1990s: the resurgence of the Left

The electoral victories of the centre–left Olive Tree coalition in 1996, and of Tony Blair in May 1997, paved the way to a change in the political fortunes of the European Left. One month after the Labour Party's victory, the Socialist Party leader Lionel Jospin was elected in France. This marked the country's return to a 'pluralist Left' government and was soon followed by the formation of the red–green government led by Schrœder in Germany. By 1998, parties of the Left were in power in thirteen of the fifteen European Union countries, albeit with different weight. The Left seemed to have moved into a new and positive phase. Repeated claims at the end of the 1980s stating that the end of socialism was nigh (referring here to Ralf Dahrendorf's suggestion that the 'century of social democracy was over')[1] seemed to be misconstrued.

In some ways the situation bore strong similarities to the political atmosphere of the 1960s. As discussed earlier, after a decade of domination by the forces of the centre and centre–right in much of Europe, a whole series of studies began to appear in the late 1950s that aimed to show how the prosperity engendered by the post-war boom left little political space for parties of a Marxist stamp.[2] However, European left-wing parties were soon to undergo a sudden recovery. Where at the beginning of the 1960s, the only places where parties of the Left governed were in the Scandinavian countries, by the end of the decade the political equilibrium had changed considerably. In 1963, the first centre–left government was established in Italy; and in 1964 Wilson led the British Labour Party to victory after the Conservatives had held power for thirteen years. In 1966 the coalition government in West Germany included the SPD for the first time – a presence that would gain greater political weight with Willy Brandt's election as Chancellor three years later. In 1966 the social democrats and communists formed a 'Popular Front' government in Finland. Finally, in 1970 the Austrian socialists established a government without the Christian Democrats.[3]

There is nevertheless a substantial difference between the position of the Left in those years and that of the 1990s. The decisive factor in the left-wing parties' success during the 1960s was the obvious need of Western capitalist economies for politics of economic planning and state intervention. Those years were described by Eric Hobsbawm as the 'marriage' between capitalism and social-democracy.[4] This alliance went well beyond simply repeating turn-of-the-century attempts by many of the liberal states to broaden the basis of their political consensus. For its survival in the 1960s the capitalist system relied not only on 'social peace', but also, paradoxically, on an economic direction of a social-democratic cast, where the principal ingredients included Keynesianism, economic planning, long-term investment in research, and the like. Under these conditions the Left exercised a full 'cultural hegemony' regardless of who was in power: the British Conservatives, from the moment they returned to power in 1951, adhered strictly to Keynesian economic principles; only a few years later, de Gaulle began to promote economic planning in France. In Italy, the Christian Democrats abandoned the classic liberalism promoted by Einaudi immediately after the war. When the Left came to power throughout Europe in the 1960s, it did so, therefore, using distinctive left-wing policies.

The situation in the 1990s was profoundly different. Socialist parties returned to power but they did so with few traditional left-wing policies. It is frequently noted that today's Left is now subordinate to the hegemony of neo-liberalism.[5] The Left is therefore showing its capacity to adapt, as it has done throughout history, but with one major difference: talk of 'the crisis of the Left' continues unabated. This is a Left widely described as in retreat, on the defensive, ready to drop its ideological and cultural baggage in order to embrace doctrines and values that only a few years ago it abhorred.

Not surprisingly, the questioning of the Left–Right polarity has re-appeared to the forefront of political debate.[6] Forty years after the publication of *The End of Ideology* by Daniel Bell, the collapse of communism gave a new boost to the 'end of ideology' genre. Recast in the new 'end of history' discourse from Fukuyama's much-quoted book,[7] in a world where liberal democracy has triumphed globally and irreversibly, it is argued, little room is left for past controversies and divisions. Ideological confrontation is said to have died and been replaced by limited technocratic disputes over problem-solving.[8]

As Norberto Bobbio has pointed out, Left and Right are questioned in periods characterised by a great degree of consensus, that is, when one side holds hegemonic strength both politically and electorally. Those on the winning side, dusting off the end of the rhetoric of ideology, triumphantly insist there is no alternative left but theirs; those on the losing side are more than happy to get rid of labels associated with defeat.[9] When the Left/Right dichotomy was first questioned in the 1950s and 1960s, the Right was still expiating the inter-war failure of orthodox monetary policies and the defeat of totalitarian regimes during World War II. Here, no alternatives seemed to exist equalling Keynesian politics. The welfare state and public spending were the new mantra that all post-war European political parties, irrespective of their colour, pursued. In what went down in history as the 'age of consensus', many began to question the relevance and significance of Left and Right. Today, the crisis of the Keynesian model, the collapse of communism, and the overall hegemony of neo-liberalism which followed suit have created a new unbalanced power between Left and Right, albeit this time to the latter's advantage. While for most of the post-war years the Right was regarded with negative connotations, particularly in those countries such as Italy which had experienced authoritarian regimes during the inter-war years, the opposite is true today. Today it is the Left that is tainted with evils such as infringement of basic liberties, bureaucracy, inefficiency and defeat. It is against this background that many left-wing parties now seem very keen on using alternative labels to describe themselves such as 'left of centre', 'radical–centre', 'centre–left', 'radical' or 'progressive'.

This is not to say that they are prepared to accept the 'end of the Left' rhetoric. As a matter of fact, it is claimed that the collapse of communism far from depriving it of its *raison d'être*, has instead strengthened the case for social democracy. Social-democratic parties, it is argued, have always been in the forefront of those who condemned really-existing socialism as a deviance and betrayal of left-wing values. As Tony Blair put it, the fall of the Berlin Wall did not signal the death of the Left; rather, it opened a new era for progressive politics.[10] It is accepted that old lines along which Left and Right used to divide in the past, such as antagonism to capitalism and the degree of state intervention in the economy, have become redundant; however, socialists' commitment to equality – 'the socialist value par excellence', as Tony Wright has argued[11] – is said to make the Left/Right dichotomy still relevant.[12] In so far as socialism is intended as 'ethical', it is therefore said to be far from dead. In this respect it should be pointed out that Anthony Giddens's 'Third Way' is not conceived, as some commentators have misleadingly suggested,[13] as a third way beyond Left and Right as if the two categories were not valid anymore.

Rather, it is thought of as a renewal of social democracy and its adaptation to the social, economic and cultural processes of globalisation; a third way between the old social-democratic model and neo-liberalism. In other words, a third way within, and not beyond, the Left.

The revival of ethical socialism

As Tony Blair has often reiterated, of all the varieties of socialism that developed during the last century, the only one that has survived the collapse of the Berlin Wall is 'ethical' socialism. That is, as he put it, 'the only serious view of the Left's future that can remain'.[14] Socialism should be about values and not 'an economic dogma':[15] old ideologies and fixed political projects should make headway through inspired pragmatism. This is why the Third Way should be conceived as 'work in progress',[16] 'a permanent revisionism', and a continual search for better means to meet Labour's goals.[17] What matters, 'is what works'.[18]

This brand of socialism has deep origins in the ideological past of the Labour Party. Its values are derived from the utopian and Christian socialism of thinkers such as the inter-war Scottish moral philosopher John Macmurray and, to some extent, figures such as R. H. Tawney, who emphasised solidarity, community and mutual co-operation.[19] As Blair pointed out, in the footsteps of earlier centre–right revisionists, the time has come to discard a scientific view of socialism based on a notion of economic determinism and a particular view of class.[20] The six lines in his Fabian pamphlet *Socialism* in which he dismisses the relevance of Marxism could well be regarded as a sign of the times.[21] The demolition of central Marxist tenets like the 'collapse' or the 'pauperisation' theories had required far longer sections in Anthony Crosland's *The Future of Socialism* and Douglas Jay's *Socialism in the New Society*.[22] In contrast, criticising 'The Mirage of Marxism'[23] today is like knocking down an open door.

A critique of Marxism and 'scientific socialism' is of vital importance particularly for those parties such as the DS (the PDS since 1998)[24] whose ideological communist past is still one of the favourite political cards played by its opponents during elections as a way of de-legitimising them. If for the leadership of Communist Refoundation Marxist and neo-Marxist notions such as the uneven development of capitalism remain 'ideas which will never die', as the title of a book published in 2000 by Fausto Bertinotti declared,[25] for the majority of the new DS they would be better shelved. As the then secretary of the party Walter Veltroni put it at the first DS Congress in 2000, the only thing one can save of

Marx is his dialectic notion of modernity. As for the remainder of his economic and social analysis, he argued, new times have made it redundant. In this respect, it is quite revealing that throughout his entire speech, the word 'capitalism' was not mentioned once.[26]

The PCI, even before its 'social-democratic' rebirth in 1991, had long distanced itself from Leninism, the Stalinist horrors and 'really-existing socialism'. Togliatti's route throughout the post-war years was to call for an 'Italian road to socialism'. The launch of Eurocommunism in 1973 by Enrico Berlinguer was an explicit reiteration of the same concept. The latter was symbolically followed in a few years by the 'break' with the Soviet Union over the Afghan invasion in 1979. In 1981, after condemning Jaruzelski's proclamation of a state of emergency in Poland, Berlinguer declared the end of the 'propulsive force beginning with the October revolution'.[27] When Occhetto made his suggestions for the party's refoundation in the 1989 speech at the Bolognina he declared that the PCI was the child of the French, and not the October, revolution.

When it comes to the party's specific legacy and the number of attempts made by PCI leaders in the post-war years towards formulating an 'Italian road to socialism', greater caution has been evident. From the beginning of the new course started by Occhetto in 1987, Togliatti and Berlinguer's legacy have come under some criticism and reconsideration; it never, however, took the shape of a total demolition. A number of reasons account for this: firstly, before the socialists dissolved in 1993, there was the predominant fear that Craxi's party, which since 1976 had harshly attacked the communists' ideological legacy and post-war ambivalence, might have capitalised on any sign of ceding. Criticising Togliatti would have been an implicit acceptance of the socialists' argument whereby no real distinction existed between Italian and Soviet communism. Secondly, as was the case with Nenni's PSI in 1956, the PCI leadership could not ignore the resistance posed by the inner left-wing factions to shelve the party's history and past symbols. A harsh attack with regard to past communist identity, it was argued, would have dramatically split the party. The breakaway by Communist Refoundation that followed the foundation of the PDS in 1991 showed that such fears were not unfounded.[28]

The decision to keep a reduced version of the old PCI hammer and sickle at the bottom of the new PDS's logo of the oak tree (where the choice of a tree alluded to the French Revolution's tree of liberty) testified to the awareness of the party's leadership of the enormous weight placed upon symbols both within the latter's political apparatus and by its members. In 1998 a completely new logo replaced both: a red carnation.

On the whole, the party adopted a compromising attitude towards its past. This was made easier by the 'duplicity' which characterised the PCI's strategy throughout the post-war years. While any revolutionary connotations within their theoretical and political legacy might be discarded, there still remained a reformist 'democratic heritage'[29] which could be saved. As far as Palmiro Togliatti was concerned, it was his role in the anti-fascist coalition that helped consolidate the newly founded post-war Italian Republic and its Constitution. As for Enrico Berlinguer, although his strategy has been the object of widespread criticism, the party will never 'forget Berlinguer', as ex-PDS deputy Miriam Mafai, a well-known commentator for the newspaper *La Repubblica*, urged in a polemical pamphlet published in 1996.[30] Not only, it is argued, was he a charismatic and popular leader whom people loved (as the title of a famous film by Roberto Benigni *Berlinguer ti voglio bene* declares) but, in D'Alema's words, there are some elements of his thinking that are still valid. These are the importance attributed to the alliance with the Catholic world to avoid its shift towards the Right, his concern with new social movements and new political issues such as gender and environment, and last but not least, the centrality attached to the 'moral question' that the anti-corruption 'Clean Hands' operation, which took place after 1993, has made more topical than ever.[31]

Even the legacy of Antonio Gramsci, rediscovered now as a forerunning 'liberal',[32] has been preserved. The abundant and fragmentary quality of his works have rendered their interpretation 'open' and 'problematic' for years. They have permitted, in fact, 'multiple uses' in connection with diverse cultural and political turns. Since the years between the two world wars, the communists have proposed renewed readings of the Sardinian intellectual to the extent that, as Guido Liguori wrote, the history of the PCI itself could be reconstructed through them.[33] The end of historical communism has resulted in further interpretations of Gramsci, opening a new season of analysis and reflection. Since 1991, the Gramsci Institute has been working on a new 'national' edition of his complete works, a project which, in so far as it attempts to reinterpret Gramscian thinking in the direction of a 'post-communist' Gramsci, critical *ante litteram* of communism, has aroused more than a few debates between intellectuals from the Old Guard, including Valentino Gerratana.[34]

Selective readings of a past legacy went hand in hand with the revival or 'appropriation', of more acceptable traditions. More than ever before, especially after the fall of 'really-existing socialism' and the new ideological–cultural context of the post-1980s, which saw neo-liberal thought gaining increasing hegemony, it has become vital for ex-communist parties to liberate themselves from heavy ideological burdens and instead draw on theoretical debates that reinforce their own 'liberal' credentials.

Parties such as the DS have for some time pursued a growing interest in reformist political–cultural traditions such as that of Catholic democracy as represented by figures like Giuseppe Dossetti, or the liberal–socialist one that draws in traditional values such as social justice and equality, as well as the equally important 'rediscovered' values of democracy and liberty. In particular, the liberal–socialist Rossellian heritage has become an increasingly important reference point, signalling a 'revenge of history' on behalf of political experiences and currents of thought that were the 'Cinderella' in Italian political and cultural debates for years. This is for the Communists' heirs a true 'Copernican revolution'.[35] As we saw in Chapter 1, with the Italian socialists' autonomist turn and the revisionist season that preceded the first centre–left governments, there was a reawakening of interest in Actionism (from the short-lived Action Party, 1942–7) and, in particular, for the lessons of Carlo Rosselli (who incidentally used Tawney as an important reference point). As far as the PCI was concerned, however, actionist ideas remained marginal to communist thinking until recently. Only after the collapse of the Soviet Union and 'really-existing socialism' did doors open for urgent research on alternative forms of socialism, and only since then have theoretical works by thinkers such as Rosselli begun to witness a new relevance and centrality in post-communist political discourse.[36]

With the fall of historic communism came the birth of some movements in Italy that explicitly reclaimed Rosselli's liberal socialism: the Action Movement of Justice and Liberty, founded on 29 April 1994, was one.[37] The political fortune of these groups has remained very limited; however, the growing hegemony of liberal socialism as a doctrine on already existent Left formations seems indisputable. Liberal socialism is a major source of inspiration for the diverse movements and runaway groups from the old Italian Socialist Party, such as Enrico Boselli's Italian Socialists (SI).[38] One such group of the centrist area of the DS calls itself, significantly, 'Association for Equal Liberty' (*Associazione Libertà Eguale*), implicitly referring to a key concept of liberal socialist tradition. Lastly, Rosselli's thought also represents the doctrinal reference for Valdo Spini's Labour Federation (founded in 1994) that entered the DS in 1998.[39]

In February 1999, Spini's Labour Federation was amongst the organisers of a conference entitled 'Socialism and Liberty: Remembering

Carlo Rosselli'[40] in which key figures from both the political world and the intelligentsia of the ex-PCI participated. Spini opened the conference with a speech entitled 'Rosselli's topicality: from Liberal Socialism to a "second phase" in the construction of a New European Socialist Party in Italy'. Biagio de Giovanni followed this with an account entitled 'Liberalism and Socialism: The culture of the Left between and beyond Revisionism'. Other speeches included Fabio Mussi's 'Socialism and new orientations of democratic thought' and Giorgio Napolitano's 'Socialism and liberty in a future European Left'. The conference ended with a significant speech by Walter Veltroni that continued with his 'appropriation' campaign in regards to the actionist memory that had opened with his controversial speech in 1998 when he was elected secretary of the party. In this he condemned Togliattian communism (unrecoverable because it was stained by totalitarianism) and urged instead a revival of the liberal democratic roots of the actionist tradition which he still considered vital.[41] The incompatibility between communism and liberty, and the idea of Rosselli's socialism as the 'New *Esperanto*' of the Left, was later again reiterated by Veltroni during the DS's Congress in Lingotto in January 2000.[42] This congress, in Veltroni's words, was supposed to put an end to the post-transition psychosis which had followed Occhetto's speech at the Bolognina and, by defining once and for all 'what the devil is the Left in Italy', to give the party a new soul and identity that wasn't merely 'post' something. Entering into direct polemics with Togliatti's definition of Rosselli as 'an amateur player', Veltroni affirmed that, if the new frontier that the DS envisaged for its generation wanted to be the 'globalisation of fundamental individual rights', the Rossellian heritage should certainly be considered a point of inspiration more suitable than the communist legacy.[43] 'We aren't dealing with an operation of appearances', as the Right would like, continued Veltroni, but an 'intellectually honest operation' that tries to recuperate the 'best parts and traditions of the Left' by integrating those aspects of the ex-PCI's cultural baggage that are still valid (including the eternal Gramsci) with political cultures other than the Marxist tradition, such as the doctrines of liberal socialism.[44]

The 'instrumentalisation' and revival of ideas elaborated in a radically diverse historical context has provoked a lot of suspicion and criticism concerning an operation that rarely defeats anti-historicism.[45] While it is beyond the scope of this book to consider the merits or relevance of the lessons left by these thinkers – these are up to political philosophers to assess – it is worth examining the reasons why, apart from their intrinsic value, ideas of the founder of *Giustizia e Libertà* have become the objects of growing interest. The reasons are clear. Firstly, Rosselli's revisionism is not within the Marxist tradition but was intended to over-come it; in this sense it has been described as post-Marxism.[46] Rosselli's proposal is for an ethical socialism, which is the only type of socialism that survived the fall of the Berlin Wall and is 'acceptable' today. By refusing a deterministic concept of history, Rosselli's socialism is not a closed system like Marxism. Rather it is an ideal, the attainment of which is not fatalistically determined but is instead the result of an 'ethical commitment'. Furthermore, Rosselli's liberal socialism proposes ideas that are topical today such as 'equal liberty', an idea of liberty that seeks to reconcile individual autonomy with social justice.[47] Another topical theme is the centrality Rosselli accords to the individual; for Rosselli, the individual and society precede the State. This remains one of the central themes not only in the doctrine elaborated by the founder of the GL but in the entire actionist tradition.

Rosselli speaks of a 'co-operative individual' who is ethically orien-tated. Even here, he undoubtedly offers useful insights for a Left that, while centring its political discourse on the individual, refuses to accept the neo-liberal notion of the individual as an isolated, self-centred atom. Where neo-liberals envisage individuals as separate economic actors that maximise profit in the market place, for the Left, individuals are instead conceived as naturally co-operative and linked by moral obligations.[48] In a world of high reflexivity, it is now accepted by left-wing parties that an individual must achieve a certain degree of autonomy of action as a con-dition of being able to survive and forge a life. Autonomy, however, as Blair put it, is not the same as egoism, but implies reciprocity and inter-dependence.[49]

The question of how to regain a sense of community and renew social solidarity without reverting to old 'statist solutions' is at the heart of third way politics. State action based on low public spending and taxes requires ethically oriented and responsible citizens who are able to look after themselves and are prepared to take over many of the caring roles which the state used to provide. It is against this background that the interest shown by some British 'thirdwayers', *in primis* Tony Blair, for Communitarianism[50] – with its emphasis on solidarity and reciprocity and the importance attached to civic obligations and responsibilities as the corollary of social rights and entitlements – should be considered. Since the 1960s, as the Labour leader put it, the pendulum has swung towards a more individualistic ethos. This explains why so many sec-tions of the Left were captivated by the elegance and power of John Rawls's analyses. Yet, his 'highly individualistic view of the world', Blair continues, should be contrasted with a notion of citizens as part of a community, a concept of Britain as a team rather than as 'a collection of selfish players' where notions of mutuality and interdependence are not 'abstract ideals' but 'facts of life'.[51]

Blair's kind of communitarism, so clearly influenced by his Christian beliefs, raises a great deal of suspicion in large sectors of the British progressive intelligentsia and political elite. This includes, for instance, Gordon Brown, who, when questioning old beliefs and policies, has so far seemed more inclined to rely upon liberal and radical thinking as a source of inspiration for the party's new course.[52] The reservations with which the British and Italian Left regard their own pasts, has, in fact, not only opened the way for a revival of ethical and liberal socialism but has also led to a 'renewal of interests' for the radical–liberal vein.

Towards 'radical' politics

Another writer in whom there has been a revival of interest in recent years among some factions of the Italian Left is Piero Gobetti. Gobetti is known as a fundamental contributor to the renewal of Italian liberal thinking, not only by claiming liberalism's minimal tasks (Gobetti was one of the first intellectuals and writers of the liberal area who took a position against fascism), but also by pushing for a new and more enlarged interpretation of its objectives.[53]

Paolo Flores D'Arcais's, article entitled 'The Actionist Alternative' which appeared in 1991 in *Micromega* (a journal that from its birth in 1986 has played a bridging role between the so-called 'submerged liberal Left' and the PCI), was, in this respect, a significant turning point. It argued that the Italian Left must 'break with its communist, Marxist–Leninist past and all its duplicity, including international restraints that had kept it behind'.[54] The Gobettian heritage was seen as the only alternative for the PCI's heirs after the crisis of really-existing socialism. A new edition of Gobetti's *Liberal Revolution* was published in 1995 with an introduction by Flores D'Arcais. This marked the definite 'appropriation' of Gobetti's legacy on behalf of some sections within the Italian Left (in which the editor of *Micromega* can be considered the most representative voice) who have long urged for a transformation of the ex-PCI into 'a new liberal post-communist Left that renounces its past' (*in primis* the Togliattian patrimony) and puts liberty at the centre of its political discourse.[55]

Another important reference point that has for some time been gaining attention is the American tradition of liberal thought, as, for example, the theory of justice by John Rawls, which has often been seen as a new version of social liberalism. There have also been contributions by

Italian left-wing scholars in the area of political philosophy, such as these of Salvatore Veca and Sebastiano Maffettone.[56] It is also worth remembering here that many DS members, including the ex-leader Walter Veltroni, particularly admired John F. Kennedy and the tradition of US democratic thought.[57]

Another tradition that has been the focus of increasing interest in recent years has been that of reformist liberal political thought. In 1995, the first Italian publication of *Liberalism* by Hobhouse was issued with an introduction by Franco Sbarberi; the latter, while establishing a parallel with the theoretical elaborations of Rosselli, defined the English philosopher as 'the most consistent supporter of the comprehensive melting between liberalism and socialism'.[58] Moreover, New Liberal[59] figures such as Karl Popper,[60] Robert Dahl, Ralf Dahrendorf, Isaiah Berlin and the Nobel Prize winner Amartya Sen, have emerged after a forty years' silence.[61] To date, almost all have been translated into Italian and have 'spilt into' the speeches and writings produced by many DS political figures.[62] Since 1989 the newspaper *l'Unità* has provided articles and interviews by these authors and other 'theorists' of liberal democracy such as Edgar Morin and Maurice Duverger. The latter was also a candidate in the PCI list during the European elections in June 1989.

The Italian DS have not limited themselves in recent years to the recovery of a liberal discourse, but have also claimed for themselves the mantle of 'Liberal Party'. The Gobettian theme of a Left paradoxically more liberal and modern than the Right now seems to be more topical than ever: the DS challenge daily the coalition parties of the centre–right on the issue of liberty, not only proposing a more extensive concept of this but by setting themselves up as the representatives of 'true liberals'. The presence within Berlusconi's centre–right government of the heirs of the old MSI, the plebiscitary tendency in which Berlusconi has often been accused, his attacks on the judiciary, the conflict of interests that remain unresolved and the alliance with a party such as the Northern League that does not disguise its xenophobia, are all themes in which the Left continues to systematically point out the dangers for the future of Italian democracy posed by their adversaries. At his appointment as leader of the centre–left coalition in the 2001 elections, Francesco Rutelli polemically reminded Fini, the AN leader, of the debt to liberty he and his coalition's members owed to those who battled against fascism. Here Rutelli encouraged the Left to 'recover the word liberty' making it part of the Olive Tree coalition banner and no longer that of the Polo alliance.[63] As D'Alema put it in *La sinistra che cambia* ('the Left that changes'), the Left should embark on the 'constitutionalisation' and democratisation of the Right.[64]

A similar debate would be inconceivable in Great Britain. With the exception of the Thatcher years, relations between political parties have always been characterised by a far more pronounced bipartisan spirit. Reciprocal delegitimation over basic principles is, in other words, banned by the political game. No party needs to reaffirm its liberal credentials with the kind of anxiety shown by the Italians. Rather, they are taken for granted. In Britain too, the transition from 'old' to New Labour has paved the way to a new attitude towards liberal culture. However, when Blair claims to be a modern twenty-first century liberal, he does not refer to the Labour Party's adherence to a package of basic rights which the British system has been long consolidating, but rather to a set of policies which reflect a greater concern with new and advanced rights in the civil sphere and a retreat from collectivism in favour of individual's rights.

Compared with parties of the European Left, Labour has always had the most pronounced 'liberal' conscience. One should not forget that the ideological origins of the party rest with Fabianism, which was in turn influenced by Bentham's utilitarianism and the New Liberalism of the turn of the last century. The 'liberal conscience' of Labour has not always been consistent. It was particularly strong during the 1950s as a consequence of the hegemony then exercised by centre–right revisionists such as Crosland. It became weaker not long afterwards, with the ascent to leadership of the technocratic centre–left under Wilson, whose purported politics of planning often represented a breach of civil liberties to his internal adversaries. However, the rediscovery, indeed exaltation, of the individual during the Thatcher years, meant that Labour had to beat Thatcherism on its own turf, and without a doubt led the party towards a new sensitivity in regards to typical liberal values.

As Tony Wright put it, as opposed to the number of labels, such as 'market socialism' or 'liberal communitarianism', which have been used to denote Blair's new philosophy, it is 'social liberalism' that today best expresses what New Labour politics is about. According to this position, socialism is a 'doctrine of community and responsibility, with a liberal reminder of the danger of an overweening state and the importance of individuals pursuing their own purposes in their own way'.[65]

Intellectuals such as Will Hutton, John Gray, Ralf Dahrendorf and Harold Perkin, who all contributed significantly to the reshaping of British progressive politics and the transition from Old to New Labour, fit into a new intellectual and political paradigm which combines insights of traditional social-democratic thinking with notions drawn from social liberalism.[66] The split between these two traditions, as Blair pointed out, did much to weaken progressive politics in Western democracies and has today been deprived by history of any justification. The Third Way, as he put it, 'draws vitality from uniting the two great streams of left-of-centre thought – democratic socialism and liberalism'.[67]

As a result of the merger of the Liberals with the Social Democratic Party (SDP) in 1988, liberalism and social democracy are separated today in the UK by the narrowest divide in political history;[68] the New Labour course and the Liberal Democrats' shift to the left have, in fact, produced a considerable convergence between the two political parties on a common progressive agenda. In the run up to the 1997 elections, Blair's party developed a constitutional reform agenda that bore striking similarities with proposals long advocated by Paddy Ashdown's party: Scottish and Welsh devolution, the reform of the House of Lords, the introduction of a Bill of Rights and the incorporation into the electoral system of some elements of proportional representation. The relationship between Labour and the Liberal Democrats came so close that, as Paddy Ashdown later recalled,[69] joint plans were considered. After more than forty years of Crosland's proposal of a joint liberal–labour alliance, the prospect of a marriage between social democracy and liberalism seemed to have been revived again.[70]

New Labour's *rapprochement* with the liberal milieu did not need, in fact, a formal merger with the Liberal Democrats. As a matter of fact, Blair's party has been appropriating the Liberal Democrats' traditional values, language and ideas over the last five years. Even the expression 'third way', as Liberal Democrats argue, was first invented by them.[71] The focus on the symbiotic relationship between a strong civil society and an active state, the decline of class-based politics and the diminishing relevance of the Left–Right divide, were all themes of a number of Liberal Democrat policy statements and pamphlets over the past decade.[72] Similarly, the emphasis on voluntary activity through local communities, education and training, and partnership between state and private companies, is also a common ground.[73]

Together with appropriating the liberal repertoire, New Labour was also successful in stealing the political space traditionally occupied by the Liberal Democrats: Blair's repositioning of its party on the centre ground from 1994 pushed the Lib–Dems to the left, which produced a major political realignment within British politics. This was fully apparent at the 2001 general election when Charles Kennedy, Paddy Ashdown's successor, decided to play the role of the tax and spend party as opposed to what was generally described as New Labour's neo-liberalism.

Towards a post-materialist agenda

One important area where the neo-revisionist Left and the liberal-inspired political parties increasingly converge today is their respective libertarian agendas. Never before have the European socialist and social-democratic parties been deprived of real margins of manoeuvre in the economic–social sphere as they have today. As a result, they tend to shift their battle towards more advanced themes such as civil rights, distinguishing themselves increasingly from their adversaries of the centre and centre–right by concentrating on libertarian and post-materialist agendas. This is also consistent with the undisputed centrality attached by neo-revisionists to the individual as opposed to class.

Significantly, as Veltroni argued at the DS Congress in Lingotto in January 2000, the frontier for a 'new Left' should be 'the universalisation of fundamental individual rights'. The individual and society, he said, should precede the state; it is the individual and no longer a class that should act as a paradigm inspirator of politics; an individual who should be emancipated and defended as much as possible from unjustifiable interference from the state. In the 'post-materialist' society – as Luciano Violante, a prominent DS figure has written – the emancipation of individuals does not solely signify liberation from need. The more people the welfare state has conquered, the more a situation of well-being persists. In addition, the more materialist values are substituted with different values, the greater the tendency to refuse any limits upon individual self-realisation becomes.[74] As Anthony Giddens has remarked, the political outlook of the Left has always been closely bound up with the idea of emancipation. However, emancipation means freedoms of various kinds: freedom from the constraints of material deprivation, but also from the arbitrary hold of tradition, from arbitrary power.[75]

Individualism was long anathema within traditional Left discourse. This underlay the difficulty of coming to terms with phenomena such as consumerism, regarded as the antithesis of the collectivist ethos central to socialist parties' ideology. As we saw in Chapter 2, initially the affluent society was regarded with hostility derived from concern over its effects on social solidarity. Electoral calculations eventually prevailed over moral condemnation. No spin doctors were needed in order to understand that electoral messages aimed at convincing people to dispose of their newly purchased cars for the sake of their soul would be suicidal. This is something that even Christian democratic parties, which shared socialists' uneasiness towards the consumer society, accepted. However, the accommodation to 'hedonism' and individual ethos remained pragmatic and instrumental. No theoretical justification or fully-fledged endorsement was ever attempted.

The ideological impact of the 'me first' culture, reinforced by the growing success of neo-liberal experiments in the 1980s in all its national variations, forced an overall reassessment and reconsideration of left-wing parties' hostility towards what had long been simplistically dismissed as disruptive self-seeking and selfish tendencies. Individualism could not remain an exclusive property of the Right; the time had come, it was argued, to catch up with the people's newly emerging aspirations for self-fulfilment. 'New Individualism',[76] which – according to third way rhetoric – is supposed to be a break from both social-democratic collectivism and a blind acceptance of market individualism[77] should be accepted, it is argued, as a liberating phenomenon. In so far as it is conducive to a 'reflexive society', where individuals are increasingly free from tradition and the fixities of the past, it should be welcomed and encouraged.[78] Fears that this might exert disruptive effects on social solidarity and political participation are acknowledged, but the clock, it is argued, cannot be turned back and alternative means to secure them need to be found.

As far as social cohesion is concerned, the very idea of an 'enabling state', which is central to socialists' neo-revisionism, is supposed to entail a notion, if somewhat voluntaristic, of a society comprised of more responsible citizens capable of looking after themselves and who are less dependent on the hierarchical state (that is, top–down state action).

As for the dangers in terms of political alienation and disentanglement, further democratisation, decentralisation and devolution are seen as the key ingredients of a third-way-inspired response.[79] In a society where tradition and custom are losing their hold, the only route towards establishing authority, as Giddens put it, is by recasting it on a more active and participatory basis that allows for greater democratisation.[80]

Western societies today face widespread disillusionment with parliamentary politics and the democratic processes. This has resulted in increasingly lower voter turn-out and a decreasing level of trust in politicians in recent years. Political apathy is a phenomenon that goes back, as we saw in earlier chapters, to the late 1950s. However, people's remoteness from politics has been further aggravated since then. This is well illustrated by the use of formulas to describe it which go far beyond the earlier softer one of *depolitisation*. As in the title of the oft-quoted book by Geoff Mulgan (the former Director of the think tank Demos and adviser to Tony Blair), we live today in an 'anti-political age': indifference has given way to hostility.[81]

The need to connect people to politics is one of the most frequent refrains made by contemporary politicians. It is within this context that the growing concern of both New Labour and the Italian DS with regards to electoral, institutional, and constitutional reforms should be viewed. The latter have all been at the core of a number of books published over the last ten years by left-wing scholars and politicians in both countries, all arguing that institutional and constitutional reforms are needed in order to respond to growing dissatisfaction with the institutional structure.[82] Sometimes pejoratively described – quite rightly – as 'institutional reductionism', the underlying assumption is that all social and political crises affecting Western countries in recent years can be explained by their institutional structures. Under the slogan of 'returning power to the people' and the need for recasting the state/ citizen relationship on a more participatory basis, both the Italian and British Left have abandoned the centralist attitude that characterised the European Left until recently and promoted reforms in a federalist and decentralising vein. Just as New Labour during its first term granted greater autonomy to Scotland and Wales, in Italy the Amato centre–left government put forward in March 2001 a major institutional reform which envisaged a significant reorganisation of the present regional arrangements. It might be worth noting that for all the genuine concern over people's apathy, the growing electoral strength of parties such as the Northern League in Italy and the Scottish Nationalist Party in the UK, also played a crucial role in pushing issues such as devolution to the centre of New Labour and the DS's political agenda.

The socialist neo-revisionist parties' acceptance of the rising importance of individualism has gone hand-in-hand with an increasing sensibility for new individualist politics and the tainted 'permissive society'. This was facilitated by generational change: most of today's prominent socialist leaders were deeply imbued with the new individualist ethos of the 1960s and 1970s and far more at ease than their fathers were in dealing with post-traditional society.[83]

In spite of rhetorical commitment to equal opportunity, feminist issues long played a marginal role in socialist and social-democratic parties' political agenda. While much of feminist thought has been sympathetic to the Left, or at least not overtly hostile, European socialists were long indifferent to non-class specific interests of women, showing a rather exclusive focus upon the workplace (historically dominated by men) and sticking to a definition of social rights based on male employment patterns. Emancipation was long conceived as a gender-neutral liberation from capitalists' 'exploitation' ignoring other more intimate forms of oppression (for instance, within the home). However, neo-revisionist socialist parties seem to show a greater commitment to gender issues today. As will be seen in the next chapter, the traditional gender gap and women's tendencies to vote Right have been on the decline since the 1970s. If not only out of electoral calculations, the 'needs of women' have been making increasingly great incursions in left-wing parties' agendas.[84]

It goes without saying that no revolution has been either promised or carried out beyond that of a soft reformism. The libertarian radicalism of left-wing intellectuals such as Ulrich Beck and Anthony Giddens could never be completely adopted by parties such as New Labour or the DS; the latter are very aware of the need not to compromise their broad electoral appeal by endorsing too advanced or unpopular causes. Issues that pressure groups, mainly composed of highly educated middle-class activists, propose hardly match ordinary people's common sense. Left-wing parties know well that endorsing civil rights campaigns for minorities who are often discriminated against (for example, ethnic minorities or homosexuals), can be electorally very risky. As Martin Seymour Lipset noted in his analyses on authoritarianism and low-income classes, the latter tend to be progressive on economic and social issues, but generally, conservative in terms of moral and family issues.[85] One further reason that explains socialist parties' hesitations when faced with the promotion of civil rights is that, although they might seem to be 'cost free' legislation, in fact they are not. The socialisation of the 'professionists of love'[86] and anti-discriminatory laws that enhance the number of women entering the labour market require thorough reforms of the welfare state and greater investments in facilities such as childcare. Lastly, it should not be forgotten that the alliance with Catholic-inspired political parties which underlies the electoral strategy of parties such as the DS acts as a further restraint to more radical policies on family matters and civil rights issues.

Unlike the 'needs' of women, ecological issues, another theme central to postmaterialist politics, have so far remained rather marginal to the agenda of both British Labour and the Italian DS.

As we saw earlier, socialists have long held a critical, though favourable, approach to technological progress. No inherent mechanism was said to exist that would automatically secure social progress; only if directed, it was argued, would scientific innovation be conducive to advancement for all. However, an almost exclusive concern for its possible economic and social effects long prevailed. Hardly any consideration was paid to the problems and limitations of modernising processes related to the environment. With few exceptions, socialists and social democrats long held an anthropocentric ethic that assumed nature was a material resource to be manipulated according to potentially endless human needs and desires. Furthermore, environmental policies were seen as irreconcilable with their focus on manufacturing and labour-intensive production as well as traditional concern with economic growth and full employment. Unemployment, taxes and health care were thought to be the 'real' issues socialists should address. As one trade union leader put it, quite rightly, why should his members 'worry about holes in the ozone layer when they have holes in their roof?'[87]

When confronted in the 1980s with the electoral growth and popularity of environmental movements – which by and large draw on a left-wing constituency – socialists could not help but reconsider their insensitivity towards ecological issues and attempt to integrate them into social-democratic politics.

As Giddens points out in *The Third Way*, providing citizens with security has long been a concern of the social democrats. The latter saw the welfare state as the main vehicle for providing such security, but one of the main lessons to be drawn from ecology is that just as much attention needs to be given to ecological risks.[88] The problem is that the endorsement of ecological ideas does itself bear some 'risks'. If libertarian policies might become electorally damaging, the same applies to green politics. During periods of economic recession or crisis, 'post-materialist' preoccupations are easily swept aside by more basic economic concerns.[89] Furthermore, the so-called post-materialist electorate, though quite vociferous and politically active, still remains a minority phenomenon. 'Sustainable development', a slogan that can be easily sold to vast electoral constituencies (particularly in the wake of ecological disasters), when turned into concrete legislation (for example carbon and petrol taxation or measures to facilitate traffic restraints), might prove very unpopular. The right to use a car wherever and whenever needed, whether to take children to schools or to set off to the office in comfort every morning, seems to be the last global 'cause' left, capable of unifying citizens throughout the industrialised world. Lastly, for all the ecological awareness which neo-revisionists today claim to possess, measures of active government and planning in the environmental sphere are often hard to reconcile with the business-friendly politics which socialist and social-democratic parties have been building over the past years.

It is for all these reasons that the degree to which socialist parties have endorsed 'green agendas' varies considerably. If not urged by electoral considerations, parties tend to avoid unpalatable and electorally risky policies as much as they can; it is only where ecological issues took on a hegemonic role within national political debate that neo-revisionist parties turned into champions of the Green cause. The SPD's 'greening'[90] in the 1980s is quite exemplary in this respect. Challenged by one of the most powerful green movements in Europe, German socialists developed a programme of eco-social democracy that was one of the most ambitious attempts to integrate the environment into left-wing politics. By contrast, parties such as New Labour and the DS, less threatened than their German counterparts by the growth of green politics, have so far kept ecology a low priority. Penalised by the first-past-the-post electoral system, the British Greens, who at the 1989 European Parliament elections (contested with a voting system of proportional representation) gained 15 per cent, have so far been able to exert very little weight on national politics. Similarly in Italy, the Green Party has never posed a real threat to the existing parties of the Left. Founded in 1985, it never took off. Deeply divided and fragmented, it failed to capitalise on the breakdown of traditional political parties after 1992 and has remained a small party with a tiny electoral constituency (representing approximately 3 per cent). Even under exceptional circumstances – such as the mad cow crisis during the 2001 elections – the party proved unable to expand its constituency. The Green presence in the programme of the 1996 Olive tree centre–left coalition should be understood more as the need to keep a useful ally on board rather than a result of the influence of green thinking on national political debate.

The new modernisers

Another key characteristic of the new progressive agenda which socialist and social-democratic parties have been developing over the last few years is the centrality placed upon discourses of 'modernity'.

In the footsteps of Wilson's leitmotif of the 'white heat of technological revolution', New Labour manifestos and documents exhibit a relentless rhetoric of 'modernisation', a term that Tony Blair used 87 times in 53 speeches between 1997 and 1999. The latter has become a typical 'new Labour word', if not distinctive theme.[91] The term 'new' appeared 107 times in the *Road to the Manifesto* document and 37 times in Blair's address to the 1995 party conference.[92] In the run-up to the 1997 election, Blair promised a 'cool' Britannia; by following in the footsteps of the famous picture of Wilson's handshake with the Beatles in the 1960s, he tried to make his point by posing in numerous photographs with the Spice Girls. As he put it in *New Britain: My Vision of a Young Country*, New Labour in power would modernise and re-energise Great Britain by making it a 'young' country again. New Labour's policies should not be regarded only as 'a programme for government', he wrote, but rather as a 'mission of national renewal'.[93]

If the old politics of the Left stood for old industry, New Labour politics, maintains Blair, puts new information and promotion of its economy at the centre of its political agenda.[94] More than half of employees in Britain now work in information processing and 80 per cent of all the information stored anywhere in the world is in English. These are massive markets where Britain holds a decisive competitive advantage.[95] Great Britain, the argument goes, should be investing in the new electronic superhighways; satellite and telecommunications technology that act as the nerve-centre of a new information economy will do for the next century what roads and railways did for the nineteenth and twentieth centuries.[96] The government should play a vital role, it is argued, in encouraging long-term research and investment in new technologies by boosting its scientific base, as well as helping citizens to acquire the necessary skills to succeed in the modern economy.[97] In 1997, the Blair government appointed the first e-minister in British political history.

Modernity and modernisation also seem to be the leitmotif of the DS, though, given the substantial dissimilarities between the structure of the British and the Italian economies, with an obvious difference. As a result of the steady growth of wages in the 1960s, the profitability of Italian industry declined considerably by the 1970s. One way out would have been to adopt a strategy aimed at strengthening labour-saving science-based high technology sectors. This was a strategy also made urgent by the growing globalisation of world markets and the increasing threat posed by newly emerging manufacture-based economies. However, the Italian economy opted to remain heavily reliant on traditional industrial sectors with low technological content and productivity rates, such as textiles, clothing and shoes. Competition with the newly industrialised Third World developing countries was kept up by decentralising production and creating medium and small-sized firms which circumvented trade union constraints and tax regulations, resulting in keeping the cost of labour and prices very low. It was the so-called 'third Italy' (mainly located in the North-east and the North-centre), from the famous description coined by Bagnasco,[98] that, incidentally, contributed to Italy's economic recovery in the 1980s. This did very little to fill the gap between Italy and other advanced economies like Britain, France and Germany, which by contrast were more successful during the same period in shifting their production from traditional to high technological sectors.[99] While modernisation for Great Britain means new and more significant investment in technology and competitiveness, for Italy it predominantly means resolving the profound historical defects of the Italian economy; that is, substituting its infamous *capitalismo straccione* (beggar capitalism) with a 'normal capitalism' and, above all, undertaking a true liberal reform of the market. The end result should guarantee clarity and competition and put an end to the oligarchic arrangement of Italian capitalism. Modernisation is intended, in other words, to further the direction of a modern and 'normal' country, as implied by Massimo D'Alema's book, *Un paese normale.*[100]

As we saw in earlier chapters, during the 1960s and what was then called the 'second industrial revolution', the discourse of modernity was already the fulcrum of socialist revisionism. 'The white heat of the technological revolution' was the celebrated slogan coined by Wilson during the campaign that brought Labour to Downing Street in 1964. In those years it was quite easy for parties like Labour to represent themselves as the party of 'modernity', as opposed to an 'old' Conservative Party which, against the background of a swinging London, seemed more and more anachronistic and inadequate. Much the same applies to the present era. Over the 1970s and 1980s Labour was increasingly associated with old and exhausted policies. After 1979, the flag of modernity was firmly in the hands of Margaret Thatcher, if only for her identification with an uncompromising fight against old industrial Britain. In this respect the leadership of Tony Blair signalled a turning point. Together with the dilution of the party's working class image, he did his upmost to plug New Labour into the 'new economy' and become the party of the 'new middle classes'. As will be seen in the next chapter, he recruited new and younger party members, as well as MPs (the average age of the new Labour MP who entered the first Labour government of 1997 was 44, including five in their thirties). The Labour Party, as Tony Blair promised his electors, was a party that was younger and better equipped than the Conservative opposition and would guide Britain through the challenges posed by the 'post-industrial revolution' under way.[101]

By that time, Conservatives were a party that appeared tired. Indeed, the impetus given by Margaret Thatcher had subsided. John Major's resignation and the election of William Hague as leader in 1997, a young leader but certainly not somebody at the cutting edge of a new generation, did very little to make the Conservative Party a credible moderniser (it is worth remembering that the average age of party members is sixty years old). For all its efforts, the party did not manage to get rid of its image as a party of the aristocracy, countryside, traditions and traditional values. The new leader, Ian Duncan Smith, who was elected in September 2001 seems unlikely to promise much change in this regard.

As with Tony Blair and his acolytes, the leadership of the DS belongs to a generation in their forties and fifties – the 'Berlinguer boys' as the title of a book by Pietro Folena's refers.[102] The concomitant discontinuity with culture, methods, and mentalities of the past should help them make the promise of party renewal, and in particular of the country, more credible than if it had been put forward by the old apparatus. The centre–right coalition led by the media tycoon Silvio Berlusconi is far better than their British counterparts at projecting a modern right-wing ideal. Berlusconi is over seventy years old but portrays himself as young, especially with regards to his lifestyle. He has a new family with a younger wife and young children and does not hesitate to use camera filters which make him appear younger. He is a self-made man with no aristocratic posture or snobbishness. In addition, he is comfortable with the English language, a language that many opponents on the Left often still find quite hard to master and he is fond of 'modern' slogans such as 'what matters is the three I's' where I stands for *Inglese* (English), Internet, and *Impresa* (business).

It is however, by insisting on a notion of modernisation as the completion of the 'unfinished liberal revolution',[103] that the Left seeks to monopolise the modernity discourse. Reviving Gobetti's damning analysis on the inter-war liberal political elite and his harsh attack on the deficiencies and weaknesses of the Italian bourgeoisie, the Italian Left still insists on the 'absolute underdeveloped character' of the latter. The 'missing liberal bourgeoisie' argument remains a central theme to the DS's political rhetoric, as well as its implicit assumption that it is down to the Italian Left to carry out the liberal revolution that has so far failed to emerge.

In the 1960s, Ernesto Rossi and the friends of *Il Mondo*, which included Riccardo Lombardi's socialist autonomist group, claimed the seal of 'true liberals' for themselves by presenting the nationalisation of electricity in its anti-monopolist function as a choice for liberty and a prerequisite for a true regime of competition. Today the Left is taking an analogous step by attacking Berlusconi for the monopolistic character of his media empire and by suggesting that they are the only coalition capable of resolving the deep flaws which have historically existed in the Italian economy by giving life to liberal market reforms that clearly guarantee effective competition and put an end to the oligarchic order of Italian capitalism.

The 'new global social question'

If the final destination of the new European Left still appears somewhat unclear, there is little doubt about its origins. Whatever text or official document of New Labour or the PDS/DS might be considered, they all acknowledge the profound changes that have taken place over the last twenty years: entry into Europe, the globalisation of the market, and the decline of Fordist models of production have all radically changed the context of Left politics. These changes imply a crisis for the national state, at least as an economic unit, and thus the end of the mechanisms and instruments with which the Left has balanced and tempered capitalist development of the twentieth century.

Analysis of the profound transformations taking place has given rise to two different interpretations within the European Left. As we saw in earlier chapters, in the wake of debates in the 1950s and 60s within the PSI over structural reforms, faith expressed by men such as Riccardo Lombardi and Antonio Giolitti in the 'revolutionary' potential of structural reforms was counterposed by the claim of inner party leftist factions that no socialist imprint could ever be made upon the so-called second industrial revolution. This argument was also put forward at the same times by the faction around Ingrao during its clash within the PCI with Amendola's compromising attitude towards neo-capitalism.

A similar divide between a 'governing' Left, confident in the corrective potential of state intervention, and a more radical Left which has been critical not only of deterministic approaches which too easily equate technological progress with social progress, but of any strategy based upon the idea of reform, now characterises the European Left's debate on globalisation and post-Fordism.

On one side is a Left that sees the processes of globalisation as ultimate proof of the need for an alternative to the present social model: with the end of the virtuous circle of production–employment–consumption, and thus also of the positive relationship between economic growth and social well-being, the margins for successful reformist strategy, it is argued, have disappeared. This is the position of a significant body of work by Italian intellectuals such as Rossana Rossanda, Pietro Ingrao, Marco Revelli, and Giorgio Lunghini.[104] On the British side, the *New Left Review*, which has become the focus for an incisive intelligentsia, maintains a similarly radical critique of Labour policies. Also noteworthy is the special one-off issue of *Marxism Today* in December 1998 that reflected upon the positions of those who, while recognising the need for the Left to rethink itself, are critical of Tony Blair's project and what they consider the thirdwayers' surrender to neo-liberalism.[105]

As discussed earlier, intellectuals such as Stuart Hall and Eric Hobsbawm made important contributions to the demolition of Labour's 'old conservativism' in the 1980s; however, when it came to reconstruction, as was the case with the end of the short-lived convergence between Wilsonism and the New Left, irreconcilable divergences emerged. A very similar process occurred in Italy where Occhetto's change of course against unreconstructed orthodox groups such as Cossutta's faction was supported by the libertarian neo-communist faction that centred around Ingrao. The latter found common ground with the centrist neo-revisionist neo-berlinguerian group on a more realistic analysis of post-Fordism and the importance attached to issues such as inner-party democracy, gender and environmental politics. However, once the party's old leadership was defeated and it was apparent where Occhetto's demolition of past policies was leading, differences with the New Leftist *ingraiani* began to emerge.

Globalisation, radical new Leftists such as George Monbiot argue,[106] means that the space for different models of capitalism has disappeared. Institutions can no longer make a difference, as had long been the case – hence the distinction made in the past between market-led Anglo-American, 'Rhineland' stakeholder German, or Japanese models of capitalism. The neo-liberal capitalist world order can no longer be reformed from within and can only be changed by creating alternatives to dominant market-led capitalism.[107]

It is important to note that there is a substantial difference between the British and the Italian cases. In Britain those whose aspirations include creating an alternative to present social models tend to form part of an intellectual circle. While they may have high theoretical profiles, they possess little political influence. In Italy, their counterparts have considerable political weight and are centred inside the Communist Refoundation party. Although the latter is a small party, it is an alliance partner that is essential to the electoral success of the centre–left coalition. This fact was demonstrated in the 1994 and 2001 elections when the failure to reach an agreement with Communist Refoundation resulted in the defeat of the whole coalition. It should also be remembered that the first centre–left government led by Prodi fell in 1998 following the decision by Fausto Bertinotti, Refoundation's leader, to withdraw his party's support from the cabinet.

The second major response of the Left to the profound economic changes of recent years is that of parties like the DS and New Labour. This is a Left which still believes in the progressive character of the modernisation process, in the possibility of influencing the course of the existing model of social development, a Left which still feels confident about the potential for future progress – though naturally only if that future is guided by parties of the Left.[108] Unlike those who tend to dismiss globalisation as a myth and a neo-liberal invention instrumental to apathy and consensus, neo-revisionist social-democratic parties regard globalisation as a reality with which they still have to come to terms.

The epochal tones which characterise discussions on its potentially drastic effects and implications are reminiscent of debates on automation that took place during the 1950s and 1960s; this is not, it is argued, just a period of change but rather a period 'of historical transition'.[109] Globalisation, it is said, has had a major impact not only on the nation–state and its governing power but also on everyday peoples' life-style and society as whole. It is primarily responsible for the process of detraditionalisation under way and the resulting increase in risk and uncertainty.[110] The increasing flexibility of the labour market is also considered by neo-revisionists as a glaring example of a phenomenon brought about by globalisation, which if not regulated might entail seriously disruptive consequences. As the proportion of permanent staff within large firms shrinks and more people become contract workers, freelance workers, and 'temps', the individual absorbs risks and shocks that were once absorbed by the firm. This new contingency has been destructive to personal security, social solidarity and ultimately to society itself, especially at the bottom end in terms of decreases in standards of living and employment security.[111] Technological change, it is argued, threatens to deliver economic and social consequences that, if left to the private determination of the market, seem set to produce casualties of an intolerable and almost unimaginable nature.

Just as automation offered a new case for socialism in the 1960s, so, according to neo-revisionist discourse and rhetoric, does globalisation today. As Tony Wright pointed out, 'the suggestion that it can safely be left "to the market" is genuinely frightening; there is no less need for socialism in the condition of the world at the end of the twentieth century'.[112]

The clearest and most perilous indication of the conflict between the private rationality of market capitalism and universal human rationality rests in the sphere of the physical environment itself.[113] But space for corrective manoeuvres and regulation, neo-revisionists argue – echoing earlier revisionists' optimism on governability – does exist. Once regulated, globalisation can become an undeniable means of progress and advancement for all. For all the Jeremiahs who would like to turn back the clock, globalisation is said, in fact, to be a good thing. As Charles Leadbeater put it in *Living on Thin Air* (a book that is considered amongst one of the reference texts of New Labour revisionism), the Left should not retreat from modernisation, but rather create the organisations, public and private, economic and social to unleash and spread the benefits of the 'knowledge economy'.[114]

The globalisation of the economy, culture, and communications are all processes that must be seen as 'the great fact of progress' in that they offer the potential to emancipate vast numbers of individuals excluded from any redistributional processes. According to this view, what faces the Left of the twenty-first century, in the words of Massimo D'Alema, is 'a new, original social question, characterised by its global dimensions'.[115] The triumph of the democratic Left of the twentieth century was to learn how to regulate Western capitalism, reducing its distortions and injustices. The Left of this century must prepare itself to govern through a new and larger process, ensuring that the broader scale is itself an aspect of broader progress.

But can globalisation be regulated? As opposed to the pessimism displayed by radical new Leftists, neo-revisionists seem fairly optimistic about it. This is not surprising. Once you campaign for government on a left-wing agenda it would be absurd to do it while warning your electorate in advance that there will be little you can do to carry out the promises of change included in your programme. For all the talk of a 'runaway' world,[116] as was the case with 'automation' forty years ago, globalisation is, in fact, regarded and presented as something which can be mastered. The collapse of the social-democratic paradigm does not mean, it is argued, the subordination of the Left to the technocratic right, as critics on the left affirm. While globalisation's pervasiveness cannot be ignored, its constraints on national governments should not be overestimated.

As Anthony Giddens noted, the Left should refrain from what he describes as a 'new medievalism', that is 'a confession of impotence in the face of forces larger than us'.[117] Globalisation is quite often spoken of as if it were a force of nature, but as he argues, nations will continue to retain considerable governmental, economic and cultural power over their citizens in the foreseeable future.[118] Neither globalisation nor capitalism deprives politics of the ability and the responsibility of choice. Citizens can still choose between a 'neo-liberal' (American) and a 'social market' (social-democratic European) form of capitalism.[119]

A new 'European' road to socialism

Given that globalisation is regarded as something that can be regulated, the framework *par excellence* into which the Left is investing both great hopes and great resources is the European Union. This is truly a *deus ex machina* that offers a way out of the impasse in which the parties of the Socialist International found themselves as a result of the collapse of the Keynesian social-democratic paradigm. The demise of the Bretton Woods system, the introduction of flexible exchange rates, the creation of transnational credit and finance markets, as well as the end of the sovereignty of nation–states over interest rates, has not only led to a crisis of the nation–state itself, but to the end of national reforms in the European tradition. The close nexus between socialism and Europeanism and the identification of Europe as the only way out of the crisis for the parties of the Left are now ideas central to all European social-democratic parties' agenda.[120]

Particularly after the failure of the French experiment of 'Social Democracy in One Country' during 1981–2, European socialist parties realised that the future of centre–left policies could only be viable in the economic framework of the EU. As already pointed out, socialists eventually understood that the only way to match the internationalisation of capitalism was to internationalise politics.[121] The brand of politics envisioned by New Labour and the DS, as by the whole spectrum of the European Left, are only realisable, neo-revisionists argue, within the framework of European integration – provided, of course, that the Left is in a position to model the Union according to its own criteria. This is the 'challenge', D'Alema declared,[122] facing the European Left: to construct a new political order which is supranational and allows for co-ordinated action in matters such as work and unemployment, common legislation on social rights, and the harmonisation of taxation systems in order to prevent evasion and overcome intolerable disparities in the levels of pressure on markets and enterprise. In this regard, the Socialist International began to be thought of as a means to a new 'European road to socialism'.

The PCI, taking a different stance on this from all other Western European communist parties since 1962, adopted an increasingly positive attitude towards the process of European integration. From then, the EEC began to be regarded as the precondition for Italy's modernisation and economic growth.[123] Europe was also at the centre of the party's reformulated 'Italian road to socialism' – Eurocommunism – in the 1970s. However, up to the 1980s, as was the case with other socialist and social-democratic parties, the PCI's road to socialism remained a *de facto* national one. It was only after 1987, in the context of Occhetto's new course, that a supranational dimension acquired a key centrality in the policies elaborated by the party. As the neo-revisionist leadership argued, the only way out of the crisis of the Left and the Keynesian model was a united European Left capable of transforming the institutional system of the European Union in such a way that it could become a viable means to a new European Keynesianism.[124]

Europe and the EU is the area where New Labour neo-revisionism is most removed from old revisionism.[125] Developed in a period during which the syndrome of decline was only in its initial phase, the 'future of socialism' forecast by intellectuals such as Anthony Crosland in the 1950s was closely tied to a national framework in which the Keynesian recipe was still bearing fruit in terms of both prosperity and redistribution. It was also a vision that saw Britain playing a prominent role internationally, but within the Commonwealth rather than Europe. An insular vision also underlay the 1983 election manifesto and the party's commitment to Britain's withdrawal from the European Community.

The attitude of New Labour towards Europe signalled a real break with the past. The party today recognises Europe as the only framework within which the European Left can have a future.[126] Only a a more united Europe, it is argued, can provide socialists with a response to globalisation.[127] One of the first initiatives of the first Blair government was to repeal the decision taken by the previous Conservative governments to opt out of the Social Chapter. It goes without saying that New Labour's stance on Europe still differs quite substantially from its continental counterparts. Unlike its Italian counterparts, Labour faces a strong eurosceptic attitude among the public. This is especially true during elections when the question over Europe becomes a 'hot' issue. The hesitancy displayed by the party's leadership towards EMU is quite telling in this regard. Although accepted in principle, no clear date has been set on when to join. Furthermore, New Labour is firmly against tax harmonisation and the reduction of national veto on tax matters, a proposal that relies on the support of other European socialist figures like

Jospin and Schroeder. It has also always been hostile towards any suggestion of an expansive revision of the Dublin stability pact or any direct investment towards job creation, as suggested by the past Jospin French government.[128] As Blair put it at the Malmo gathering of European socialist parties in 1997, rather than importing 'euro-sclerosis', New Labour should instead try to influence its European counterparts with its recipe of labour market flexibility and welfare to workfare reform.[129]

Governing globalisation? Supply-side versus distributional socialism

If globalisation can be regulated, as neo-revisionists maintain, what is the recipe for new politics with which the Left proposes to 'govern globalisation' as it takes place? Are these the politics of a Left that is really only playing second fiddle to the technocratic Right, as its critics maintain? Or do they really amount to a 'third way' between subjection to neo-liberalism and a now obsolete social-democratic model?

An examination of the economic policies of New Labour and the PDS/DS makes it clear that both adhere unconditionally to the policies of low inflation, low budget deficits and low pay rises that are now *de rigueur* for any country that wishes to remain competitive in a global market. Orthodox management of the economy, with priority given to fiscal discipline and balanced budgets, is now taken for granted. The first decision of the newly elected Labour cabinet in 1997 was to increase the independence of the Bank of England. This was a clear signal to the City that the party had finally broken with previous traditional instruments of financial management, that is, tax and spend policies.

The message certainly got through. When standing for a second term in 2001, Blair's party received full endorsement from the conservative press, for example the *Economist* and the *Financial Times*, which went so far as to describe the Labour Party as the 'only credible conservative government currently available'. Labour macroeconomic policies, an *Economist* article read, 'has been more orthodox than its Tory predecessors, with more fiscal discipline and the welcome granting of independence to the Bank of England'.[130] Similarly praised by international economic circles and the press was the policy of austerity which the three successive centre–left governments pursued from 1996 to 2001 and which resulted in the successful entry of Italy into the EU's monetary union in May 1998. This undoubtedly gave the bigger party within the coalition, the DS, increased legitimacy and credibility. As this was the latter's first experience in government since 1947 – when its predecessor

PCI was part of a DC-led coalition – it was important for the DS to prove that its social-democratic conversion had not ended with old-fashioned demand management policies but had instead been carried further in the neo-revisionist deflationary creed.

Since the late 1980s European socialist parties have replaced a Keynesian agenda with so-called supply-side socialism. As the Blair–Schroeder/Third Way document states, this is an agenda which rules out 1970s-style reliance on deficit spending, high levels of government borrowing and heavy-handed state intervention.[131] Competitiveness and profitability should, it is argued, be a more immediate concern than unemployment and under-consumption; the best way to create jobs is to 'build competitive industries that can succeed throughout the world'. Socialist governments' primary objective is hence said to be to increase production efficiency, reduce unit costs and enhance national competitiveness.[132] Flexible markets are now described as 'a modern social democratic aim'. The days when trade unions were at the heart of socialists' programmes now seem a distant memory. Not only did New Labour abstain from reversing any parts of the industrial relations legislation implemented by earlier conservative governments, but it also made clear to its union partners that labour market flexibility would remain an important element of the new party's political agenda. The corporate management of the economy and state involvement in industry, which characterised past Labour governments, particularly those between 1974–9, are today thoroughly rejected. As Blair put it, New Labour would not return to 'tripartite institutions or beer and sandwiches at number Ten':[133] it is not for government, he maintains, 'to second guess employment decisions taken by companies on commercial grounds'.[134]

While seeking distance from its historical special relationship with the trade unions, New Labour has contemporaneously put considerable effort into building trusting partnerships with business. As Blair and Schroeder wrote in their joint Third Way declaration, in the past social democrats became identified with high taxes, especially on business. Modern social democrats have modified this picture by recognising that 'in the right circumstances' tax reform and tax cuts can play a critical part in meeting their wider social objectives'.[135] Corporate tax cuts, it is argued, raise profitability and strengthen incentives to invest.

The Thatcher governments implemented fundamental changes in labour legislation and successfully curtailed a great deal of trade unions' powers. When dealing with unpalatable policies such as labour market deregulation, the question for Blair's first Cabinet was hence one of defending the status quo and the 'achievements' of the earlier conservative governments, rather than pushing for new legislation. None of his continental counterparts was faced with such an easy task. The problem confronting the Italian, French, and German left-wing governments in the mid-1990s was one of demolition rather than preservation.

A greater flexibility of the labour market was indicated as one of the priorities of the Olive Tree government from its inception in 1996.[136] Part-time work in Italy is one of the lowest within the EU; in 1992 part-time employment as a percentage of total employment was 5.9 per cent, less than half of similar figures in France (12.7 per cent) and Germany (14.1 per cent). In Britain, the figure is one quarter of the work force (23.5 per cent), one of the highest together with Northern Scandinavian countries.[137] Italy suffered, it was argued, from a very rigid labour market which went back to its 1970 *Statuto dei Lavoratori* (Statute of Workers), a significant body of quite advanced labour laws approved by parliament in the wake of the Hot Autumn that shifted the country's political balance in favour of the trade unions. All three Italian centre–left governments which came to power after 1996 knew that any reform attempts would meet a great deal of resistance by organised labour. Italian trade unions, like those of other Southern European countries, have been traditionally less cohesive and politically homogeneous than their Northern European counterparts. Their fragmentation has always ruled out any close alignment or 'axis' with the government. As was the case with past Italian governments, the Olive Tree cabinets could not count on organised labour as a reliable and acquiescent ally. It should also be remembered that one of the very first decisions taken by the newly founded PDS in 1991 was to dissolve the party's faction within the CGIL. This turned the party's relationship with the latter into a more independent but also more uncertain one.[138]

Since 1993 trade unions have accepted a far more conciliatory approach based on consultation, which was suspended only during the Berlusconi government in response to the antagonistic attitude that the centre–right coalition mistakenly adopted towards it. A number of agreements over delicate issues, such as incomes policy and labour market reform, were achieved. In December 1998, during the D'Alema government, the Social Pact (*Patto Sociale*) was signed; this was the last of three national agreements of the 1990s that were explicitly inspired by a model of economic governance based on *concertation*.[139] With regard to the question of Italian labour market rigidities, hirings on fixed-term contracts, and other temporary work schemes have increased significantly: 85 out of 100 new posts created in the third quarter of 1999 were in so-called atypical forms of employment.[140] Nevertheless, a main obstacle to further labour market liberalisation and flexibility has been an unemployment benefit system which, as will be seen below, is totally inadequate for the spread of new types of contract and the greater instability the latter entail for the workforce. The growth of so-called 'atypical work' and the steady increase in the share of employment in small firms (almost 50 per cent is in firms with less than 15 employees, where the strictest employment protection norms do not apply) have put the present unemployment benefit system under strain as new categories of workers are pushing to get more protection from the risk of job loss.

Competitiveness, efficiency and profitability as well as the need to develop 'a culture of enterprise' thus now dominate European Left discourse. As opposed to their past identification with distribution issues, socialist parties stress their competent economic management and commitment to economic growth; as their motto states, 'Caring is not enough unless you can pay for it'.[141] As argued earlier, the Left, or at least the element that has made a clear choice to participate in government, has long understood that the main condition for a more generous and humane capitalism is a healthy economy. As the inter-war years proved, economies in disarray are anything but advantageous to the Left; on the contrary, the Left had its best moments during the so-called 'Golden Age of Capitalism' (1945–70). It is for this reason that the principal preoccupation of any leftist party in power has always been the effective running of the economy. Those who have charged governments of the Left with economic incompetence, and their leaders with the destruction of the national economy (an accusation frequently levelled in the past at the Labour Party), fail to take into account that it was only with the recent resurrection of neo-liberal economic doctrines that Keynesian policies began to be seen as destructive. For many decades beforehand such policies were regarded as the best formula for guiding capitalism into a new phase of expansion. The best proof of this is the fact that all parties, regardless of their political hue, faithfully adhered to them. The priority given to employment rather than inflation until about twenty years ago was not a costly sacrifice to a matter of principle by the parties of the Left, but rather a winning formula emerging from the crisis of the 1930s that saved capitalism from what could have been the end foreseen by Marx. The great fortune of the parties of the Left during the post-war years was, in fact, that the policies indicated by Keynes perfectly matched their primary objectives: full employment and a more equal distribution of resources, as well as the guarantee of certain essential rights such as education and health care.

Far from being uniquely concerned with distribution, with just a few exceptions (for example centre–right revisionists *à la* Crosland during the early phase in the booming 1950s), socialists and social democrats hardly took for granted economic efficiency of a market economy.[142] When faced with tough choices, they opt for economic growth, as the widespread acceptance of monetarism in the mid-1970s testifies.

Indeed, this continuity should not obscure the fact that there is a substantial difference between today's Left and yesterday's Left. While in the past the parties of the Left dedicated themselves to directing their respective economies, they also maintained the prospect of an alternative system. Today the Left has renounced any such prospect and has fully embraced the principles of the market economy. This sets the neo-revisionism of the 1990s apart from any previous brand of socialist revisionism: capitalism is no longer a transitory phase, destined sooner or later to disappear and leave the way free for a socialist society. Capitalism has become a system of production destined to last for the foreseeable future, a system that can be tempered but not changed.

As the programme of the PDS in 1994 affirmed, the party accepts the market economy as the fundamental basis of economic organisation. At the same time a far more favourable and flexible attitude towards privatisation has been adopted. Though not comparable with the massive sale of public assets that occurred during the Thatcher governments, the first privatisations in Italy were also carried out in the 1980s during the five party coalition government led by Craxi. The soaring public debt, and the growing pressures exerted on Italy by the international community to reduce it, resulted in the pruning of the IRI's group and the sale of some important public holdings such as the car company Alfa Romeo to Fiat in 1986.[143] That was only the beginning. During the 1992 Amato government, the five main shareholding companies, ENI petroleum, EFIM, ENEL, INA, and IRI were restructured into two larger shared-based companies with the goal of preparing them for eventual privatisation. The paradox was that the massive sale of a large part of IRI's public holdings was eventually carried out during the Olive Tree Prodi government in 1998 with the full support of the former communists PDS/DS, the largest party of the coalition.[144]

When Labour returned to power in 1997, there was hardly anything left of the public sector. As with the question of labour flexibility, where very little remained to be done beyond maintaining legislation inherited by the Conservative government, the question facing Blair's cabinet in 1997 was not privatisation, but rather re-nationalisation. That is, whether Labour should return any public assets – for example the railways – which the Conservatives had privatised during their eighteen years of government, into public hands. This is what the Labour Left was urging. As a point of fact, that was never an option. New Labour was a *new*[145] party which had made a clear break with past policies and there was no other item from their past agenda which was more uncompromisingly rejected than nationalisation.

Overall, nationalisation had ceased to be a core element of the Labour agenda since the mid-1950s when more flexible forms of social ownership made their way into the party's policy documents. However, with the ascendancy of the Hard Left in the 1980s, old-style nationalisation was again revived. It was central to the Alternative Economic Strategy devised by Stuart Holland and eventually endorsed by the party again as official policy once die-hard Keynesians were defeated: the 1983 Electoral manifesto committed Labour to the re-nationalisation of all firms and industries privatised by the Conservatives.[146] That was a manifesto that was later described by commentators as the 'longest suicide note in history'. What made it the beginning of the end for 'Old Labour' was its stance on nationalisation which, as studies on electoral behaviour had shown since the 1950s, was an electoral liability which heavily affected Labour's share at the polls. No wonder that a resolute battle against it became the number one priority of the party's 'modernisers' in the years to follow. Under the leadership of Neil Kinnock's Soft Left and later openly neo-revisionist leaders such as John Smith and Tony Blair, nationalisation was increasingly diluted and eventually discarded. With the replacement of the old Clause IV with a new statement of democratic socialist values in 1995, Labour's Bad Godesberg and Blair's major image coup (after managing to do what other previous leaders either had never dared or failed to do), was to put an end to any ambivalence in this regard.[147] Since 1997, the party's position on industrial policy has been to advocate joint public–private partnerships. The private sector is keenly wooed as it was under successive Conservative governments. The new socialism as defined by Blair is one which 'no longer confuses means such as wholesale nationalisation with ends, that is a fairer society and more productive economy. It can move beyond the battle between public and private sector and see the two as working in partnership'.[148]

While questioning their past hostility towards privatisation, both the DS and New Labour have been redrawing the lines between public and private, with the relationship between the market and the state ending up under radical review. The state, as an entity, has long held an undisputed centrality in socialist and social-democratic thinking. It was long regarded as a powerful agent of social change. This model of directive control characterised not just Soviet communism but also various forms of top–down socialism such as Fabianism.[149] In contrast, today the role of the state within society as well as within the economy has been confined to a minimalist one of regulation.

As a result of the increased awareness of the practical shortcomings of the programme of nationalisation which left-wing governments such as that of Attlee from 1945 to 1951 had pursued, a period of thorough reconsideration of the role of public ownership opened in the following years. As discussed earlier, issues like accountability and the efficiency of the public sector were central to technocratic socialist revisionism. However, for all the acceptance of the limitations of public intervention, the role the state should play in the economy was never questioned. A mixed economy and the existence of a strong public sector, though reinvented in the form of competitive public enterprise or state shareholding, were long considered a crucial lever of socio-economic development as well as a precondition for balanced economic growth and a more equal society.

Things have now changed dramatically. Following the failings of Keynesian welfarism and the disrepute into which 'big government' fell over the last twenty years, all Western European left-wing parties embarked on a thorough re-assessment of this past centrality in their policies on state intervention. The disengagement of socialism from notorious 'statism' (*statalismo*), the reforms of public services and the role of government are high on any neo-revisionist policy agenda.

The classic neo-liberal critique of 'big government' has now become an integral part of the Left's repertoire. States, it is argued, can develop private interests of their own and have tendencies which range from the inflexible bureaucratic to the blatantly oppressive: 'both states and markets can be totalitarian if they invade territory that is not their own'.[150] As the Blair–Schroeder Third Way document reads:

> the belief that the state should address damaging market failures all too often led to a disproportionate expansion of the government's reach and the bureaucracy that went with it. The balance between the individual and the collective was distorted. Values that are important to citizens, such as personal achievement and success, entrepreneurial spirit, individual responsibility and community spirit were too often subordinated to universal social safeguards.[151]

As Blair put it, for years the economic framework of the British Left was dominated by questions of public ownership; markets were very poorly understood, their obvious limits leading the Left to neglect their great potential for enhancing choice, quality and innovation.[152] The ability of national governments to fine-tune the economy in order to secure growth and jobs, the third-wayers' argument maintains, has been exaggerated. At the same time, the importance of individual and business enterprise to the creation of wealth has been undervalued; the weaknesses of markets have been overstated and their strengths underestimated.[153]

The neo-liberal assumption that 'private is good' has now entered progressive thinking: state intervention is regarded suspiciously, as private business was until a few years ago. Private sector management and competitive markets have been introduced into the public sector as a guarantee of efficiency. Planning has become a tainted word; the word 'regulation' is used instead, with macro-economic management giving way to micro-economic structural and sectorial improvements. New progressive politics should not stand, third-wayers maintain, for rigid forms of state ownership or provision; it should instead be pragmatic in determining whether public or private means are the best delivery mechanism. In fact, for all their new contended pragmatism, the impression is that the often uncritical endorsement currently displayed in the private sector by parties like New Labour is equivalent to the ideological commitment shown in the past for nationalisation. As Matthew Taylor, the IPPR Director (hardly suspected of being a die-hard socialist) put it when commenting on the second Labour government's determination to go ahead with plans to privatise the London Underground and the National Air Traffic Systems, Blair and his advisers seem to behave as 'prisoners of dogma'.[154] The increasingly apparent shortcomings of nationalised industry pushed many to urge the party to reconsider its unconditional faith and trust in this means; similarly, the failure of the privatised railways and of other private finance initiatives such as the installation of an IT system at the Passport Agency contracted to Siemens have increased the number of those who look critically at Labour's infatuation with the private sector. However, even where general common sense would suggest a greater caution in endorsing privatisation plans, as the IPPR report 'Building Better Partnerships' published in June 2001 states, Labour has stuck to its PPE commitment (Private Partnership Economy) as 'it was the only game in town'.[155]

The problem is that efficiency arguments alone do not explain the disengagement of European left-wing parties from past policies of state intervention. Two more factors should be considered. Firstly, the image factor.

Nationalisation was one of the three items of the notorious 'socialist trilogy', the other two being trade union rights and unilateral disarmament, which communication experts urged Labour to drop in order to make itself electable once again. Similarly in Italy, the infamous *cosa pubblica* (public assets) is something with which no party except Communist Refoundation, feels at ease with today. Even more so, the DS, seeking to distance itself from its communist past, has made a resolute rejection of state intervention and the so-called *Statalismo*, a pejorative way of describing a favourable attitude towards the public sector that since the early 1990s has become one of the most popular targets of the Italian centre–right. If state assets in Italy during the 1950s were associated with inefficiency and regarded as nothing more than a residue of fascist days, its reputation did not improve as the years went by. In the wake of the Clean Hands Operation in the 1990s, the public sector became, the epitome of corruption and tainted 'partitocracy'; it was identified as a parasitic clientele system and as such came to be regarded as an obstacle to modernity and economic prosperity. The increasingly hegemonic neo-liberal critique of big government enhanced by the success of 'Reaganomics' found a very fertile terrain within Italian public opinion. The latter had long been aware of ongoing corruption but unaware of its scale until the Clean Hands Operation; Since then anti-statism has successfully mixed with the populism of parties such as the Northern League. Secondly, for a full understanding of the increasing reliance of left-wing parties on the private sector, economic factors should also be considered. For parties which rule out any income tax increases and deficit spending, schemes that promote private/public partnership and the increased involvement of private capital in basic structural investments[156] is an obvious arrangement to resort to when public funds are short.

Against a background of overall rejection of past forms of state intervention, a minimalist notion of the state is therefore emerging. Its tasks are now confined to regulating markets in the public interest and fostering competition when monopoly threatens. In the third-wayers' rhetoric this is what is described as 'active government';[157] that is, a government whose role should be to provide the essential framework for a market economy, to promote competition – by supporting, for instance, new technologies and research – and to ensure labour standards and environment regulation. And that is all. As Blair and Schröeder wrote, the state 'should not row but steer; not so much control, as challenge'.[158] Socialists, it is argued, have to accept that while doing all it can to support enterprise, government cannot be a substitute for it. The essential function of markets must be complemented and improved by political action, not hampered by it.[159] Broad ranges of agents and associations are said to have an equal status today alongside the state as potential agents of change: the local community, the religious establishment, voluntary associations, corporations, supranational bodies. As Blair put it in his *Third Way*, in deciding where to act on behalf of the national community, whether as regulator or provider, 'governments must be acutely sensitive not to stifle worthwhile activity by local communities and voluntary sectors'.[160] The 'grievous twentieth century error of the fundamentalist Left', his argument runs, was the belief that the state should replace civil society. A key challenge to progressive politics is 'to use the state as an enabling force, protecting effective communities and voluntary organisations by encouraging their growth to tackle new needs, in partnership as appropriate'.[161] As Luciano Violante has written, the task for the Left is to push for a definite passage from the 'Big Brother' state that aimed to define the destiny of all citizens, to the 'enabling state', a state that sets the conditions for citizens to build their future alone leaving them free to make their own choices in an autonomous way. Whilst the 'old' state required faithfulness, the new one requires responsibility.[162]

From welfare to workfare

The Left's reconciliation with the market economy has done more than prompt a rethinking of the role of the state in the economy; it has also led to a profound revision of attitudes to the welfare state, reform of which is central to the policy agenda of neo-revisionist socialist parties such as the DS and New Labour.

In contrast to widespread beliefs, Italy's percentage of public spending to GDP stands below the European average (47 per cent of the GDP). The same applies to Britain: overall public spending (notably in areas like health and education) grew slowly in the years under the first New Labour government, reaching almost 38 per cent of the country's GDP in 2001, which is still almost 10 points below the average of EU countries.[163] If Labour fulfils its commitment to increase it by 3.5 per cent, as indicated in its 2001 electoral manifesto, public spending will reach 41 per cent. The question that then faces the Italian and British neo-revisionists, as well as most socialist parties, is not cutting public expenditures, but rather how to redirect resources in such a way that 'big' spending becomes effective spending, to use one of the favourite slogans of Tony Blair.[164]

The welfare state, it is argued, should respond to the fundamental transformations that have been underpinning the economy and society over the last twenty years. Changes in work organisation, working life transformations, new patterns in ageing, family structures and the changing role of women, have all been radically transforming welfare needs, particularly during the active, adult period of the life-cycle.[165] Furthermore, 'downsizing', 'delayering' and 'outsourcing' impinge upon a welfare system that was tailored to a fairly distinct labour market and that today seems increasingly inadequate.[166] As David Marquand pointed out, 'if the emblematic figure of the 1960s was the affluent worker, today's are the redundant middle manager, the driven contract worker and the excluded, antisocial, inner-city youth'.[167]

Where to draw resources and how to redirect them are issues that vary from country to country depending on national specificities. Each European state has, in other words, its own so-called 'welfare scroungers'; in Holland it is disabled people whose rates until recently far exceeded plausible figures, and in the UK single mothers before 1997 absorbed 10 per cent of overall social spending. As far as Italy is concerned, the number one target is pensioners, who have long profited from an extremely generous retirement scheme with a proportion of spending allocated to it that far exceeds the European average. Unlike the United Kingdom, Italian pensions are financed by the contributions of those currently working. Against a background of a declining and ageing population, it was thus a system which called for a major rethink. Since the early 1990s, in the wake of the new austerity policies implicit in Italy's acceptance of Maastricht criteria, pension reform has been central to the political agenda of any Italian government, irrespective of its colour. Seniority pensions have, in particular, come under attack (the latter enabled employees to retire at any age so long as they had paid contributions for 35 years). Some initial, though insufficient, changes to the existing legislation were implemented in 1992 when an increase in the retirement age and the number of years necessary to qualify for a pension were carried out. In 1994, the Berlusconi government attempted to take pension reform even further and scrap seniority pensions altogether. However, the attempt failed under what commentators described as the largest demonstration in post-war Italian history. That was a lesson which later governments learned. After this point, a more conciliatory approach with the trade unions was pursued. Pension reform was eventually carried out in 1995 by Dini's technocratic Government that had the parliamentary support of the centre–left coalition. For all its limitations and weaknesses (a revision was planned for 2001), it has been described as 'one of the most radical reforms in the history of the welfare state'.[168]

Turning to Labour, once it was back in power in 1997, it was spared the embarrassment of any unpopular reform with regard to the pension issue. The earlier conservative governments had, in fact, already implemented important changes in the pension system such as the introduction of 'means testing' and the end of an earnings-related index for pensions. As the Borrie Commission on Social Justice (set up by the then Labour leader John Smith) report suggested in 1994, a Labour government would be unlikely to reverse any of this legislation. Once again, it was ratification instead of demolition.

Neo-revisionist parties' welfare reforms are greatly influenced by the re-assessment of traditional ideas of the Left such as equality and social justice. The idea of a welfare state as an instrument of redistribution and 'levelling' is no longer favourable: once the market economy was accepted in principle, the Left also had to accept its inevitable corollaries, above all the inequalities that it implies. When it comes to defining exactly what kind of equality the Left stands for today, very ambiguous formulas are put forward. Blair's statements and speeches on this issue are a case in point. Addressing the Labour Party conference in September 2000, Blair argued that the goal for Britain was nothing short of 'true equality'; what this meant exactly was left to its audience to interpret and to scholars to decipher. If one examines Blair's writings and declarations, his notion of equality seems to be, in fact, quite minimalist, one which does not go beyond recognition for equality of opportunity.[169] As Gordon Brown put it, this is 'the essence of equality':[170] the overall objective of progressive politics, as it is often argued, is a society where the basic rights and conditions of all citizens are as equal as possible. Labour will do what it can to reduce differences in individuals' starting positions and to improve prospects at the bottom end by giving individuals not just a single opportunity to succeed at the age of 16 but a lifetime of recurrent permanent opportunities; beyond that, it is necessary to accept broad market outcomes. The time has come for the Left, socialist neo-revisionists maintain, to distance itself from 'utopian egalitarianism'. One wonders whether any social-democratic party in the past ever stood for this kind of egalitarism. However, caricaturing the past is a precondition for presenting contemporary policies as a real novelty and breaking with what political parties want to leave behind.

As Luciano Violante argued in *Le due libertà*, the modern Left does not aim to render all equal; it should rather be concerned with the 'start up conditions' and try as much as it can to remove the handicaps and obstacles that impede competition. The state can no longer guide the citizen from the cradle to the grave; it should instead teach its citizens to cross the street, providing the best possible conditions for them to do so.[171] Consistent with the centrality given to individuals and self-promotion, welfare, neo-revisionists claim, should be reconsidered in such a way as not to stifle individuals' merit but to reward effort and responsibility instead.[172]

Clearly the assumption underlying neo-revisionists' faith in the abilities of equal opportunity policies to secure a more just society is that present day society is characterised by unprecedented social mobility; this is a recurrent theme in third-wayers' discourse. Images of increasingly shorter ladders to success are now part of the Third Way's iconography and, in some respects, mythology. Poverty and wealth, they claim, should be regarded as transitory phenomena. As Anthony Giddens put it, 'poor do not stay poor for long and rich do not stay rich for long'. This is why equality and inequality should be redefined, he claims, to mean respectively social inclusion and exclusion, with economic inequality referring not to gradations in income and wealth as everybody previously supposed, but to situations in which the poor are cut off from social and economic opportunities.[173]

Another distinctive feature characterising neo-revisionists' welfare reforms is a new productivist approach underlying them as opposed to the past's main focus on redistribution. The distinction between the 'levellers' and the 'investors' strategy was made clear in the Borrie report on Social Justice.[174] 'Levellers', the document read, 'are pessimists' who 'are concerned with the distribution of wealth to the neglect of the production; they develop policies for social justice independent of the economy'.[175] In contrast, 'investors' 'combine the ethics of community with the dynamics of a market economy'; they invest in people by means of the extension of economic opportunity in this way providing 'the basis for prosperity as well as social justice'.[176] They therefore reject what they see as the negative focus of the Beveridge welfare state as an insurance against want, disease and squalor. Instead, reforms should be carried out towards a 'positive welfare state', a 'social investment state', which, while investing in human capital, does not confine itself to equalising life chances but aims at improving the functioning of the markets.[177] The state, third-wayers argue, must become an active agent for employment and not merely the passive recipient of the casualties of economic failure; similarly, social provisions should be transformed from a safety net of entitlements into a springboard to personal responsibility.[178]

The emphasis on 'equality of opportunity' as well as a greater integration of social policies with economic policies explains the importance attached to education, which is today a key priority to the neo-revisionists' political agenda. The Olive Tree programme indicated a combination of supply-side provisions in regard to education and training as the chief means of their fight against unemployment, particularly as it concerned youth.[179] Greater investment in education is seen as crucial to advanced economies. As Blair put it, the success of a modern economy is built on the skill and talent of its workforce; 'know-how' is the key to overcoming competition from low-wage or low-skill competitors.[180] At the same time, education is also the key to any successful strategy aimed at enhancing equality of opportunities. Given that it is dependent on the individual to make headway, the best way for the state to intervene and to advance the individual's ability to prosper within the new economy is to provide him/her with lifetime access to education.[181]

The notion of the 'enabling state' is the key word to understanding today's neo-revisionists' welfare policies. In Gordon Brown's words, the key motto should not be what the state can do for you but what the state can enable you to do for yourself. This is the logic that underlies proposals such as baby bonds that have been growing in popularity both within New Labour and the DS. Responsibility is the other key word to remember when assessing welfare rethinking under way within the Left. For too long, claims Blair in *The Third Way*, 'responsibility and duty were the preserve of the Right'.[182] For too long, he continues, the demand for rights from the state was separated from the duties of citizenship and 'the imperative for mutual responsibility on the part of individuals and institutions'.[183] Third-way politics looks for a new relationship between the individual and the community, a redefinition of rights and obligations. As Giddens put it, there should be 'no rights without responsibilities'.[184] One of the main ideas guiding the current revision of welfare policies, also derived from neo-liberal thinking, is the concept of a 'culture of dependence'. Although perhaps most pronounced in Italy, the critique of the so-called *stato assistenziale* (state of dependence) is a problem that is felt in all European countries, Great Britain included. Welfare should be reviewed, it is argued, in the light of its possible adverse effects and restructured so that it does not create 'dependence'. Under the slogan 'from welfare to workfare', Labour has, since its return to office, carried out a set of policies which testify to the Left's awareness of the inherent risks within past welfare policies, particularly when they became disincentives to return to work.

In line with the 'making work pay' philosophy, Labour reintroduced the national minimum wage with the clear objective of making working worthwhile for low-income workers forced off the welfare state and the benefit system. Similarly, the objective of the massive New Deal for Young People under 25 programme launched in 1998 (which offered increased opportunities for education and job training) was to bring youths, single parents and the long-term unemployed into the work force. Other measures such as the Working Families Tax Credit (with tax credits for every family with full-time earnings), or tax reforms to make it more attractive to employ people, were designed to take people off the benefit system and bring them back to work.[185] The British unemployment benefit regime has become increasingly tight through a series of changes since 1986. However, it is since the New Labour government came to power in May 1997 that a quite new line of thought has come to the fore – that people ought not to remain unemployed beyond a certain time limit. Since 1998 benefit recipients have been formally expected to be 'actively seeking work'.[186] Right to benefits must be matched by an obligation to find a job, if jobs exist: once the state is channelling offers of work to everyone within the first year of unemployment, that should be the maximum period for which benefits are available.

The New Deal is largely regarded, not unfairly, as the most distinctive achievement of the first Blair government. Since April 1998, 170 000 young people have found work, and long-term unemployment among young people has been almost eliminated. Great Britain's unemployment rate in 2000 was almost half of the European average, ranging around 4–5 per cent. Not surprisingly, the New Deal experiment has become a reference point for all those EU countries, particularly in Southern Europe, which still struggle with high unemployment rates; certainly it has become so for Italy, which in 2000 still suffered from an unemployment rate of 12 per cent. The joint bilateral document entitled ' "Welfare to Work" and the Fight against Long-term Unemployment' commissioned by the D'Alema and Blair governments in 1999 and published in 2000, reflects clearly the growing interest of Italian centre–leftists for the 'welfare to work' British model.[187]

Long-term unemployment and non-participation have very different causes in different parts of Europe. In Northern Europe, including the UK, they result mainly from the dysfunctional structuring of the welfare system, in which huge sums are spent on long-term benefits which encourage inactivity and exclusion. By contrast, in Italy a number of other factors should be considered: on the one hand, centralised collective bargaining institutions which do not allow wages to compensate for lower productivity levels *vis-à-vis* other regions, discouraging job creation outside the state sector and inflating the ranks of the underground economy. On the other hand, there is very low labour mobility: Italian unemployment benefits target adult males with relatively long work records while young people receive state support only indirectly via their families. Youth migration from southern Italian regions suffering from high unemployment rates is prevented because the (largely in-kind) income support provided to the family is conditional on sharing the same dwelling.

Thus the problem facing the Italian centre–left governments was not that of redesigning the system of benefits and tightening it so that people would be brought back to work, but rather, in some respects, one of creating a comprehensive unemployment benefit system itself. This was seen as crucial for increasing the 'employability' of millions of working age people who, for the dysfunctional structural reasons explained above, were not even looking for work. Thus parliament gave the government a broad mandate to introduce a uniform unemployment benefit system replacing the many different schemes then in place. However, this could well be regarded as the 'missed reform' of the centre–left legislature. The policy response has not been a change in the overall design of benefits, but simply a selective extension of the policy instruments used in the past to deal with redundancies, and the creation of new unemployment benefit schemes accessible to workers already inside the job market. Furthermore, while some progress has been made in the direction of improving the information system of the Public Employment Service (PES), no pressure is put on those registered, not even on those claiming benefits, to seek a job. Employment subsidies are the dominant form of active policy in Italy and have so far proved hardly effective to stimulate additional outflows from unemployment.[188]

Despite the failure to implement significant legislation once in power, 'welfare to work' policies remain central to the DS's policy agenda and rhetoric. Following in the footsteps of Clinton's famous statement that 'the best anti-poverty program is still a job'[189] and 'work, work and work again', as in the slogan of the Dutch social democrats, work is a key element to third way politics.[190] Work, as Giddens put it, remains central to self-esteem and standards of living.[191] While this may well be so, it should also be added that a society with a high employment ratio does not spend huge sums on social benefits.

The new task the Left has set is the creation of a welfare state that provides assistance but also returns responsibility to the individual whose rights are balanced by duties to the 'community'. One of the most characteristic Blairite slogans is the need to shelve the 'something for nothing culture'. The Labour leader has made concepts of community and responsibility (for oneself and others) as core elements in both the 1997 and 2001 election campaigns. Once in office, some of the programmes that his ministers launched had a communitarian ring to them, such as community policing or the decision by Gordon Brown to encourage charitable giving and volunteerism by scrapping the £250 minimum limit for donations to attract tax relief.[192] In the US example of 'mutual help groups' on problems such as alcoholism, depression, breast cancer and domestic violence, policies are being examined which promote self-reliance and self-care (for example, by means of improved patient information). This, it is hoped, will encourage people to take more responsibility for themselves (quitting smoking, reducing alcohol abuse, doing exercise) and for one another. Whether it is a matter of childcare or protecting the environment, people, neo-revisionists claim, need to assume responsibility.[193]

New Labour's emphasis on responsibility, the need for strong communities and stable families, as well as for active policies on youth crime, school truancy, and inadequate parenting have raised, not surprisingly, some suspicion and criticism.[194] Libertarians are not the only ones to feel uneasy with New Labour's new welfare thinking; it has also been accused of falling short of traditional socialist goals such as reducing inequalities. As Peter Towsend put it, there is little point in enhancing people's opportunities to climb ladders 'if the ladders grow ever longer, the gap between rungs wider, and the chances of falling greater'.[195]

One aspect of Marxist theory which earlier 1950s–60s revisionists challenged was the pauperisation theory: against a background of increasing social mobility, as Crosland wrote in 1956,[196] inequalities would soon disappear. Forty years later, after eighteen years of conservative governments, left-leaning intellectuals seem to be less optimistic: as David Marquand wrote in 1997, 'immiseration of the proletariat' has returned.[197] The average real income of the bottom tenth of the population fell in Britain by 14 per cent between 1979 and 1991 while that of the richest rose by 50 per cent.[198] The New Labour governments have so far only slightly altered the sorry legacy of the Thatcher years. Labour's electoral slogan during the 1997 election promised that 'Things could only get better'. Things did indeed get better for many. As a 2001 Report by the Institute of Fiscal Studies put it, the first Blair cabinet was the most redistributive government Britain has ever had; the degree of redistribution to the bottom 10 per cent was the greatest for a quarter

of a century. However, although the direct effect of government measures, such as the *Working Families Tax Credit*, was to reduce inequality,
the underlying distribution of income widened enough to more than
offset the effects of tax and benefits changes in the first three years of
the parliament;[199] at the time of writing, 25 per cent of the British adult
population lives below the poverty line as opposed to 9 per cent in
1979.[200] Since being back in office in 1997, Labour, which had spent the
last ten years trying to convince the British electorate that it was no
longer a 'tax and spend' party, ruled out any significant change to the
tax structure that Conservatives laid down in the late 1980s. This
sharply constrained its freedom of manoeuvre and above all militated
against any attempt to significantly reduce the inequality gap. In the
run-up to the 2001 elections Labour reiterated its commitment not to
increase income tax, leaving the Liberal Democrats alone to advocate it
for those earning more than £100,000, under the slogan 'You can't get
something for nothing'. Blair knows well that income tax is a very delicate question, one that pollsters have long warned political parties to be
very cautious about. A firm pledge not to alter it is said to be the precondition to keep the middle classes on board and, as will be seen in the
next chapter, this is a key object of New Labour politics. The so-called
'Mondeo Man' has in fact for some years now become the number one
target of Blair's middle-class oriented electoral strategy.

5
Moving to the Centre: Socialists Get Rid of the Cloth Cap

The idea of the disappearance of class, or at least the progressive and irreversible attenuation of class difference and antagonism, has always been a fundamental idea of socialist revisionism in its various phases. The Left, in other words, has constantly had to adapt to the development of a social structure that did not reflect the proletarianisation foreseen by vulgar Marxism. Today as never before, socialist parties face the need to cement their consensus among the middle classes.

Over the past twenty years, as a result of the crisis of Fordism and the rapid ascendancy of the so-called New Economy, trends which have long been under way, notably the growth of the tertiary sector and the shrinking of the traditional working class, have accelerated. In the 1970s British market researchers divided society into an approximate 60–40 split between working and middle class; today, depending on definitions, the proportion has been reversed with manual workers falling to a figure slightly more than one-third of the workforce.[1] In Italy the percentage of those employed in both industry and agriculture declined consistently throughout the 1980s and 1990s with the tertiary sector accounting for over 50 per cent the active population. A traditional working class that included 45.9 per cent of total employment in 1976 decreased to 35.4 per cent in 1989, and 32.7 per cent in 1994.[2] As Achille Occhetto put it in making his case for 'change or die', communist bastions such as Sesto San Giovanni (an industrial area in Milan's periphery) which boasted 24 000 workers concentrated in four or five big factories in the past, now have no more than 2500 workers, all of which are dispersed into hundreds of small factories.[3]

155

The decline of the working-class vote

Not only has the traditional working class been on the decline, but it also seems increasingly less inclined to vote for left-wing parties. In 1996, the PDS was still the party with a proportionally high percentage of working class vote (29.1 per cent),[4] followed by the Northern League and Communist Refoundation. However, against a background of an overall electoral decline of the party since 1979, it has also suffered each year from a significant decrease within the manual workers' vote.[5] At the 2001 elections Forza Italia scored 30.6 per cent of the working class vote which slightly exceeded that of the DS and Communist Refoundation combined, respectively 16.4 per cent and 11.5 per cent.[6] Similarly, the Labour Party has been affected throughout the 1980s by a gradual and steady drain of the so-called 'aspirational workers'.[7]

A number of factors account for what seems to be the end of the 'special relationship' between socialist parties and their 'natural' electoral constituency. First, there is an acceleration of the process of *dépolitisation*, a term Western sociology has used since the late 1950s to explain the crisis of political militancy and of parties' presses. As we saw in earlier chapters, factors such as the 'end of ideology', described by Daniel Bell,[8] and the spread of a consumerist society contributed to defusing the post-war climate of ideological confrontation. The end result was the weakening of collective identities and class solidarity. More prevalent today than ever before, the new reality after the end of the Cold War is a society characterised by 'contented majorities'.[9] Furthermore, we are now living, as Geoff Mulgan argues, in an 'anti-political age' where past allegiances and division are losing relevance and where the number of those who distrust parties and traditional parliamentary politics is growing.[10]

This is well illustrated by the increasing abstention rates that characterise European politics. As a partial consequence of the first-past-the-post electoral system, election turnout has always been quite low in Britain. However, its decline has accelerated over the last fifteen years, reaching a peak of 40 per cent at the 2001 election. This was a record figure that had not been experienced since the 1918 election. Italy's abstention rates have always been quite low. However, as a result of the number of electoral reforms carried out from the early 1990s, which were conducive towards a majoritarian electoral system, voting/abstention patterns have been steadily increasing.[11]

Abstention particularly affects the so-called *underclass*. There has been a growing concern in Europe, specifically in Great Britain, that there might be a reproduction of an American-type system that combines

social and political exclusion with a *de facto* gradual disenfranchise-
ment of lower social strata. What is often noted is that a low turn-out in
deprived areas cannot be explained by political apathy alone; rather,
it originates from the disenchantment and disillusionment of large
sections of traditional left-wing voters towards a Left many regard as
betraying its traditional values and goals. Significantly, American
democrats and New Labour, when elaborating electoral strategies, dis-
tinguish 'apathetic' voters from what communication experts describe
as a 'cynical' electorate, to be addressed with specific and reassuring
'left-wing' messages.

Another factor that social scientists emphasise in explaining the
decline of the working-class vote for left-wing parties is 'class realignment'. Ralf Dahrendorf, in *Class and Class Conflict in Industrial Society*,
published in 1959,[12] illustrated the heterogeneity and composite nature
of the working class in the wake of the post-war economic miracle. If in
those years a car, a washing machine and a refrigerator were enough to
weaken class consciousness, the demise of the working class as a distinctive socio-political entity is said to have run its course today. Growing
rates of home ownership among manual workers and the spread of
middle-class consumption habits, such as travelling to remote exotic
islands made possible by inexpensive last minute package holidays, have
further accelerated trends long under way such as instrumentalism, privatisation and individualism.[13] Class solidarity seems to many a relic of
the past. Moreover, against a background of growing unemployment,
which is almost four times higher today than post-war rates, and labour
market 'decomposition' deregulation and flexibility, today's working
class is fragmented and heterogenous; this is clearly evident in the crisis
of traditional trade unions. Giulio Sapelli in *L'Italia inafferrabile* (1989)
described Italian society as 'the Tower of Babel' affected by a growing
process of 'disassociationalism'.[14]

In countries such as the United Kingdom where class voting has
always been traditionally strong,[15] the 'betrayal' of the working class
(to the advantage of the Conservatives) has had a serious effect on
the Labour Party, and this has been reflected in a steady decline of its
working-class vote since the 1980s. Today four out of five of the British
electorate has a mixed social background.[16] The massive entry of women
into the labour market, mainly in the tertiary sector and the newly
emerging new economy sectors, has deproletarianised a significant
number of families. The so-called 'aspirational worker' – an updated
version of the 'affluent worker' – associating Labour with the traditional
working class, the have-nots and the underdog, has, since the late 1970s,

identified with the Conservatives as the best political force capable of meeting their aspirations for social advancement.[17] The electoral and political success of Margaret Thatcher in the 1980s largely rested on a love affair with these social strata.[18]

The 'middle-classisation' of third way politics

In the light of the above considerations, socialist and social-democratic parties accelerated their transformation into catch-all parties. Old class rhetoric has been shelved for good. No longer are 'they' (the bourgeoisie) the enemies or 'temporary street companions' (a typical expression used by the Italian Marxist Left); it is the 'individual' and no longer the 'class' which neo-revisionist parties now address in their policies and electoral messages. By drawing on well-known analyses by sociologists such as Ronald Inglehart, we are said to live in a 'post-materialist society'[19] where class conflict has lost its relevance and emancipation can no longer be intended as the sole material emancipation from basic needs. It is argued that the more societies turn into affluent societies, the more materialist values make and lead the way to post-materialist aspirations. This results in a rejection of any constraints placed upon individual self-fulfilment. Together with Inglehart's work, other books such as Martin Seymour Lipset's *Political Man* (1983), Bauman's *Memories of Class* (1982) or Gorz's *Farewell to the Working Class* (1982),[20] have all highlighted the growing influence exerted on electoral behaviour by post-industrial cleavages (gender or ethnic identity) as opposed to traditional class issues; the increased importance acquired by 'new politics' issues such as the environment or civil rights is said to have surpassed traditional socio-economic ones.

Former antagonism between labour and capital, and consequently between the working class and the bourgeoisie, it is argued, have led to new types of conflicts: between the long-term unemployed and workers with secure employment; dependent workers and autonomous workers; young people and old people; the public and private sector; men and women; Northern and Southern Italy; the Scottish, Welsh, and English in the United Kingdom; as well as between multinational companies and environmental movements. The traditional class concept has today become one used only by a few die-hard and 'clinging' nostalgics. As Tony Blair put it, we live in a classless society characterised by unprecedented social mobility. This is a society where, as third-wayers describe it, there are no losers but simply potential winners. It is precisely this new meritocratic society that is said to offer thousands of opportunities or 'ladders' through which everybody, irrespective of their social background, can advance. In this respect, the neo-revisionists term 'underclass' refers to a minority isolated from the mainstream.[21]

To be a 'people's party' is not just the aspiration of New Labour; it is a trend which involves the entire European Left. Even the Italian DS has for some time ceased to express its ideas in terms of social class. The idea of the primary role of the working class is regarded as outdated as that of class solidarity. For Labour the new social referent is 'community'. Similarly, the Italian Left speaks of the 'social fabric made of cells whose cement is not that of class solidarity, but the idea of belonging to a community'.[22] Just as in the late 1950s when the first works arguing the demise of class conflict were published and there were sections within the Left – that is, the neo-Marxist New Left – that rejected the contended disappearance of class, so today there is still a radical Left which dismisses the idea of a classless society as empty rhetoric. Whatever the case may be, it is nevertheless clear that what Marx defined as class-consciousness is now very weak. This is a fact that parties that want to win elections cannot afford to overlook.

Given that class rhetoric and the cloth cap image have been discarded, European socialist parties have also had to reinforce their appeal to the middle classes. During the 2001 electoral campaign, the Forza Italia leader Silvio Berlusconi brilliantly reinvented himself as the 'working class', the 'successful entrepreneur', the 'artisan' and the 'peasant' candidate dependent upon on the audience whom he addressed. Through reinvention, Berlusconi has illustrated well that one of the preconditions of political parties' appeal is to facilitate mechanisms of identification between them and the electorate. This is what Massimo D'Alema meant when he wrote that the DS should aspire today 'to represent labour and the working world beyond the narrow class horizon'. Modern labour, as he put it, is now as a result of post-Fordist restructuring 'post-blue collar workers': that is, a labour force which is no longer located just in the factory but includes Chinese manual workers as well as those who work at home with their computer.[23] It is these new social strata, he wrote, which the Italian Left can no longer afford to ignore.

The need to win the electoral consent of the emerging new middle classes has been central to Labour's restyling operation of the last fifteen years. In the wake of the seemingly irreversible electoral decline which the party suffered throughout the 1980s, the number of those urging Labour to eliminate its traditional image as the working-class party increased. By 1989 the infamous 'socialist trilogy', that is nationalisation, trade union rights and unilateral disarmament, has been dropped.[24]

Labour defeat at the 1992 election allowed for the Conservative Party's fourth consecutive return to office. The argument of 'modernisers', that change should be pushed further, grew stronger. The swing of the pendulum theory, which in 1959 dominated discussions on Labour's third subsequent electoral *débâcle*, found its way again within inner party national political debate. The arguments of Anthony Crosland's *Can Labour Win?* published thirty years earlier came to the fore again:[25] Conservatives' dominance could be reversed, it was contended, only if Labour was electable again. Labour should bring further its 'middle-classisation' and eliminate its reputation of being the party of the underdogs. It was in this climate that the battle against Clause Four gained new strength and was eventually won by Tony Blair in 1995.

The abandonment of class-based policies went hand in hand with a drastic restyling of the party's image. Research on voting behaviour has long shown the extent to which 'synoptic' images of the parties may count more in voting decisions than the policies themselves.[26] Thus, although the name was never formally changed, in all party speeches and documents 'New' Labour replaced Labour. This should have signalled a clear break with the past and sent the message that a new beginning was dawning. Under the close guidance of communication experts, Labour leadership was told to shelve extravagant ties and trade unionist-style clothes and instead wear elegant and more business-like suits. Furthermore, as far as electoral broadcasts were concerned, it was suggested that derelict houses and deprived areas should be replaced by more glamorous New Economy sets and testimonials of the same calibre of Virgin tycoon Richard Branson. Last but not least, it was thought more advantageous to move the party's congress from Bournemouth, the epitome of the working-class holiday resort with its fish and chips and kitsch promenade, to the far more middle class and respectable Brighton.[27]

Tony Blair, with his public school background and impeccable Oxbridge accent, together with his past career as a lawyer, is the embodiment of the new middle class which New Labour aims to attract. A shift towards a deproletarianisation of the party ranks has also been under way. Labour has long elected a higher number of working-class candidates compared than its European counterparts; however, since the 1960s the working-class component of the party's parliamentary group has been on the decline. Efforts to increase the party's electoral appeal within the middle classes have not been in vain. According to a survey carried out just before the election in 1997, the percentage of the electorate closely identifying Labour with the underdog and the working class decreased from 47 per cent in 1987 to 34 per cent.[28]

Even the Italian DS have moved steadily towards a greater 'middle-classisation'. As argued in earlier chapters, class voting has always been a far less pronounced phenomenon in Italy when compared with other countries, notably Britain. The image problems of the party have been more related to its communist past rather than its labourite nature, which, admittedly, has never been strong. Most of the party's leaders and cadres have always been drawn mainly from the middle class. In 1987 MPs with a working-class background represented 3.8 per cent; a percentage that further declined to 1.7 per cent in 1994.[29] As was the case with the PSI after the Nenni's turning in 1956, the PDS/DS move towards the centre has been driven mainly by the need to be accepted in the family of European social-democratic parties as well as the urgency to increase their legitimacy and respectability in a political system where alliances are crucial to win elections; that is, to put an end to the *Conventio ad Excludendum*, a tacit agreement which ruled out communists' participation in government during the Cold War years. This resulted in the 1989 decisions to change its name from Italian Communist Party to Democratic Party of the Left and to replace the embarrassing hammer and sickle with a more presentable oak tree.

It is quite apparent however, the extent to which even the Italian PDS/DS has tried to replace traditional class division with a new dichotomy of progress–modernity/conservatism–tradition. Capitalist restructuring, as D'Alema argued, entailed a thorough reshaping of social groupings and produced new cross-cutting alignments alongside the conservative–progress division. The class-ridden notion of politics which identified progress with a quasi-motionless progressive working class and also a quasi (motionless) reactionary bourgeoisie is no longer valid today. The latter includes progressive elements whereas the working class might comprise conservative fractions as long as they resist the advances brought about by technological innovation. This is why, in D'Alema's words, the DS should now aspire to represent the New Economy's most dynamic and modern entrepreneurial sectors.[30] As New Labour opted to move their congress to the more decorous Brighton, similarly the DS moved their 2000 'Convention' – as they glamorously renamed their congress, borrowing the American expression – from the popular Rimini to Turin – an old working-class city but also the symbol of the new post-Fordist and post-industrial reality – and specifically the Lingotto, the old Fiat factory which the well-known architect Renzo Piano recently refurbished and converted into an extra-modern congress centre.

The ability of left-wing parties to make incursions into the middle-class vote is not solely dependent on the 'deproletarianisation' of their image. The building up of solid credentials as competent and reliable political forces is also regarded as of key importance. By the 1992 elections Labour had already moved a long way from the kind of 'loony' and divided Left, as it was described in the tabloid press in the 1980s. Important policy changes had been carried out and party factionalism and trade union powers had been put under control. However, it still lost. Labour, social scientists argued, seemed to lose out particularly on matters of competence. On the basis of surveys about voters' main issue concerns (education and unemployment), Labour should have gained a handsome victory in 1992. However, parties offer a service, namely to govern a country, and must persuade voters that they can do it competently. As Dennis Kavanagh put it, voting for a party may be more like choosing a doctor or solicitor where a client relies on the professional's competence and reputation. Voters are interested, he argues, in a party's image, particularly such features as its perceived trustworthiness, potential governmental competence, ability to manage the economy and the likelihood that it will keep promises. A problem for Labour in 1987 and 1992 was that, for all its popularity on a number of issues, many voters simply did not trust it, particularly with regards to economics. This was an electoral liability which Conservatives in the 1992 elections were quite good at exploiting: during the first two months of 1992 they produced 21 publications on the theme 'You can't trust Labour'.[31]

In this respect, the 1997 Labour government marked a real turning point. Under the severe and rigorous management of the Chancellor of the Exchequer, Gordon Brown, the first Blair government in 2001 asked for a second mandate boasting an inflation rate of 1 per cent and an unemployment rate of approximately 4 per cent (both the figures were half the European average). After five years of unabated economic growth, the syndrome of the 'incapable but good-hearted party' seemed to be over. In a survey carried out for the 2001 election, more than 50 per cent of the British electorate indicated Labour as the most reliable and competent party on economic issues.[32]

Another factor that greatly contributes to winning elections is unity. This is another test that New Labour passed brilliantly. As a result of a number of far-reaching internal reforms regarding the inner voting system carried out since the mid-1980s, the hard Trotskyite Left was totally annihilated and a small amount of resistance was left to contrast neo-revisionists' ascendancy within the inner party. Blair has increasingly adopted a 'presidential' and centralising style:[33] all messages and sound bites produced by the party are strictly controlled by close advisers such as Philip Gould or Alistair Campbell – also described as *Control Freaks* as the title of a book by Nicholas Jones reads.[34] In the 2001 New Labour Electoral Manifesto there were no pictures of other party members, except for Tony Blair.[35]

The Italian DS and its Olive Tree coalition allies seem to be fairly aware that unity and competence are two fundamental ingredients of electoral victory and success.[36] The first centre–left Prodi government appointed to the Ministry of Treasury, the former governor of the Bank of Italy, Azeglio Ciampi, was later elected President of the Republic. As Veltroni wrote in *Governare a sinistra* (1997), in the past the possibility of the Left in power evoked 'images of instability, the flight of capital, unchecked spending, and "big government". Today, even in Italy "left" means stability, confidence, responsibility, low inflation, and low interest rates.' [37]

The creation of Forza Italia, a party led by a leader whose favourite leitmotif is his background of being a self-made man and his promise that Italy would be successfully run as his economic empire, made it even more urgent for the DS and its coalition allies to stress their credentials as being competent and reliable parties. Not surprisingly, when standing for a second mandate in 2001, the electoral card which the coalition decided to play was Italy's entry into the Euro – admittedly one of the most important achievements of the centre–left legislature – in spite of the austerity and neo-liberal policies with which it was associated. In the end, the election was lost. The coalition had, in fact, fared quite well on matters of competence but scored very few points on two other ingredients which are equally important to win an election: unity and consistency. In spite of the abolition of the rule of democratic centralism in 1989, throughout the 1990s the DS has been a fairly united party with no major conflicts between the leadership and the inner Left. Deprived of its most radical elements as a result of the split of Communist Refoundation, the party acted throughout the legislature in a 'close the ranks' spirit. However, this counted very little as in fact bitter contrasts and tensions afflicted the centre–left coalition throughout the duration of the legislature, as is well illustrated by the succession of three different prime ministers over its five years' life-span. No last minute 'crocodile tears' or declarations of unity could defuse the electorate's perception of what had in fact been a quarrelsome and unstable coalition.

Shortcomings and inconsistencies apart, the effort aimed at a 'deproletarianisation' of their party's image has not been in vain but has instead allowed both the DS and New Labour to make substantial incursions into the middle-class vote. Labour's share of the British vote in 1964 (44.8 per cent) was almost identical to the one in 1997 (44.3 per cent). However, while in 1964 votes among white-collar/white-blouse workers amounted to 22 per cent, their percentage increased to 39 per cent in 1997.[38] In the 1996 elections the PDS gained 19.9 per cent of its support from self-employed workers and entrepreneurs; only four points less than its opponent, Forza Italia.[39]

European socialist parties' increasing support among the middle classes is also explained by the fact that there has been an increase among those classified as bourgeois 'with hearts to the left'. If the 1980s went down in history as the Yuppies' decade, the 1990s will probably be associated with the ascendancy of 'Bobos', the Bohemian Bourgeois, from the title of the best-selling book by the American journalist David Brooks, *Bobos in Paradise*.[40] They are the updated version of what were in the past labelled as *radical chic* in Italy, *Gauche Caviar* in France and *Champagne socialists* in Great Britain. They are seen as a group of half Hippies/half Yuppies belonging to the middle class who endorse a 'bohemian' unconventional lifestyle and set of values. They are a critical 'neo-bourgeoisie', the epitome of what sociologists such as Ulrich Beck or Anthony Giddens have described as the 'reflexive society': socially conscious and environmentally aware, as they are the greatest consumers of the extraordinarily expensive organic food. They also tend to reject the traditional family and moral values cherished by their parents. Their libertarian and post-materialist inclinations identify them with the Left in its modernised neo-revisionist variant. The new young leadership of parties such as the DS and New Labour and their European counterparts share a similar 'Bobo' culture. Consider, for example, D'Alema's love of sailing as opposed to Berlusconi's mega yachts or the preference of some Olive Tree figures like Francesco Rutelli for a scooter rather than the large official blue cars as a way of reaching parliament.

Another factor that explains the increase in the vote of neo-revisionist parties within the middle class is their growing popularity among women. Women's past electoral preference for centrist and conservative parties – what used be described as the traditional gender gap – has reversed since the mid-1960s: since 1979 the overall gender gap has been only 3 per cent on average and has become statistically insignificant. As a result of the sexual and cultural revolution, feminism, secularisation, higher education levels, increased participation in the labour market – particularly in sectors such as the public services or education which are traditional strongholds of the Left – a new modern gender gap has developed with an increasingly higher percentage of women voting Left.[41]

Particularly from a long-term perspective, once the older generation has been replaced by the new one, the women's vote is seen as a priority electoral target for socialist and social-democratic parties. This becomes clear when considering the efforts made by most parties to increase their appeal among women by employing a strategy to feminise the party's apparatus and parliamentary group. The number of New Labour female MPs grew from 37 in the 1992 election to 102 in the 1997 election, amounting to one fourth of the total elected deputies. It is what Clare Short described as a 'quiet revolution' in the Labour Party.[42] Italian politics have always seen a very low number of women elected to parliament. After the May 2001 election women comprised less than 8 per cent of the Senate and slightly more than 10 per cent of the House. Although far from equalling Northern European standards, this signalled a significant improvement on the past; in the 1975 election only 3.8 per cent of those elected to the parliament were women.[43] Furthermore, the percentage of women within the PDS/DS (21 per cent in 1996 election and 14.5 per cent in 2001 election) is far higher than the national average.[44]

Attracting women voters has also been achieved by promoting policies and strategies that clearly target them. The leitmotif of the DS ex-Minister for Social Affairs, Livia Turco, during the third centre–left Amato government advocated 'a more maternal social state'. It has given special allowances to those who have a third child. In addition, it has awarded insurance coverage to pregnant women whether employed or not. In fact, considerable advantages have been given to families by creating nurseries, especially in areas where the latter were non-existent. The 8 March 2000 law now allows both parents with small children to take a leave of absence from work.[45] At the same time, during the first New Labour government, divorced women gained the right to a share of their ex-husbands' occupational pensions for the first time. Paid maternity leave, although remaining the lowest rate in Europe, was doubled to eighteen weeks. Policies such as the National Childcare Strategy were launched creating affordable childcare for all 0–14 years olds who needed it; an area where Britain lagged far behind other EU members. The achievements were far from being revolutionary.[46] However, it was a step forward and above all a clear attempt to send a message to women that Labour cared about them.

Thus, working against a background of a decline in the working-class vote, the new middle class and women seemed to be the new electoral constituencies that neo-revisionists looked to for electoral growth in the years to come. According to the critics of the Third Way, all this will lead to the demise of the Left and is the very reason it came into existence. Democratic politics, it is argued, is inherently argumentative in its nature; to be a catch-all party, a party that can cater to all interests, is impossible and mystifying.[47] If the Left moves to the centre, it will inevitably sacrifice the protection and promotion of those in a more deprived social stratum to which it has traditionally promised a fairer and more just society. Particularly in countries such as Italy where the 'new' reflexive middle classes are still by and large a minority phenomenon and largely outnumbered by a more traditional bourgeoisie consisting of small retailers and entrepreneurs, the middle-class strategy of parties like the DS might prove a veritable 'Faustian deal'. In some respects, the dilemma facing them today resembles the one with which Italian socialists were confronted in the 1960s. Structural reforms, it was then argued, would appeal to new dynamic urban professional sectors; however, it was soon apparent that these strata amounted to a very small percentage of the total electorate compared to the traditional middle class, a far more vociferous and electorally influential group; this resulted in a great deal of resistance posed to reforms and any attempt to 'rationalise' the productive system.

The increasing need for the party's messages and policies to appeal to the middle class also carries some political risks. Discontented British traditional left-wing voters have little alternative but to abstain, which has so far barely affected New Labour. The working class in Britain is predominantly concentrated in safe seats which means that a low turn-out does not make a great deal of difference to the party's overall seats. In contrast, the DS have a party on their left – Communist Refoundation – which has so far proved quite good at capitalising on their 'betrayal' of a more radical electorate: traditional working-class sectors, but above all students and the young.

'Selling' politics: the ascendancy of spin-doctors

The increased importance attached to the image of parties such as New Labour and the DS has gone hand in hand with a growing professionalisation of their electoral campaigns as well as an increasingly large role played by political communication experts in the packaging of the two parties' messages.

For a long time, British Labour resisted political marketing and what was regarded as an unacceptable attempt to sell politics like 'soap powder'.[48] A tendency to create more professional campaigns emerged within the Labour Party in the late 1950s. The 1959 and 1964 elections were the first televised elections. This not only called for improved telegenic skills, but also for an overall reconsideration of the electoral campaign itself. As the years went by, conducting elections increasingly became a matter to be approached 'scientifically', something that could not be left to the good will and improvisation of activists and militants. The spread of TV called for a completely revised attitude towards running electoral campaigns resulting in an awareness of the new challenge with which political parties were faced. Following increasingly vociferous complaints about the ineffectiveness of the party's propaganda, Labour established a Publicity and Political Education Sub-Committee in 1955.[49] Subsequent years were marked by growing attention to opinion polls and a concern with the production of public opinion surveys. Research on political attitudes was conducted, such as Mark Abrams survey on the reasons behind Labour's 1959 electoral defeat,[50] in an attempt to furnish the party with useful guidelines in order to draft policy statements and election manifestos.[51]

Since then, Labour leaders have become increasingly aware of the importance of professional advice. If compared with the manner in which the Conservative Party conducted elections, however, their approach remained quite amateurish. Since the mid-1970s, whilst Conservatives invested an increasing amount of money in professional communication – appointing in 1977 Saatchi & Saatchi, an agency with a reputation for being aggressive, publicity conscious, energetic and creative – Labour Party members and officials continued to be unsympathetic to modern media techniques and communication professionals. Their suggestions were often either dismissed or challenged with competing advice by different sections of Transport House.[52] The peak was reached in 1983 when the party entered the election without thorough preparation: the entire campaign was put in the hands of a small advertising agency just a few months before the elections and a scant interest was shown in opinion polls.[53] Labour lost badly and learned the lesson. The 1987 election was a breakthrough in the party's adoption of modern communication methods. Peter Mandelson, who had a background in television, was appointed as the party's Director of Campaigns and Communications in October 1985. A new Shadow Communications Agency was established in 1986 to which Philip Gould, who had worked for the Clinton campaign, was appointed.[54] The era of spin-doctors, focus groups and sound bites was opening up.[55]

Based on the American model, the British electoral campaign is now fully managed and packaged by communication experts who set target priorities and produce messages on the basis of market research-style survey. Since 1997, the budget to conduct focus groups of some ministries has more than tripled. After all, as a conservative minister put it in 1988, 'politics is like the corn flakes; you don't sell it without publicity'[56] When TV debates made their appearance, they represented a new challenge for every party. Macmillan is reported to have described the moments before appearing on TV as 'worse than waiting to go over the top in the trenches in 1916'.[57] As an NEC minute of 1954 put it, TV programmes were not easy for those who took part: participants were required to demonstrate 'quick thinking and the ability to argue the point briefly and effectively'. Mental agility, coupled with 'political pugnacity and a real desire to disagree', as the document continued to report, were essential skills that politicians needed to develop if an opposing argument was to be met and a different viewpoint was to be expressed and successfully demolished in about one minute.[58] Today, things have changed significantly and the 'trenches' syndrome seems to be fully overcome. At the 2001 election, the leaders of the main parties have all shown (as noted by commentators) excellent television skills, an undoubtedly large capacity to speak in sound bites, and excellent confrontational skills such as those required to stand up to British TV journalists like Jeremy Paxman, who are far more confrontational than most of their European counterparts, let alone those from Italy.[59]

Although later than in the UK, electioneering has also been going through a process of professionalisation in Italy. For a long time the Italian Left (both socialists and communists) showed little interest in opinion polls and communication strategies. As was the case with the Labour Party, there was much ideological resistance to what was dismissed as an unacceptable 'marketisation' of politics. Further, the later spread of TV delayed the crisis of traditional canvassing. In a survey focusing on the means of propaganda and their effectiveness conducted after the 1958 Italian elections, it was demonstrated that radio and TV contributed to the shaping of opinions or voting patterns in only 23 per cent of the population and tended to be influential almost exclusively within the centre or centre–right electorate. The majority of the population was still greatly influenced by the canvassing of individual militants.[60] Things began to change in the early 1960s. Studies such as Alberto Spreafico and Joseph La Palombara (eds) *Elezioni e comportamento politico in Italia* (1963, translated as 'Elections and electoral behaviour in Italy'),[61] numerous research articles on electoral behaviour which appeared in journals like *Tempi Moderni*[62] and the works of political scientists such as Giorgio Galli and Giovanni Sartori, illustrate the extent to which electoral behaviour was also beginning to attract considerable attention in Italy. Although Italy lacked any tradition of studies in this field, with the improvement of research methodologies in social sciences, electoral behaviour soon became a major focus of interest in academic study.[63]

However, the relatively stable electorate that characterised Italian politics during the so-called First Republic meant that up to the early 1990s parties showed only a modest interest in opinion polls and communication techniques.[64] It was only following the collapse of the old party system after 1992 that a greater concern began to be reflected in electoral behaviour studies and opinion polls. The monopoly on the vote once held by the DC–PCI–PSI, which in 1976 was 82.7 per cent, passed in 1992 to 59.4 per cent, proving the electorate increasingly mobile.[65] The rise of the Northern League, the demise of the Italian Socialist Party (whose electoral share passed from 13.6 per cent in 1992 to 1.5 per cent at the local election just one year later) were all examples to many of the extent of volatility which now characterised the Italian political system. This was further exemplified by the 21 per cent result gained in 1994 by Forza Italia, a party that had been founded just a few months before the elections. A careful analysis of voting patterns of the last two elections (1996 and 2001) shows how mobility tends to occur more within the two main centre–left and centre–right coalitions than between the coalitions themselves.[66] However, this does not make the competition between individual parties even within the same coalition less urgent.

The entry into politics of media tycoon Berlusconi, who founded his party from a market research and focus group firm, paved the way for a new era in Italian politics where communication methods became increasingly important. In 1994 the centre–left *Progressisti* coalition was caught totally unprepared, and contested elections in a very amateurish way.[67] However, later electoral campaigns showed that the lesson had been learned. For their campaign in the 2001 election, the centre–left Olive Tree electoral alliance hired well-known political communication experts such as Tal Silberstein, who was one of the closest advisers to the Al Gore electoral team during the American presidential elections that had just been contested.

The DS have also accelerated their transformation into a 'lighter' party. Since the XVIII congress of 1989, the neo-revisionist group of the *quarantenni* addressed the issue of the need for internal reforms conducive to the replacement of Togliatti's mass party by a new more flexible and competent type of 'cadre' party; the final goal being the construction of a 'flexible party'.[68] This new type of party was eventually created at the Rimini congress in 1991; the party's apparatus was reduced by two-thirds and the local branches were halved in size.[69] At the same time the party's membership drastically declined; throughout the 1980s the PCI lost almost a quarter of its membership. In 1989 there were 1 424 000 members. When the PDS was founded in 1991, only a quarter of them adhered to the new party that suffered from a steady and further gradual decline of its membership in the years to follow. When Occhetto resigned from the party's leadership in 1994, the PDS had 698 212 members, a figure which further shrunk to 600 000 in 1998.[70] Labour experienced a similar drain of its membership. In the 1950s the Labour Party claimed about a million individual members, a figure that fell to about 300 000 in 1997.[71] It might be worth noting that both the DS and New Labour have made some efforts to reverse this trend. Although local canvassing has dramatically declined over the last twenty years, on some occasions constituency election campaigning in target seats has become crucial. As recent studies carried out in Britain have shown, it can significantly affect election outcomes in key seats. Not surprisingly, the Labour Party's greatest recruitment efforts have been directed towards electorally important areas in the Midlands and the South from where 60 per cent of the new members originate.[72] Moreover, recruitment of new members is also seen as a way to replace the old party's membership with a new one that is more in tune with the neo-revisionist project that both parties have been pursuing. This was crucial for New Labour particularly following the introduction of one member–one vote. New members in recent years have tended to be younger (their average age being 39, which is significantly younger than both Tories' average age of 62 and the Liberal Democrats' of 55). Furthermore, most are university educated and professionally employed.[73] The DS was also successful in replacing old members with new ones. Two-thirds of the 1989 PCI membership consisted of traditional working class and pensioners. In 1988 only 2.1 per cent of the party's members were less than 25 years old. A generational and 'genetic' renewal was of the greatest urgency for the sake of the party image and survival. By 1994, one-third of its membership had been newly recruited resulting in the party becoming more socially heterogeneous.[74]

The altered voters/militants ratio and the 'lightening' of the party's organisation that both the British Labour and the Italian DS experienced went hand in hand with the growing personalisation of their politics. A tendency towards a certain personalisation of the party, especially when compared with the rest of Europe, has always been a characteristic of British politics and is related to the two-party system. The most obvious reflection of the phenomenon is the large number of biographies and autobiographies traditionally published about British politicians – far more than for their European counterparts. *Tony Blair Prime Minister*, *Tony Blair: the Moderniser*, *The Blair Agenda*, *Blair's Hundred Days*, and *Who is Tony Blair?*[75] are just a few recently published works on Tony Blair. Even when the aim has been to analyse the ideas of New Labour, the British political starting point is Tony Blair and the 'Blair Revolution'.[76]

A greater personalisation of political parties' life has also been taking place in Italy. Since 1994 and Berlusconi's entry into politics, TV has become the dominant medium through which elections have been contested. The new sound-bite media communication implies that a movement exists towards an enormous concentration of decision-making power in the hands of the leader and a growing personification of political messages;[77] this was also given impetus by the number of electoral reforms carried out in the early 1990s, both of which have resulted in a closer identification between the electorate and the coalition's leader.[78] The intimate pictures of Achille Occhetto kissing his wife and of his exuberant sailing vacation were an attempt by the PDS leadership to respond to the highly personalised Berlusconi's *Polo delle Libertà* electoral campaign in 1994 and would have been inconceivable during the old PCI years. Both Togliatti and Berlinguer were high profile leaders who were strongly identified with the party's image in the years during their leadership. However, they never used their private lives to increase their appeal.[79]

Personalisation is an issue of some embarrassment in Italy: the 'monopolisation' of the PSI by the party leader was one of the distinctive features of the tainted *Craxismo*.[80] Besides, a party like the DS which emphasises its break from the communist past and rules such as democratic centralism cannot but show some uneasiness with utilising practices that reflect scant interest for democratic consultation. In 1994 Massimo D'Alema, when stepping forward as the candidate for the party's leadership, condemned Occhetto's unilateral style of party management, well illustrated by his manner of taking decisions such as changing the party's name without previous consultation.[81] However, D'Alema would soon realise that sound-bite communication politics do not leave much room for the complexities of party consultation and he was to be similarly, if not more so, personalistic and centralising. The introduction of the direct election of the party leader carried out at the PDS Congress (22–4 February 1997) was a further step towards the 'party leader' for which Occhetto was blamed. Similarly, the 1998 creation of the DS was a top–down operation as much as it had been at the Bolognina.[82]

Epilogue

In the new millennium we now see a Left that has radically transformed itself from the first socialist parties founded at the end of the nineteenth century. Undoubtedly, today's Left would be unrecognisable to its predecessors. Important totems such as nationalisation of the means of production or the centrality attached to the working class in the parties' strategies and programmes have been dropped. The role that the state should play in the economy has also been thoroughly reconsidered, together with traditional concepts such as that of equality. The latter, while still remaining a distinctive left-wing value, has today gone through a fundamental change as far as its meaning and interpretation are concerned.

However, the very aim of comparing the recent wave of neo-revisionism with that which took place in the 1950s and 1960s was to show that the former was not a last minute change; it was just a further, and presumably not a last, step taken along a continual path of re-assessment and adjustment of policies and ideas that socialist parties have been carrying out since their inception. The fact that capitalism, the very system they were born to oppose, has been constantly evolving and has gone through fundamental transformations throughout the century could not leave socialists unaffected. In essence, they had no other option but to constantly adapt their means and strategies to what turned out to be a continually changing 'enemy'.

Indeed, one fundamental difference that sets today's 'third way' apart from any earlier revisionism is the renunciation of the long-term aspiration of replacing capitalism with socialism. The latter is the distinctive feature of contemporary neo-revisionism. For all their pragmatism and moderation, no socialist parties had previously questioned that in the end – however distant this might be was seen as irrelevant – a better and more equal society would replace what was regarded as an inherently unjust model (namely, the free market economy). In contrast, capitalism is regarded today as something to be tamed, reformed and regulated but not replaced. Following the collapse of really-existing socialism, it is now accepted as the only game in town. The argument underlying previous revisionist attempts since Bernstein's nineteenth-century 'heresies' was that socialists should always search for better means in order to meet their goals. Those who recently re-polished this motto to explain the rationale behind neo-revisionism fail to mention the fact that this time not only have the means, but also the goal itself, changed. The search for a 'third way' is no longer an alternative between communism and capitalism. Instead, it is now regarded as something to be found inside the capitalist model.

Therefore, the Left now faces the hard task of extracting from capitalism the kind of more equal and just society which for the past one hundred years they had believed to be incompatible with that very system. At some point during the 'Golden Age' (1945 to the mid-1970s), the reconciliation of a profit-led economy with social justice seemed realistically achievable. In the age of welfare capitalism, Keynesian policies seemed to fulfil both capitalism's requirements for growth and expansion, as well as traditional socialists' objectives for redistribution and greater equality. It was during this phase that Keynesianism began to pass for socialism, resulting in evolutionary socialism – such as that professed by centre–right revisionists like Anthony Crosland – came back in fashion to establish an unchallenged, although short-lived, dominance within many socialist parties' policies and agendas.

However, that era has now ended. The collapse of the social capitalism model has now given way to the dominance of a new, though similarly pervasive, set of policies and parameters present within neo-liberal agendas. Similar to the years before the mid-1970s when welfare politics were pursued by and large by all parties irrespective of their colour, today very little room for manoeuvre seems to exist for alternatives beyond neo-liberalism. The decline of the Fordist model of production and the globalisation of markets have all radically changed the context of left-wing politics. These changes portend a crisis for the nation-state, at least as an economic unit, and thus the end of mechanisms and means with which the Left has balanced and tempered capitalist development during the past century. Economies are increasingly interdependent. Today not only 'national' roads to socialism, but also to capitalism, seem difficult to pursue. This is a reality with which parties that aspire to govern have had to come to terms. Policies of low inflation, low budget deficits and low pay rises are now *de rigueur* for any country that wishes to remain competitive in global markets. Against this background, objectives for full employment, along with greater social protection and greater equality, often seem to be more voluntary aspirations than goals that can be realistically met.

Consensus for collective and redistributive policies, which was very strong in the years immediately after the end of World War II, has been declining since the new individualistic ethos has replaced the past collective spirit. In this regard, a passage by Roy Jenkins in the *New Fabian Essays* (1952), is striking for its predictive capability. As he put it, in an increasingly 'bourgeoisiefied' society, many will believe themselves to be on the wrong side of the line around which further measures of redistribution will take place. As he stated, any egalitarian that believed that the forces of history were working inexorably towards this goal was living in a fool's paradise.[1]

Within the context of growing 'Darwinian affluence',[2] it is increasingly difficult for parties or coalitions that today aspire to return to power to preach values of solidarity and equality. We are faced with the paradox that when socialists carry out policies that are clearly redistributive in kind, they tend to understate it. When the British Press heralded Gordon Brown's first Budget in 1997 as one of the most redistributive since 1945, New Labour's reaction was that of embarrassment and denial. When standing in elections, left-wing parties prefer highlighting their economic achievements such as low inflation rates or, as was the case with the Italian centre–Left coalition in the run-up to the 2001 election, entry into the EMU.

Shortly after his election in 1997, Tony Blair declared that New Labour's return to power not only signified governmental change but also an overall transformation of the country's political culture. However, anything but this has been the case. Left-wing parties do redistribute, but they do not admit it. Under the severe *diktat* of focus groups' results, far from 'shaping' public opinion they seem to be lagging behind it. This might sound fairly obvious to many. After all, the function of political parties should not be that of providing citizens with 'visions', but instead with responses to concrete and practical problems. As politics textbooks explain, parties are there to capture political demands emerging within society and offer them political representation. However, left-wing parties long held the aspiration of not just meeting people's material needs but also – one might argue quite paternalistically – guiding those very people to better understand what their needs should be. This applies to socialism in all its variants. Utopian socialists, Marxists and Fabians, all believed that not only should socialists' policies contribute to the creation of a more just society but they should also facilitate a more ethically oriented society where people were made more aware of where, in fact, their 'true' interests lay. This was what 'organic' intellectuals, in Gramsci's words, were supposed to do. The fact that socialists now 'market' their policies like any other political party, signals a significant break with the past and one of the very objectives they were born to fulfil.

'Big vision' politics has run its course. Not only have ideologies been shelved but the word 'ideology' itself has become one that politicians feel uneasy with. Instead, they prefer talking about 'public philosophies'. In the past, the existence of long-term goals could make militants and the electorate pragmatically accept anything that happened in between; however, in so far as politics is now about day-to-day short-term improvements, loyalties have become much weaker and more volatile. Electorates are more impatient and more 'reflexive'. What voters expect from parties is not a ready-made packaged *weltanschauung* pointing them to a 'better future', but rather practical and immediate answers on what matters to them, which is something they want to decide by themselves. Not surprisingly, the relationships between intellectuals and left-wing parties have been going through a fundamental change over the last ten years. The wide-ranging intellectual has fallen into disgrace. Greater importance is now attached to specialised knowledge, practical reasoning and solutions rather than big ideas, resulting in political philosophers giving way to sociologists, political scientists or economists as the new 'gurus' from whom left-wing politicians seek guidance.

The idea that the aspirations of the Left today embody a third way in politics has been met with scepticism, to say the least. Anthony Giddens's *Third Way* manifesto attracted so much criticism that he felt he should publish a sequel to his book two years later – *The Third Way and its Critics*[3] – where he would try to make his point again in a more persuasive manner. However, for all the efforts made to present it as a 'solid' philosophy, today's variant of the 'Third Way' has been dismissed by commentators as vague, fuzzy and a masterpiece of ambiguity. As the *Economist* wrote, 'trying to pin down an exact meaning is like wrestling an inflatable man. If you get a grip on one limb, all the hot air rushes to another.'[4] To many, 'third way politics' is nothing other than a potent recipe for gaining power; or as Stuart Hall stated, 'the great moving nowhere show'.[5] Admittedly, the truth lies somewhere in between: while failing to be the revolutionary new route the Left claims to have found, it is also an exaggeration to dismiss today's left-wing politics as 'reheated Thatcherism'. All the more so now that 'Thatcherism' has given way in right-wing parties' agenda to softer centrist policies such as those pursued by the Partido Popular under Aznar in Spain. Differences between right-wing and left-wing parties, although minimal, do still exist. It might be worth remembering here that critics on the Left have always attacked social democrats in power as being 'betrayers'. Those who are today nostalgic for the time when the Left was a 'true Left' forget that those post-war social-democratic governments' experiences which are now looked at with a 'never will be again' spirit, were as fiercely accused of surrender as those of neo-revisionists' are today. Political parties face constraints once in office and compromises have always been inherent in social-democratic politics. What perhaps might be argued is that those constraints now often tend to be overestimated, resulting in socialist parties' easy 'surrender' even where some room for manoeuvre might still exist.

Scholars and commentators over the last few years have been engaged over the unresolved issue whether it was socialism which most changed capitalism or vice versa. There is no doubt that socialism, in all its variants – Marxist, liberal socialist, and so on – has played an important role in the past towards modifying capitalism. Especially after the Great Slump in 1929 and the success demonstrated by the Soviet system, capitalism resulted, as Roberto Guiducci wrote in 1956, in adopting *Capital* as 'its best medical text'[6] and transformed itself from a 'short and devouring maggot' into a 'gaily-coloured and agile butterfly'.[7] In its new post-war variant of regulated social capitalism, it ended up incorporating 'socialist' elements that were regarded as vital to its political and economic stability as well as to its further expansion. However, when it comes to more recent years, the balance seems to have been reversed with socialist parties becoming more and more free market devotees and pro-business in their frame of mind.

That said, for all the disappointment this has provoked in the traditional left-wing electorate, it should also be noted that, just as socialism once saved capitalism, now capitalism has returned the favour fifty years later. Neo-liberal critiques spurred from the crisis of the old Keynesian welfare state contributed to a more than auspicious re-assessment by parties of the Socialist International on a number of issues. Think, for example, of the recognition of the shortcomings and limitations of past forms of public intervention with their inflexibility and inefficiency, or the redefinition of the relationship between the market and the state in such a way to strike a better balance between the individual and the collective. All this helped the Left to recover politically and electorally in the 1990s after the long, gloomy 1980s.

It is the capacity of the Left to adapt to new scenarios that has permitted European socialist parties to survive a century of great transformations and to prove unfounded the repeated announcements of its imminent demise. The neo-revisionism in which the major parties of the Left are currently involved may well help to guarantee them another hundred years. The question then remains: at what price?

Notes

Introduction

1 E. Bernstein, *Evolutionary Socialism* (New York: Schocken Books, 1963).
2 See D. Sassoon, *One Hundred Years of Socialism* (London: Tauris, 1996), p. 241.
3 *Ibid.*, p. 722.
4 J. Schneer, *Labour's Conscience. The Labour Left 1945–1951* (London: Unwin Hyman, 1988), p. 10.
5 See Sassoon (1996) on this, *op. cit.*, p. 432.
6 See I. Favretto, 'La svolta autonomista del PSI vista oltremanica: il partito laburista, il Foreign Office e il centro–sinistra', *Italia Contemporanea*, no. 202 (March 1996), pp. 5–44.
7 Interview with Antonio Giolitti, Rome, December 1995.
8 P. Glotz, *Manifesto per Una Nuova Sinistra Europea* (Milano: Feltrinelli, 1986).
9 G. Tamburrano, *Storia e Cronaca del Centro–Sinistra* (Milano: Rizzoli, 1984), p. 233.
10 M. Degl'Innocenti, *Storia del PSI. Dal dopoguerra a oggi* (Roma-Bari: Laterza, 1993), p. 408.
11 I. Diamanti, 'Dossier: DS, quel piccolo PCI', in *La Repubblica*, 15 November 2001, pp. 28–9.
12 *Ibid.*
13 See S. Bartolini, *The Political Mobilization of the European Left, 1860–1980. The Class Cleavage* (Cambridge: Cambridge University Press, 2000).

1 Rethinking Socialism

1 See, for instance, P. Armstrong, A. Glyn, J. Harrison, *Capitalism since 1945* (Oxford: Basil Blackwell, 1991), p. 117; and E. Hobsbawn, *Age of Extremes* (London: Michael Joseph, 1994), p. 263.
2 G. Therborn, *European Modernity and Beyond. The Trajectory of European Societies 1945–2000* (London: Sage, 1995), p. 349.
3 A. Maddison, *The World Economy in the 20th Century* (Paris: Organisation for Economic Co-operation and Development, 1989), pp. 31–41.
4 Hobsbawm (1994), *op. cit.*, p. 268.
5 Maddison (1989), *op. cit.*, p. 96.
6 Hobsbawm (1994), *op. cit.*, p. 261.
7 A. Shonfield, *Modern Capitalism. The Changing Balance of Public and Private Power* (Oxford: Oxford University Press, 1965), p. 3.
8 *Ibid.*, pp. 3–7.
9 *Ibid.*, p. 7.
10 P. Armstrong, A. Glyn, J. H. Armstrong (1991), *op. cit.*, p. 137.
11 *Ibid.*, p. 138.

12 S. Padgett and W. Paterson, *A History of Social Democracy in Postwar Europe* (London and New York: Longman, 1991), p. 186.
13 A. Przeworski, *Capitalism and Social Democracy* (Cambridge: Cambridge University Press, 1985), p. 148.
14 Hobsbawm (1994), *op. cit.*, p. 270.
15 Shonfield (1965), *op. cit.*, pp. 65–6.
16 A. Crosland, *The Future of Socialism* (London: Jonathan Cape, 1956).
17 Sassoon (1996), *op. cit.*, p. 241.
18 Padgett and Paterson (1991), *op. cit.*, p. 22.
19 *Ibid.*, pp. 22–3.
20 See N. Ellison, *Egalitarian Thought and Labour Politics* (London: LSE/ Routledge, 1994), pp. 26–9. See also E. Durbin, *New Jerusalem: the Labour Party and the Economics of Democratic Socialism* (London: Routledge and Kegan Paul, 1985), p. 131.
21 Ellison (1994), *op. cit.*, p. 31.
22 R. Crossman (ed.), *The New Fabian Essays* (London: Turnstile Press, 1952).
23 R. A. Attlee, Preface, in Crossman (ed.), *New Fabian Essays*, *op. cit.*, pp. vii–viii, p. vii; see also K. O. Morgan, *The People's Peace. British History 1945–1990* (Oxford: Oxford University Press, 1992 [1st edn 1990]), pp. 124–5.
24 P. Flora, F. Kraus, W. Pfenning, *State Economy and Society in Western Europe 1815–1975*, Vol. I–II, *The Growth of Industrial Societies and Capitalist Economies* (Frankfurt: Campus Verlag; London: Macmillan Press; Chicago: St James Press, 1987), Vol. I, p. 442.
25 R. Crosland, 'The Transition from Capitalism', in Crossman (ed.) (1952), *op. cit.*, pp. 33–69. See also G. Myrdal, *Beyond the Welfare State* (London: 1960).
26 Crosland (1956), *op. cit.*, p. 18.
27 See J. Burnham, *The Managerial Revolution* (London: Putnam, 1942), a book which was an important point of reference for centre–right revisionists.
28 Labour Party, *Industry and Society*, NEC policy document, 1957, pp. 16, 18.
29 Ellison (1994), *op. cit.*, p. 75.
30 Crosland (1956), *op. cit.*, p. 500.
31 *Ibid.*, p. 502.
32 See 'Labour Manifesto 1951' and 'Labour Manifesto 1955', in F. Craig (ed.), *British General Election Manifestos, 1900–1974* (London: Macmillan, 1974), pp. 147–50 and pp. 176–82.
33 Labour Party, *Planning for Progress*, NEC policy document, 1958.
34 See for a similar assessment on *Planning for Progress*, N. Thompson, *Political Economy and the Labour Party* (London: UCL Press, 1996), pp. 180–2.
35 See Labour Party, *Industry and Society*, *op. cit.*, pp. 42–5; 'Labour Manifesto 1959', in Craig (ed.) (1974), *op. cit.*, pp. 200, 202; and Labour Party, *Planning for Progress*, *op. cit.*, p. 9.
36 Crosland (1956), *op. cit.*, p. 169; similar arguments were first put forward in Crosland, 'The Transition from Capitalism', *op. cit.*, pp. 61–2. See also D. Jay, *Socialism in the New Society* (London: Longman, 1962), p. 345.
37 Crosland (1952), *op. cit.*, p. 37.
38 R. Crossman, 'Towards a New Philosophy of Socialism', in Crossman (ed.)(1952), *op. cit.*, pp. 25–7.

39 R. Crossman, *Socialism and the New Despotism*, Fabian Tract no. 298, November 1955, p. 11. See also A. Bevan, *In Place of Fear* (New York: Monthly Review Press, 1964 (1st edn London: Heinemann, 1952), pp. 135–7.

40 T. Balogh, *Planning for Progress. A Strategy for Labour*, Fabian Tract no. 346, July 1963, p. 2.

41 J. K. Galbraith, *The Affluent Society* (London: Hamish Hamilton, 1958).

42 R. Crossman, *Labour and the Affluent Society*, Fabian Tract no. 325, June 1960, p. 10.

43 V. Bogdanor, R. Skidelsky, *The Age of Affluence 1951–1964* (London: Macmillan, 1970), p. 15.

44 M. Chesi, 'Rassegna di interpretazioni sullo sviluppo economico italiano nel secondo dopoguerra', *Società e Storia*, no. 41 (July–September 1988) pp. 669–91, p. 669.

45 A. Maddison, *Phases of Capitalist Development* (Oxford: Oxford University Press, 1982), p. 97.

46 P. Flora, F. Kraus and W. Pfenning (1987), *op. cit.*, Table: Origin and Use of National Product: United Kingdom, p. 436; Sweden, p. 430; Italy, p. 420; Germany, p. 415; France, p. 413.

47 *Ibid.*, Table: The Development of the Labour Force (percent distribution by sector): Italy, p. 551.

48 B. R. Mitchell, *European Historical Statistics 1750–1975* (London: Macmillan, 1981, 2nd revised edn (first published in 1975)), table C2, p. 178, Unemployment (Numbers in Thousands and Percentage of Appropriate Workforce), pp. 178–9.

49 G. Sapelli, *L'Italia inafferrabile* (Venezia: Marsilio, 1989), p. 17.

50 See A. Salsano, *Il Neocapitalismo. Progetti ed ideologia, in Storia d'Italia*, Vol. 5, part 1 (Torino: Einaudi, 1972), pp. 888–909, pp. 898–903.

51 C. Daneo, *La politica economica della Ricostruzione* (Torino: Einaudi, 1975), pp. 46–7.

52 Sassoon (1996), *op. cit.*, pp. 117–18.

53 Degl' Innocenti (1993), *op. cit.*, p. 34.

54 A. Giolitti, 'Politica ed economia nella lotta di classe. Un'intervista con Antonio Giolitti', *Mondo Operaio*, Vol. X (September 1957), pp. 2–4, p. 3.

55 See on this, for instance, F. Coen, 'Temi e problemi della nostra politica', *Mondo Operaio*, Vol. XII (December 1959), pp. 7–12, p. 11.

56 *Unione Popolare* (UP) and the *Unione Socialista Indipendente* (USI) both merged with the PSI in 1957. See G. Galli, *I partiti politici italiani* (Milano: Rizzoli, 1991), p. 113.

57 *Ibid.*, p. 132.

58 Degl'Innocenti (1993), *op. cit.*, p. 477.

59 A. Giolitti, 'Programma e formule', *Mondo Operaio*, Vol. XII (July 1959), pp. 6–9, p. 9.

60 V. Cattani, 'Ancora sul Programma', *Mondo Operaio*, Vol. XII (October 1959), pp. 43–7, pp. 43–4.

61 R. Panzieri, (edited by S. Merli), *Dopo Stalin. Una stagione della sinistra* (Venezia: Marsilio, 1986), p. xii.

62 *Ibid.*, p. xxiii.

63 F. Fortini, *Dieci Inverni 1947–1957* (Bari: DeDonato, 1973).

64 A. Pizzorno, 'I tolemaici, ovvero i migliori anni della nostra vita', *Passato e Presente*, no. 3 (May–June 1958), pp. 1–3.
65 R. Guiducci, *Socialismo e Verità* (Torino: Einaudi, 1956); A. Giolitti, *Riforme e Rivoluzione* (Torino: Einaudi, 1957).
66 R. Panzieri and L. Libertini, 'Sette tesi sul controllo operaio', *Mondo Operaio*, Vol. XI (February 1958), pp. 11–15.
67 Panzieri (1986), *op. cit.*, p. xxxi.
68 See, for instance, G. Galli, 'Tre anni di Revisionismo', *Tempi Moderni*, Vol. III (April–June 1960), pp. 56–69; see also A. Giolitti, *Lettere a Marta* (Bologna: Il Mulino, 1992).
69 See, inter alia, D. Sassoon, *La via italiana al socialismo. Il PCI dal 1944 al 1964* (Torino: Einaudi, 1980); G. Bedeschi, *La parabola del Marxismo in Italia, 1945–1983* (Roma-Bari: Laterza, 1983), p. 97; G. Vacca, *Politica e teoria nel Marxismo Italiano (1959–1969)* (Bari: De Donato, 1972).
70 B. Groppo, 'Il 1956 nella cultura politica del PCI', in B. Groppo and G. Riccamboni, *La Sinistra e il '56 in Italia e in Francia* (Padova: Liviana, 1987), pp. 189–218, pp. 202–3.
71 C. Vallauri, 'La crisi del '56 e il PSI', in G. Arfè (ed.), *Trent'anni di politica socialista (1946–1976), Atti del Convegno organizzato dall'Istituto Socialista di Studi Storici* (Roma: Mondo Operaio-Edizioni Avanti!, 1977), pp. 73–105, p. 99.
72 Panzieri (1986), *op. cit.*, p. xxviii.
73 On this question, see P. Spriano, *Le Passioni di un Decennio* (Roma: Ed. L'Unità, 1992), pp. 191–2. See also the poignant and entertaining tale by Italo Calvino, 'La Bonaccia delle Antille' (originally published in *Città Aperta* in 1957), in G. Mughini, *Il revisionismo socialista. Antologia di testi 1955–1962* (Roma: Nuova Serie dei Quaderni di Mondo Operaio, 1975).
74 L. Longo, *Revisionismo nuovo e antico* (Torino: Einaudi, 1957).
75 Istituto Gramsci (edited by), *Tendenze del Capitalismo Italiano. Atti del Convegno di Roma* (Roma: 1962).
76 A. Pesenti and V. Vitello, 'Tendenze attuali del capitalismo italiano', in Istituto Gramsci (edited by) (1962), *op. cit.*, pp. 13–96.
77 L. Barca, 'Problemi del Capitalismo di Stato e della pianificazione', Istituto Gramsci (edited by) (1962), *op. cit.*, pp. 65–106.
78 See on this P. Bagnoli (ed), Liberalsocialismo, special issue of *Il Ponte*, Vol. XLII (January–February 1986), pp. 72–3; F. D'Almeida, *Histoire et politique en France et en Italie: l'esemple des socialistes 1945–1983* (Roma: Ecole Française de Rome, 1998); and M. Mafai, *Lombardi* (Milano: Feltrinelli, 1976), p. 22.
79 Guiducci (1956), *op. cit.*, p. 73.
80 *Ibid.*, p. 83.
81 Giolitti, *Riforme e Rivoluzione*, *op. cit.*, p. 24.
82 P. Amato, *Il PSI tra Frontismo e Autonomia (1948–1954)* (Cosenza: 1958), p. 92.
83 PSI Executive Committee's report to the 32nd PSI National Congress (1957), in PSI, *Resoconto stenografico 32° Congresso Nazionale PSI, Venezia 6–10 febbraio 1957* (Milano-Roma: Edizioni Avanti!, 1957), p. 16.
84 F. Vasetti, 'Partito e tecnici', *Mondo Operaio*, Vol. X (February–March 1957) pp. 72–7, p. 72.
85 R. Panzieri, 'Capitalismo contemporaneo e controllo operaio', in Panzieri (1986), *op. cit.*, pp. 175–8, p. 175.

86   J. Strachey, *Il capitalismo contemporaneo* (Milano: Feltrinelli, 1957).
87   See, for instance, M. Dobb, 'Some Economic Revaluations', *Marxist Quarterly*, Vol. 4 (January 1957), pp. 2–7. And R. Bellamy, 'Mr. Strachey's guide to contemporary capitalism', *Marxist Quarterly*, Vol. 4 (January 1957), pp. 21–30.
88   R. Amaduzzi, in 'Capitalismo contemporaneo e controllo operaio' (Round Table organised by *Mondo Operaio* on contemporary capitalism), *Mondo Operaio*, Vol. X (December 1957), pp. 10–21. See also Giolitti, *Riforme e Rivoluzione, op. cit.*, p. 20.
89   Amaduzzi (1957), *op. cit.*, pp. 10–21.
90   Guiducci (1956), *op. cit.*, p. 145.
91   *Ibid.*, p. 136.
92   *Ibid.*, p. 161.
93   Antonio Giolitti, 'Alcune osservazioni sulle riforme di struttura', *Passato e Presente*, no. 6 (November–December 1958), pp. 677–91, p. 681.
94   Idomeneo Barbadoro, 'Sviluppo economico e lotta rivoluzionaria', *Mondo Operaio*, Vol. X (September 1957), pp. 13–15, p. 14.
95   Sassoon (1996), *op. cit.*, pp. 70–82.
96   Vallauri (1977), *op. cit.*, p. 85.
97   P. Nenni, 'Luci e ombre del congresso di Mosca', *Mondo Operaio*, Vol. IX (March 1956), pp. 146–54.
98   P. Nenni's report to the 32nd PSI National Congress (1957), in PSI, *Resoconto stenografico 32° Congresso Nazionale PSI, Venezia 6–10 febbraio 1957, op. cit.*, p. 26.
99   Vallauri (1977), *op. cit.*, p. 85.
100 A. Gramsci, 'Noterelle sulla politica del Machiavelli', copybook 13, in V. Gerratana (ed.), *Antonio Gramsci. Quaderni del Carcere*, Vol. 3 (Torino: Einaudi, 1977), pp. 1613–16. The re-interpretation of the notion of the dictatorship of the proletariat as the Gramscian notion of hegemony was central Italian 'revisionists' thinking. See Giolitti, *Riforme e Rivoluzione, op. cit.*, pp. 29–41; Guiducci (1956), *op. cit.*, pp. 228ff; see also F. Onofri 'La via sovietica (leninista) alla conquista del potere e la via italiana, aperta da Gramsci', *Nuovi Argomenti*, (November 1956–February 1957), pp. 48–85.
101 Giolitti, *Riforme e Rivoluzione, op. cit.*, pp. 35–7.
102 R. Lombardi, 'Le riforme di struttura come via democratica al socialismo', (Speech to the 35th PSI National Congress, Rome, 25–29 October 1963), in S. Colarizi (ed.), *Riccardo Lombardi, Scritti politici 1945–1963, dalla Resistenza al Centrosinistra* (Venezia: Marsilio, 1978), pp. 395–415, p. 396.
103 see Giolitti (1958), *op. cit.*
104 Archivio Centrale di Stato (Rome), Nenni Papers, 'Party' series, box no. 90, bundle no. 2215, Report to the PSI Central Committee, 9–10 April 1956.
105 The question of the new forms and function of the state acquired an undisputed centrality in *Mondo Operaio* in the years from 1956 to 1957. See *inter alia* the following articles: F. De Martino, 'Ancora dello Stato', *Mondo Operaio*, Vol. IX (July 1956), pp. 423–6; F. De Martino, 'Pretese questioni di teoria intorno ai problemi dello Stato', *Mondo Operaio*, Vol. IX (October 1956), pp. 563–6; and G. Tamburrano, 'Marx, Engels, Lenin e lo Stato', *Mondo Operaio*, Vol. IX (October 1956), pp. 566–72.
106 R. Lombardi, 'La conquista democratica dello stato', *op. cit.*, pp. 340–4. See also Riccardo Lombardi, 'La nuova politica delle alleanze' (Speech to the

33rd PSI National Congress, Naples, 15–19 January 1959), in Colarizi (ed.) (1978), *op. cit.*, pp. 293–6, p. 294.

107 F. Coen e G. Tamburrano, 'Sulla funzione e la struttura dello Stato nella moderna societá capitalistica', in Istituto Gramsci (edited by) (1962), *op. cit.*, pp. 171–90, pp. 172–3.

108 See 'Mozione della corrente autonomista' (33rd PSI National Congress, 1961), in F. Pedone, *Novant'anni di pensiero socialista attraverso i congressi del PSI 1957–1966* (Venezia: Marsilio, 1984), pp. 207–11.

109 Coen and Tamburrano (1962), *op. cit.*, pp. 176–9.

110 Giolitti, *Riforme e Rivoluzione*, *op. cit.*, p. 13.

111 Guiducci (1956), *op. cit.*, p. 161.

112 V. Strinati, *Politica e cultura nel Partito Socialista Italiano 1945–1978* (Napoli: Liguori, 1980), p. 193.

113 Emilio Lussi's speech to the 33rd PSI National Congress (1959), in PSI, *Resoconto stenografico 33° Congresso Nazionale PSI, Napoli 15–18 gennaio 1959* (Milano-Roma: Edizioni Avanti!, 1959), pp. 208–20, p. 209.

114 Archivio Centrale di Stato (Rome), Nenni Papers, 'Correspondence' series, section 1944–79, Pietro Nenni-Lelio Basso correspondence, box no. 18, bundle no. 1093, Letter from Lelio Basso to Pietro Nenni, 23 April 1959 (Milan).

115 Tullio Vecchietti's speech to the 34th PSI National Congress (1961), in PSI, *Resoconto Stenografico 34° Congresso Nazionale PSI, Milano 15–20 marzo 1961* (Milano-Roma: Edizioni Avanti!, 1961), pp. 56–80, p. 67.

116 De Martino, 'Ancora dello Stato', *op. cit.*, p. 424. See also PSI Executive Committee's report to the 32nd PSI National Congress, in PSI, *Resoconto stenografico 32° Congresso Nazionale PSI, Venezia 6–10 febbraio 1957*, *op. cit.*, p. 34.

117 Pietro Nenni's report to the 34th PSI National Congress (1961), in PSI, *Resoconto Stenografico 34° Congresso Nazionale PSI, Milano 15–20 marzo 1961*, *op. cit.*, pp. 7–54, p. 48.

118 Morgan (1992), *op. cit.*, p. 197.

119 D. Porter, 'Downhill all the way: thirteen Tory years 1951–1964', in R. Coopey, S. Fielding, N. Tiratsoo (eds), *The Wilson Governments 1964–1970* (London and New York: Pinter Publishers, 1993), pp. 10–28, p. 17–18.

120 A. Koestler, *Suicide of a Nation? An Enquiry into the State of Britain* (London: Vintage, 1994) (first published in Great Britain by Hutchinson, 1963), p. 7.

121 Morgan (1992), *op. cit.*, p. 197.

122 Koestler (1994, 1st edn 1963), *op. cit.*, p. 13.

123 M. Shanks, *The Stagnant Society*, (London: Penguin Books Ltd, 1964 [1st edn 1961]), p. 47.

124 OEEC National Account Statistics, 1955–65, Paris, 1964, Table: UK share of world exports.

125 D. Porter (1993), *op. cit.*, pp. 20–1.

126 A. Harvey, *Casualties of the Welfare State*, Fabian Tract no. 321, 1960.

127 R. Crossman, 'Scientists in Whitehall' (1963), in R. Crossman, *Planning for Freedom* (London: Hamish Hamilton, 1965), pp. 134–47, p. 136.

128 A. Crosland, *The Conservative Enemy: a Program of Radical Reform for the 1960s* (London: Jonathan Cape, 1962).

129 Balogh (1963), *op. cit.*, p. 7.

130   Ellison (1994), *op. cit.*, p. 52.
131   *Ibid.*, p. 62.
132   H. Wilson, *In Place of Dollars* (London: Tribune Monthly Publications, 1953), p. 14.
133   H. Wilson, *Post-War Economic Policies in Britain*, Fabian Tract no. 309, September 1957, pp. 8–21.
134   S. Haseler, *The Gaitskellites: Revisionism in the British Labour Party, 1951–1964* (London: 1964), p. 142.
135   *Ibid.*, p. 209.
136   See for example, C. Cook, I. Taylor (eds), *The Labour Party* (London and New York: Longman, 1980), pp. 22–3; Haseler (1964), *op. cit;* and for more recent works, A. Wright, *Socialisms Old and New* (New York and London: Routledge, 1996), p. 127; and T. Jones, *Remaking the Labour Party. From Gaitskell to Blair* (New York and London: Routledge, 1996).

2   Structural Reforms and the 'Socialist' Management of Capitalism

1   Labour Party, *Personal Freedom: Labour's Policy for the Individual and Society*, National Executive Committee (thereafter NEC) policy document, June 1956, pp. 3–32, p. 6.
2   *Ibid.*
3   Pietro Nenni's report to the 32nd PSI National Congress (1957), in PSI, *Resoconto stenografico 32° Congresso Nazionale PSI, Venezia 6–10 febbraio 1957, op. cit.*, pp. 26–8; see also on this Nenni (1956), *op. cit.*, pp. 146.
4   Crossman (1955), *op. cit.*
5   *Ibid.*, p. 2.
6   Crossman, 'Scientists in Whitehall' (1963), *op. cit.*, p. 135.
7   *Ibid.*, p. 139.
8   H. Wilson, 'Speech opening the Science Debate at the Party's Annual Conference, Scarborough, 1963', in H. Wilson, *Purpose and Politics. Selected Speeches* (London: 1964), pp. 14–27, p. 18.
9   F. Coen, 'Scienza e politica al Congresso Laburista', *Mondo Operaio*, Vol. XVI (October 1963), pp. 11–24, pp. 12–13.
10   F. Pollock, *Automazione. Conseguenze economiche e sociali* (Torino: Einaudi, 1976 [1st Italian edition 1956]), p. 102.
11   *Ibid.*, p. 25.
12   *Ibid.*, p. 178.
13   *Ibid.*, pp. 291–305.
14   See, for instance, J. Diebold, *Automation – The Advent of the Automatic Factory* (New York: Van Nostrand, 1952); or P. Drucker, *The Practice of Management* (London: Heinemann, 1955).
15   Giolitti, 'Politica ed economia nella lotta di classe. Un'intervista con Antonio Giolitti', *op. cit.*, p. 3. See also Giolitti, *Riforme e Rivoluzione, op. cit.*, p. 14.
16   V. Foa, 'Il Socialismo per un'Italia moderna', *Mondo Operaio*, Vol. X (February–March 1957), pp. 69–71, p. 69.
17   C. Wright Mills, *The Power Elite* (Oxford: Oxford University Press, 1956).

18 R. Guiducci, 'Il mito dell'industria e programma alternativo' (July–August 1959), in R. Guiducci (ed.), *New Deal Socialista*. *Valori e strumenti per un piano a lungo periodo* (Firenze: Vallecchi, 1965), pp. 32–54, p. 33.

19 R. Guiducci, 'Un piano di riforme democratiche' (May–October 1957), in Guiducci (ed.) (1965), *op. cit.*, pp. 19–31, p. 21.

20 Pietro Nenni's speech to the 32nd PSI National Congress (1957), in PSI, *Resoconto stenografico 32° Congresso Nazionale PSI, Venezia 6–10 febbraio 1957, op. cit.*, p. 23.

21 Giuseppe Bonazzi, 'Prospettive dell'automazione e via italiana al socialismo', *Mondo Operaio*, Vol. XI (August 1958), pp. 9–18. The Italian socialists' arguments clearly echoed those aforementioned of their British counterparts. See, for instance, Crossman, 'Scientists in Whitehall', *op. cit.*, or H. Wilson, 'Speech opening the Science Debate at the Party's Annual Conference Scarborough 1963', *op. cit.*

22 Sassoon (1996), *op. cit.*, pp. 193–5.

23 *Ibid.*, p. 295.

24 Wilson, 'Speech opening the Science Debate at the Party's Annual Conference, Scarborough, 1963', *op. cit.*, p. 18.

25 H. Wilson, 'Wilson Defines British Socialism' (article written for the *New York Times*, September 15, 1963), in Wilson (ed.), *Purpose and Politics...*, *op. cit.*, pp. 263–70, p. 265.

26 D. Porter (1993), *op. cit.*, p. 10.

27 *Ibid.*, p. 11.

28 S. Fielding, '"White Heat" and White Collars: the Evolution of Wilsonism', in Coopey, Fielding and Tiratsoo (eds) (1993), *op. cit.*, pp. 29–47, p. 39. On this theme see also H. Wilson, *The New Britain* (Harmondsworth: Penguin Special, 1964).

29 Archivio Centrale di Stato (Rome), Nenni Papers, 'Correspondence' series, section 1944–1979, Pietro Nenni-Roberto Guiducci correspondence, box no. 28, bundle no. 1445, Letter from Roberto Guiducci to Pietro Nenni, 4 October 1965 (Milan), p. 1.

30 *Ibid.*, p. 4.

31 My emphasis.

32 Archivio Centrale di Stato (Rome), Nenni Papers, 'Correspondence' series, section 1944–1979, Pietro Nenni-Roberto Guiducci correspondence, box no. 28, bundle no. 1445, Letter from Roberto Guiducci to Pietro Nenni, 9 May 1966 (Milan), pp. 1–2, p. 1.

33 See Wilson, 'Speech Opening the Science Debate at the Party's Annual Conference, Scarborough 1963', *op. cit.* See also Crossman, 'Scientists in Whitehall' (1963), *op. cit.*, p. 142.

34 Arnaudi's first articles on the question of science, research and the Italian delay go back to the mid-1950s. See, for instance, Carlo Arnaudi, 'La ricerca scientifica in Italia', *Attualità*, no.7 (January 1956).

35 Archivio Centrale di Stato (Rome), Nenni Papers, 'Correspondence' series, section 1944–1979, Pietro Nenni–Carlo Arnaudi correspondence, box no. 17, bundle no. 1061, copy of the letter from Carlo Arnaudi to the Prime Minister Aldo Moro, in Letter from Carlo Arnaudi to Pietro Nenni, 8 January 1964 (Rome).

36 G. Picciurro, 'Funzione Pubblica della Ricerca Scientifica', *Mondo Operaio*, Vol. XVII (April 1964), pp. 17–24, p. 18.

37 *Ibid.* See also Fondazione di Studi Storici 'Filippo Turati' (Florence), PSI Archive, 'Election Manifestos' series, 'Il Programma 1963', p. 82; and C. Arnaudi, *Per una nuova organizzazione della ricerca scientifica*, Speech to the Senate, 18 July 1962 (Roma: tipografia G. Bardi, 1962), pp. 1–35, p. 3–4.
38 C. P. Snow, *The Two Cultures and the Scientific Revolution*, the Rede Lecture 1959 (Cambridge: Cambridge University Press, 1959). *The Two Cultures* is an oft-quoted, ground-breaking book which denounced the bias against science of the British humanistic culture and argued in favour of an overall change in the national educational curriculum.
39 Morgan (1992), *op. cit.*, pp. 239–40.
40 Degl'Innocenti (1993), *op. cit.*, p. 326.
41 Archivio Centrale di Stato (Rome), Nenni Papers, 'Correspondence' series, section 1944–1979, Pietro Nenni–Carlo Arnaudi correspondence, box no. 17, bundle no. 1061, copy of the letter from Carlo Arnaudi to the Prime Minister Aldo Moro, in Letter from Carlo Arnaudi to Pietro Nenni, 8 January 1964 (Rome). The reference to the British model was a key argument employed by socialists in trying to defend and justify their proposal for a new Ministry for Scientific and Technological research against the hostility displayed by both the DC and the Confindustria towards any reform of the *status quo.* See also the articles that appeared in the *Avanti!* in 1964 before and after the Labour Party electoral victory, on Labour proposal regarding a new ministry of Technology to be set up and the reappraisal of the already existing Minister of Science. The emphasis put by Labour on the theme of science earned the British Labour Party considerable attention in the Italian press in general. See for example C. Maglietta, 'I Laburisti di fronte alla Rivoluzione Tecnologica', *Nord e Sud*, no. 50 (February 1964), pp. 47–51.
42 Archivio Centrale di Stato (Rome), Nenni Papers, 'Government' series, box no. 110, bundle no. 2363, 'Resoconto Riunione Interministeriale per la ricerca scientifica', 3 March 1964.
43 Crossman (1955), *op. cit.*, p. 15.
44 *Ibid.*
45 *Ibid.*
46 See, for instance, Labour History Archive and Study Centre (Manchester), Labour Party Archive, Research series, Re. 51–102, 1960, 'Research Department: functions and staff', May 1960.
47 See '35° Congresso Nazionale. Roma, 25–29 ottobre 1963', in F. Pedone, *Novant'anni di pensiero socialista attraverso i congressi del PSI 1957–1966* (Venezia: Marsilio, 1984), pp. 238–320, p. 282. On the same question see also PSI, *Resoconto stenografico 34° Congresso Nazionale PSI, Milano 15–20 marzo 1961, op. cit.*, p. 307.
48 Ellison (1994), *op. cit.*, p. 56.
49 See R. Lowe, *Education in the Post-War Years: a Social History* (London and New York: Routledge, 1988), p. 80; Labour Party–Labour Research Department (ed.), *Twelve Wasted Years*, September 1963, p. 209; and Labour Party, *Signposts for the Sixties*, NEC policy document, 1961, pp. 28–9. On Italy see, T. Codignola, *Nascita e morte di un Piano. Tre anni di battaglia per la scuola pubblica* (Firenze: La Nuova Italia, 1962), p. 119.
50 Sassoon (1996), *op. cit.*, p. 128.
51 Crosland (1956), *op. cit.*, p. 62.

52 Sassoon (1996), *op. cit.*, p. 137.
53 As Hugh Gaitskell wrote in 1955 'the major causes of inequality really amounted to the inheritance of wealth and the educational system', in H. Gaitskell, 'The Ideological Development of Democratic Socialism in Great Britain', *Socialist International Information*, Vol. V (24 December 1955), pp. 921–51, p. 937. See, also Labour Party, *Towards Equality: Labour's Policy for Social Justice*, NEC policy document, 1956, p. 5.
54 See, for instance, G. Petronio, 'La riforma della scuola', *Mondo Operaio*, Vol. IX (January 1956), pp. 32–7.
55 J. Bowen, *A History of Western Education*, Vol. 3, *The Modern West* (London: Methuen & Co, 1981), pp. 530–31.
56 Labour Party, *Learning to Live: a Policy for Education from Nursery School to University*, NEC policy document, 1958, p. 3.
57 G. Elliot, *Labourism and the English Genius; the Strange Death of Labour England* (London and New York: Verso, 1993), p. 76.
58 Crosland (1962), *op. cit.*, p. 174.
59 *Ibid.*, p. 176.
60 'Labour Manifesto 1964', in Craig (ed.) (1974), *op. cit.*, p. 237.
61 Lowe (1988), *op. cit.*, p. 61.
62 Labour Party, *Learning to Live*, *op. cit.*, p. 41.
63 T. Codignola, 'La Riforma Controriformistica', *Mondo Operaio*, Vol. XII (November 1959), pp. 1–7, p. 6.
64 T. Codignola, 'La battaglia socialista per la scuola', *Mondo Operaio*, Vol. XIV (January–February 1961), pp. 19–22, p. 19.
65 *Ibid.*, p. 22. See also E. Bestazzi, *La politica scolastica del PSI discussa nel Convegno Nazionale sulla Scuola 'Politica Scolastica Integrata nella Politica di Sviluppo', Roma 26–27 maggio 1962* (Roma: Fratelli Palombi Editori, 1962); and G. Recuperati, 'La politica scolastica dal centro–sinistra alla contestazione studentesca', *Studi Storici*, no. 1 (1990), pp. 235–60, p. 242.
66 Sassoon (1996), *op. cit.*, p. 150.
67 Padgett and Peterson (1991), *op. cit.*, p. 14.
68 Radio Interview reprinted in *The Listener*, 29 October 1964, quoted in Bogdanor and Skidelsky (1970), *op. cit.*, p. 100.
69 See, for instance, Fondazione di Studi Storici 'Filippo Turati' (Florence), PSI Archive, 'Proposte per una dichiarazione programmatica del PSI', (elaborated by a commission appointed in July 1956 by the party's Executive Committee and including among its members Nenni, Lombardi, Basso, Pieraccini, Mancini), or R. Lombardi, 'Schema di relazione introduttiva al Convegno delle Partecipazioni Statali', in PSI-Sezione Economica, *Convegno delle Partecipazioni Statali* (Milano: Edizioni Avanti!, 1960), pp. 7–44, p. 21.
70 V. Foa, 'L'industria di stato e i monopoli', *Mondo Operaio*, Vol. IX (May 1956), pp. 286–9.
71 A. Menichelli, 'Cultura e lotta operaia', *Mondo Operaio*, Vol. IX (August–September 1956), pp. 492–4, p. 493.
72 See, for instance, M. Abrams and R. Rose, *Must Labour Lose?* (London: Penguin Books, 1960).
73 A. Crosland, *Can Labour Win?*, Fabian Tract no. 324, May 1960, p. 14.
74 Cattani (1959), *op. cit.*, p. 44.
75 Giolitti, 'Alcune osservazioni sulle riforme di struttura', *op. cit.*, p. 686.

76 Lombardi, 'Schema di relazione introduttiva al Convegno delle Partecipazioni Statali', *op. cit.*, p. 10. See also M. Carabba, *Un ventennio di programmazione* (Bari: 1977), p. 103.

77 Wilson, 'Wilson Defines British Socialism', *op. cit.*, p. 268.

78 See Fondazione di Studi Storici 'Filippo Turati' (Florence), PSI Archive, 'Election Manifestos' series, 'Il programma 1963', p. 38.

79 See Labour Party, *Signposts for the Sixties*, *op. cit.*, pp. 19–20 and 'Labour Manifesto 1964', in Craig (ed.) (1974), *op. cit.*, p. 238.

80 Labour Party, *Challenge to Britain*, NEC policy document, 1953.

81 The principle of competitive public enterprise is restated but no specific industries are mentioned. See 'Labour Manifesto 1959', in Craig (ed.) (1974), *op. cit.*, p. 201.

82 Labour Party, *Signposts for the Sixties*, *op. cit.*, p. 15.

83 See, for instance, 'Labour Manifesto 1964', in Craig (ed.) (1974), *op. cit.*, p. 234. See also Wilson, 'Wilson Defines British Socialism', *op. cit.*, pp. 267–9.

84 Haseler (1964), *op. cit.*, p. 57. See also 'Labour Manifesto 1955', in Craig (ed.) (1974), *op. cit.*, p. 180.

85 Labour Party, *Industry and Society*, *op. cit.*, pp. 39–40.

86 H. Gaitskell, *Socialism and Nationalisation*, Fabian Tract no. 300, 1956, p. 35.

87 Crosland (1956), *op. cit.*, p. 236.

88 Labour Party, *Industry and Society*, *op. cit.*, pp. 39–40. See also Labour Manifesto 1959', in F. Craig (ed.) (1974), *op. cit.*, p. 201.

89 Wilson, 'Wilson Defines British Socialism', *op. cit.*, p. 269. See also 'Labour Manifesto 1964', in Craig (ed.) (1974), *op. cit.*, p. 237.

90 See, for instance, Labour History Archive and Study Centre (Manchester), Labour Party Archive, Finance and Economic policy Sub-Committee minutes, 21 December 1965.

91 See Giuseppe Tamburrano's speech, in PSI-Sezione Economica, *Convegno delle Partecipazioni Statali* (Milano: Edizioni Avanti!, 1960), pp. 104–5.

92 See on this the proceedings of the *Convegno per le Partecipazioni Statali* (Conference on State Shareholding) held in 1959. *Ibid.*

93 Fondazione di Studi Storici 'Filippo Turati' (Florence), PSI Archive, 'Election Manifestos' series, 'Il programma 1963', p. 37.

94 *Ibid.*

95 Labour Party–Labour Research Department (ed.), *Twelve Wasted Years*, *op. cit.*, pp. 110–11.

96 *Ibid.*, p. 111.

97 Lombardi, 'Schema di relazione introduttiva al Convegno delle Partecipazioni Statali', *op. cit.*, p. 36.

98 *Ibid.*, p. 25.

99 Sassoon (1996), *op. cit.*, p. 156. See also N. Chester, *The Nationalisation of British Industry 1945–51* (London: HMSO, 1975), p. 1075.

100 'Labour Manifesto 1964', in Craig (ed.) (1974), *op. cit.*, p. 33.

101 Labour History Archive and Study Centre (Manchester), Labour Party Archive, Finance and Economic policy Sub-Committee minutes, 1 December 1961: as the minutes read, it was time 'for Labour to work out detailed planning proposals and undertaking some in depth investigation on all aspects related to it (planning)'. At the meeting it was also agreed that studies would be made of various aspects of economic planning for the guidance of the party spokesmen

and members of a future Labour government; that the economist members of the committee (for example Nicholas Kaldor, Thomas Balogh, Robert Nield) should be invited to prepare as soon as possible, memoranda on economic planning with particular reference to overseas experience.

102 Labour Party, *Labour in the Sixties*, NEC policy document, 1960, p. 8.
103 *Ibid.*, p. 11.
104 *Ibid.*, p. 7.
105 Wilson, 'Wilson Defines What is British Socialism', *op. cit.*, p. 266.
106 'Labour Manifesto 1964', in Craig (ed.) (1974), *op. cit.*, p. 229.
107 *Ibid.*, pp. 233–4.
108 Wilson, 'Speech opening the Science Debate at the Party's Annual Conference, Scarborough, 1963', *op. cit.*, p. 18.
109 Labour Party–Labour Research Department (ed.), *Twelve Wasted Years*, *op. cit.*, pp. 17, 18, 32.
110 Labour Party, *Signposts for the Sixties*, *op. cit.*, p. 8.
111 'Labour Manifesto 1964', in Craig (ed.) (1974), *op. cit.*, p. 235.
112 P. Roggi, *Scelte politiche e teorie economiche in Italia nel quarantennio repubblicano* (Torino: Giappichelli, 1988), p. 65.
113 See, in contrast to the little attention devoted to the question of planning in the 1957 PSI National Congress's final resolution, the central place planning was given in the winning motion put forward by Autonomia in the 1959 PSI congress. 'Mozione autonomia, 33° Congresso Nazionale PSI 1959', in Pedone (ed.) (1984), *op. cit.*, p. 122.
114 *Ibid.* See also Lombardi, 'Schema della relazione introduttiva al Convegno delle Partecipazioni Statali', *op. cit.*, p. 39.
115 Carabba (1977), *op. cit.*, p. 72; see also P. Nenni, 'Relazione al Comitato Centrale del PSI, 17 ottobre 1962', in *Avanti!*, 18 October 1962, p. 2.
116 G. Fuà and P. Sylos Labini, *Idee per la programmazione economica* (Roma-Bari: Laterza, 1963), pp. 22–5.
117 *Ibid.*, pp. 28–9. See also C. D'Apice, *L'arcipelago dei consumi. Consumi e redditi delle famiglie italiane dal dopoguerra a oggi* (Bari: 1981), pp. 39–40.
118 Ugo La Malfa's 'Nota aggiuntiva' defined the economic programme of the government formed by Fanfani in March 1962. Ugo La Malfa was then the Budget Minister.
119 J. Hayward and M. Watson (eds), *Planning, Politics and Public Policy: the British, French and Italian Experiences* (Cambridge: Cambridge University Press, 1975), p. 15.
120 A. Giolitti, *Programmazione economica e progresso civile. Discorso pronunciato alla Camera dei Deputati nella seduta del 24 maggio 1962* (Roma: 1962), p. 8.
121 Bevan (1952), *op. cit.*, p. 14.
122 Italy experienced from the mid-1950s and, in particular, after 1958, a considerable growth in the consumption of consumer durables. From 1956 to 1957 money spent on TVs grew by 30 per cent. Similar figures apply to cars, washing machines, fridges, and so on: in the period 1951–62, the number of cars circulating on Italian territory almost trebled; washing machine ownership passed from 2.9 per cent (1958) to 32.2 (per cent) (1966); fridge ownership grew from 11.4 per cent (1958) to 59.9 per cent (1966). See D'Apice (1981), *op. cit.*, pp. 35ff.
123 See, for example, Crosland (1956), *op. cit.*, pp. 287–92.

124 Balogh (1963), *op. cit.*, p. 36.
125 See M. Foot, in *Tribune*, 27 March 1959.
126 Labour Party, *Labour in the Sixties*, *op. cit.*, p. 8.
127 Bonazzi (1958), *op. cit.*, pp. 17–18.
128 J. Osborne, *Look Back in Anger* (London: Faber, 1957).
129 L. Bianciardi, *La Vita Agra* (Milano: Bompiani, 1962) and L. Bianciardi, *L'Integrazione* (Milano: Bompiani, 1960).
130 H. Wilson, 'A Four Year Plan', *New Stateman and the Nation*, Vol. LXI (26 March 1961), pp. 462–8, p. 462.
131 Galbraith (1958), *op. cit.*
132 Crossman (1960), *op. cit.*, p. 10. See also for similar arguments, Balogh (1963), *op. cit.*, p. 9.
133 Crossman (1960), *op. cit.*, p. 9.
134 *Ibid.*
135 G. Ruffolo, *La Grande Impresa*, (Torino: Einaudi, 1971, 1st edn 1965), p. 174.
136 F. Coen, 'Le elezioni americane e il programma democratico', *Mondo Operaio*, Vol. XIII (September 1960), pp. 22–5.
137 Labour Party–Labour Research Department (ed.), *Twelve Wasted Years*, *op. cit.*, p. 72.
138 Fuà and Sylos Labini (1963), *op. cit.*, p. 97.
139 Labour Party–Labour Research Department (ed.), *Twelve Wasted Years*, *op. cit.*, p. 72.
140 Fuà and Sylos Labini (1963), p. 97 and the accusations of 'uninformative', 'misleading' and 'antisocial' advertising, in Labour Party–Labour Research Department (ed.), *Twelve Wasted Years*, *op. cit.*, p. 72.
141 A. Giolitti, *Un socialismo possibile* (Torino: Einaudi, 1968), p. 44.
142 Ruffolo (1971), *op. cit.*, p. 208.
143 Padgett and Paterson (1991), *op. cit.*, p. 91.
144 F. Cazzola, 'Elettori e Iscritti al PSI', in G. Sivini, *Partiti e Partecipazione Politica in Italia* (Milano: Giuffrè, 1969), pp. 189–212, pp. 204–205. After 1966, the PSI membership started growing again. However, this is explained by the new clientelistic character which the party began to acquire after a few years in government, an assumption which, in some respects, is proven by the almost exclusive growth of party membership in the South and the contemporaneous steady decline in the North: while in 1950 members from the North made up 67 per cent of the total, in 1967 they did not exceed 20 per cent. *Ibid.*, pp. 206–7.
145 See S. M. Lipset, 'The Changing Class Structure and Contemporary European Politics', in *Daedalus. Journal of the American Academy of Arts and Sciences*, Vol. 93 (Winter 1964), Special issue 'A New Europe?', pp. 271–303, p. 279. See also the results of the study titled 'Partecipazione politica a livello di base', published in *Tempi Moderni*, Vol. I (May–June 1958), pp. 150–166; the Round Table on 'La partecipazione politica e i partiti in Italia', *Tempi Moderni*, Vol. V (January–March 1962), pp. 29–76, which included among the most prominent contributors Norberto Bobbio, Joseph La Palombara, Lelio Basso and Jean Meynaud; F. Coen, 'Le strutture del PSI e degli altri partiti di massa nei rispettivi statuti', *Mondo Operaio*, Vol. XVI (May–June 1963), pp. 10–16.
146 See Cazzola (1969), *op. cit.*, p. 210.

147 D. Bell, *The End of Ideology* (New York: The Free Press, 1965 [1st edn 1962]).

148 R. Dahrendorf, *Class and Class Conflict in Industrial Society* (Stanford, California: Stanford University Press, 1961 [1st German edition 1957; 1st British edition 1959 by Routledge and Kegan Paul, London]), p. 52. See also Lipset (1964), *op. cit.*, p. 286.

149 M. Dogan, 'Europa. Comportamento elettorale degli operai dell'industria', *Tempi Moderni*, Vol. III (July–September 1960), pp. 91–4, p. 91.

150 Abrams and Rose (1960), *op. cit.*, p. 76.

151 M. Abrams, 'The Future of the Left. New Roots of Working Class Conservatism', in *Encounter*, May 1960, pp. 57–9, p. 59.

152 Fielding (1993), *op. cit.*, p. 37.

153 Nenni's speech to the 35th National Congress, in '35° Congresso Nazionale PSI. Roma, 25–29 ottobre 1963', in Pedone (ed.) (1984), *op. cit*, pp. 238–320. See also Degl'Innocenti (1993), *op. cit.*, p. 319.

154 Giolitti, 'Alcune osservazioni sulle Riforme di Struttura', *op. cit.*, p. 683; and Giolitti (1968), *op. cit.*, p. 46.

155 M. Dogan, 'La stratificazione sociale dei suffragi', in A. Spreafico and J. La Palombara, *Elezioni e Comportamento Politico in Italia*, (Milano: Edizioni di Comunità, 1963), pp. 407–74, pp. 437–44.

156 *Ibid.*, p. 454.

157 Dahrendorf (1961), *op. cit.*, p. 48.

158 *Ibid.*, pp. 49–51.

159 S. Lipset and R. Bendix, *Social Mobility in Industrial Society* (London: Heinemann, 1959 (American edition by University of California Press, Berkeley, 1959) p. 11. See also A. Pizzorno, 'The Individualistic Mobilization of Europe', in *Daedalus. Journal of the American Academy of Arts and Sciences*, Vol. 93 (Winter 1964), special issue 'A New Europe?', pp. 199–224, p. 214.

160 Lipset and Bendix (1959), *op. cit.*, pp. 17–64.

161 Dahrendorf (1961), *op. cit.*, p. 60.

162 It should be noted that, although the 1951 election was commonly regarded as the beginning of Labour decline, as a matter of fact, Labour gained more votes in 1951 (48.8 per cent) than in 1945 (48.3 per cent). It was only at the 1955 election that Labour electoral consent began to drop. See D. Butler, *British General Elections since 1945* (Oxford: Basil Blackwell, 1989), pp. 8, 13.

163 D. Kavanagh, 'Must Labour Lose Again', in D. Kavanagh (ed.), *Politics and Personalities* (Worcester: Billing & Sons, 1990), pp. 91–104, p. 95.

164 R. McKenzie and A. Silver, *Angels in Marble: Working Class Conservatives in Urban England* (London: Heinemann, 1968), p. 43.

165 Crosland (1960), *op. cit.*, pp. 1–23, p. 7.

166 See, for instance, J. Goldthorpe, *The Affluent Worker: Political Attitudes and Behaviour* (Cambridge: Cambridge University Press, 1968), p. 33; or F. Zweigg, *The Worker in an Affluent Society: Family, Life and Industry* (London: Heinemann, 1961), p. 107.

167 On this question see Abrams and Rose (1960), *op. cit.*

168 Crosland (1960), *op. cit.*, p. 2.

169 Labour History Archive and Study Centre (Manchester), Labour Party Archive, NEC minutes, 28 October 1959, 'Report of Elections Sub-Committee'. See also Crosland (1960), *op. cit.*, p. 20.

170   *Ibid.*, p. 2. See also Abrams and Rose (1960), *op. cit.*, pp. 7–8, 82.
171   Crosland (1960), *op. cit.*, p. 21.
172   Abrams and Rose (1960), *op. cit.*, p. 70.
173   See Labour History Archive and Study Centre (Manchester), Labour Party Archive, Home Policy Sub-Committee minutes, 17 June 1957 and Home policy Sub-Committee minutes, 17 September 1958.
174   Abrams and Rose (1960), *op. cit.*, p. 101.
175   Sassoon (1996), *op. cit.*, p. 673.
176   Haseler (1964), *op. cit.*, p. 163.
177   Crossman (1960), *op. cit.*, p. 6.
178   *Ibid.*, p. 5.
179   R. Titmuss, *The Irresponsible Society*, Fabian Tract no. 323, April 1960, pp. 1–20, p. 5.
180   Fielding (1993), *op. cit.*, p. 33.
181   *Ibid.*, p. 38.
182   See Lipset and Bendix (1959), *op. cit.*, p. 23.
183   *Ibid.*
184   See F. Momigliano and A. Pizzorno, 'Consumi in Italia', in F. Momigliano and A. Pizzorno, *Aspetti e problemi sociali dello sviluppo economico in Italia* (Roma-Bari: Laterza, 1959), p. 198.
185   Dogan (1960), *op. cit.*, pp. 91–4.
186   Kavanagh, 'Ideology, Sociology and Labour's strategy', in Kavanagh (1990), *op. cit.*, p. 105.
187   See Dogan (1963), *op. cit.*, p. 470. See also S. Lipset and S. Rokkan (eds), *Party Systems and Voter Alignments* (London: Collier Macmillan, 1967 (American edition, New York: Free Press, 1967), p. 177.
188   Any Western European socialist party tended to be affected by women's vote. Yet it was demonstrated that in Catholic countries the difference between electoral behaviour of men and women was much greater than in Protestant countries such as Great Britain. See Lipset and Rokkan (1967), *op. cit.*, p. 159 and Dogan (1960), *op. cit.*, p. 94.
189   Lipset and Rokkan (1967), *op. cit.*, p. 184.
190   Pizzorno (1964), *op. cit.*, p. 219.
191   Interview with Vittorio Foa, Rome, December 1995.
192   J. Foot, 'The Family and the "Economic Miracle": Social Transformation, Work, Leisure and Development at Bovisa and Comasina (Milan), 1950–1970', *Contemporary European History*, no. 4 (1995), pp. 327–38, p. 30.
193   *Ibid.*, p. 331.
194   S. Leonardi, *Progresso tecnico e Rapporti di lavoro* (Torino: Einaudi, 1956), p. 55.
195   *Ibid.*, pp. 52–65. On this question see also S. Mallet, *La Nuova Classe Operaia* (Torino: Einaudi, 1976 (1st edn 1963), pp.79–84.
196   Dogan (1963), *op. cit.*, p. 422.
197   Giolitti (1958), *op. cit.*, p. 683.
198   A. Giolitti, 'L'operaio, la grande fabbrica e il monopolio', *Mondo Operaio*, Vol. XIII (March 1960), pp. 23–6, p. 23. See also L. Cafagna, 'Fine della "classe generale" ', in L. Cafagna (ed.), *Classe Operaia, partiti politici e socialismo nella prospettiva italiana* (Milano: Feltrinelli, 1966), pp. 228–38 and Ruffolo (1971), *op. cit.*, p. 166.

199 See G. Alasia, 'Il PSI e il sindacato', *Mondo Operaio*, Vol. XVI (August–September 1963), pp. 2–6.
200 G. Tamburrano, 'Per un programma socialista di governo', *Mondo Operaio*, Vol. XII (April–May 1959), pp. 21–4, pp. 22–3.
201 Ruffolo (1971), *op. cit.*, pp. 166–7.
202 Tamburrano (1959), *op. cit.*, pp. 22–3.
203 See A. Landolfi, 'Partito Socialista Italiano: struttura, organi, dirigenti, correnti', *Tempi Moderni*, Vol. V (January–March 1962), pp. 3–45.
204 See Shanks (1964), *op. cit.*, pp. 175–6.
205 See N. Bobbio, *Politica e Cultura* (Torino: Einaudi, 1955), pp. 121–2.
206 See concluding remarks in Crosland (1956), *op. cit.*
207 Shanks (1964), *op. cit.*, p. 176.

3 The Crisis of Social-Democratic Politics

1 Tamburrano (1984), *op. cit.*, p. 276.
2 *Ibid.*, p. 164.
3 *Ibid.*, p. 200.
4 PSI-Sezione economica, *Nota sull'attuale congiuntura economica in Italia e sulle politiche per fronteggiarla* (Roma: SETI, 1963).
5 Degli Innocenti (1993), *op. cit.*, pp. 382–3. See also Carabba (1977), *op. cit.*, pp. 130–1.
6 Carabba (1977), pp. 145ff.
7 J. Leruez, *Economic Planning and Politics in Britain* (London: Martin Robertson, 1975), p. 173.
8 Ellison (1994), *op. cit.*, p. 136.
9 Leruez (1975), *op. cit.*, p. 180.
10 D. Walker, 'The First Wilson Governments, 1964–1970', in P. Hennessy and A. Seldon (eds), *Ruling Performance: British Governments from Attlee to Thatcher* (Oxford: Blackwell, 1987), pp. 186–215, p. 204. See also S. Brittan, *Steering Economy: the role of the Treasury* (London: Secker & Warburg, 1969, rev. edn (1st edn Penguin, Harmondsworth, 1964), pp. 312–13.
11 Leruez (1975), *op. cit.*, p. 180.
12 *Ibid.*, p. 170.
13 *Ibid.*, p. 213.
14 *Ibid.*
15 *Ibid.*, p. 216.
16 Walker (1987), *op. cit.*, p. 205.
17 *Ibid.*, p. 202. See also Ellison (1994), *op. cit.*, p. 145.
18 Sassoon (1996), *op. cit.*, pp. 201–3.
19 See A. Cairncross, *The British Economy since 1945* (Oxford: Basil Blackwell, 1992), pp. 106, 108, 112–14.
20 M. Shanks, *Planning and Politics. The British Experience 1960–1976* (London: George Allen & Unwin, 1977), pp. 21–2.
21 Labour Party, *Planning for Progress, op. cit.*, p. 37.
22 'Labour Manifesto 1959', in Craig (ed.) (1974), *op. cit.*, p. 202; see also 'Labour Manifesto 1964', *Ibid.*, p. 236.

23 See, for instance, Crossman, 'Towards a New Philosophy of Socialism', *op. cit.*, p. 57; Bevan (1964, 1st edn 1952), *op. cit.*, p. 138; and Gaitskell (1956), *op. cit.*, p. 31.

24 Labour History Archive and Study Centre (Manchester), Labour Party Archive, Study group on the control of industry minutes, 8 May 1958.

25 Labour History Archive and Study Centre (Manchester), Labour Party Archive, Finance and Economic policy Sub-Committee minutes, 9 November 1962.

26 K. Alexander and J. Hughes, *A Socialist Wages Plan*, New Left Discussion Pamphlets series (London: Universities and Left Review, 1959). See also M. Artis, 'Balogh's Economic Policies', *New Left Review*, no. 22 (December 1963), pp. 106–11; J. Hughes, 'An Economic Policy for Labour', *New Left Review*, no. 24 (March–April 1964), pp. 5–31.

27 Hughes (1964), *op. cit.*, pp. 24–5.

28 See, for instance, G.D.H. Cole, *What's Wrong with the Trade Unions*, Fabian Tract no. 301, September 1956, p. 25.

29 *Ibid.*, p. 5.

30 Labour History Archive and Study Centre (Manchester), Labour Party Archive, Study group on the control of industry minutes, 8 May 1958. During this meeting the revised draft of a party statement on control of industry was discussed. In the discussion, attention was drawn to 'the difficulty of phrasing any statement about wage restraint'; as the minutes read, 'there could be no agreement on the part of the unions not to put in wage demands'. The aim should be to create an atmosphere in which 'there was no need for wages to chase a rising cost of living' and 'there would be reason and moderation on the part of the trade unions'.

31 Labour Party, *Planning for Progress*, *op. cit.*, p. 37.

32 L. Minkin, *The Labour Party Conference. A Study into Politics of Intra-Party Democracy* (London: Allen Lane, 1978), p. 54.

33 Labour Party–Labour Research Department (ed.), *Twelve Wasted Years*, *op. cit.*, pp. 52–5.

34 See, for instance, Labour election manifestos in 1959 and 1964, where great emphasis was put on co-operation, consultation and agreement. In Craig (ed.) (1974), *op. cit.*, pp. 202, 236.

35 Balogh (1963), *op. cit.*, pp. 4–5.

36 *Ibid.*, p. 5.

37 'Labour Manifesto 1964', in Craig (ed.) (1974), *op. cit.*, p. 236.

38 See S. Turone, *Storia del sindacato in Italia. Dal 1943 al crollo del comunismo* (Roma-Bari, Laterza, 1992), p. 234.

39 Hayward and Watson (eds) (1975), *op. cit.*, p. 204.

40 Turone (1992), *op. cit.*, p. 286.

41 V. Spini, 'Il dibattito sulla programmazione agli inizi degli anni '60', in Arfè *et alia* (1977), *op. cit.*, pp. 187–225, p. 218.

42 Lombardi, 'Schema della relazione introduttiva al Convegno delle Partecipazioni Statali', *op. cit.*, p. 40.

43 PSI-Sezione economica, *Nota sull'attuale congiuntura economica in Italia e sulle politiche per fronteggiarla*, *op. cit.*

44 Fuà and Sylos Labini (1963), *op. cit.*, p. 32.

45 Fondazione di Studi Storici 'Filippo Turati' (Florence), PSI Archive, 'Election Manifestos' series, 'Il programma 1963', p. 27.

46 Giolitti (1968), *op. cit.*, p. 59.
47 A. Livi, 'Per una politica della corrente sindacale socialista', *Mondo Operaio*, Vol. XVII (April 1964), pp. 21–5. See also L. Lama, 'I Sindacati e la programmazione economica', *Mondo Operaio*, Vol. XV (August–September 1963), pp. 12–17, p. 15.
48 Archivio Centrale di Stato (Rome), Nenni papers, 'Correspondence' series, section 1944–1979, Pietro Nenni–Antonio Giolitti correspondence, box no. 27, bundle no. 1413, Letter from Antonio Giolitti to Pietro Nenni, 6 March 1964 (Rome), see attached, copy of the note sent to Aldo Moro by Antonio Giolitti on the relationships with the trade unions.
49 See A. Pizzorno, *I soggetti del pluralismo, classi-partiti-sindacati* (Bologna: Il Mulino, 1980), chapter IV, 'I sindacati nel sistema politico italiano: aspetti storici'. See also G. Bedani, *Politics and Ideology in the Italian Workers Movement* (Oxford: Berg Publisher, 1995).
50 F. Momigliano, *Sindacati, progresso tecnico, programmazione economica* (Torino: Einaudi, 1966), p. 56.
51 *Ibid.*, p. 58.
52 'Dichiarazione dell'onorevole Agostino Novella', in CGIL-Ufficio Studi Economici e Ufficio Stampa e Propaganda (ed.), *CGIL e Programmazione economica* (Roma: 1964), p. 28.
53 Archivio Centrale di Stato (Rome), Nenni Papers, 'Government series', box no. 110, bundle no. 2363, 'Riunione con i sindacati', 26 May 1964. See also F. Coen, 'Sindacati, Programmazione e Politica dei Redditi', *Mondo Operaio*, Vol. XVII (November–December 1963), pp. 59–62, p. 61.
54 Bedani (1995), *op. cit.*, p. 129.
55 Carabba (1977), *op. cit.*, p. 58.
56 See the agreement reached by DC, PSI, PSDI and PRI restating the trade unions' autonomy and the conviction that trade unions should make any effort to evaluate in advance action on economic development, in Archivio Centrale di Stato (Rome), Nenni Papers, 'Government series', box no. 110, bundle no. 2363, 'Riunione con i sindacati', 26 May 1964.
57 Walker (1987), *op. cit.*, p. 198.
58 Ellison (1994), *op. cit.*, p. 138.
59 *Ibid.*, pp. 139, 142.
60 Cairncross (1992), *op. cit.*, pp. 154–8.
61 Thompson (1996), *op. cit.*, p. 193.
62 Sassoon (1996), *op. cit.*, p. 286. See also D. Marquand, *The Unprincipled Society. New Demands and Old Politics* (London: Jonathan Cape, 1988).
63 See Padgett and Peterson (1991), *op. cit.*, p. 153.
64 Marquand (1988), *op. cit.*, p. 51.
65 Sassoon (1996), *op. cit.*, p. 449ff.
66 Padgett and Paterson (1991), *op. cit.*, pp. 157ff.
67 See, for instance, books such as Giolitti (1968), *op. cit.*, Ruffolo (1971, 1st edn 1965), *op. cit.*; R. Mondolfo (ed), *Bilancio del Marxismo* (Bologna: Cappelli, 1965); which all urged the party to accelerate its 'normalisation' within the social-democratic tradition by relinquishing once and for all its strict adherence to Marxism and a class-oriented politics. See also V. Dagnino, *Obsolescenza delle ideologie: per una morale socialista e libertaria* (Milano: Azione Comune, 1967); and the so-called 'books for the Socialist Unification' edited by the publisher Vallecchi: R. Guiducci and F. Onofri (eds), *Costituente*

Aperta. Le nuove frontiere del socialismo in Italia (Firenze: Vallecchi, 1966); or Guiducci (1965), *op. cit.*; P. Nenni (edited by G. Tamburrano), *Il Socialismo nella democrazia. Realtà del presente* (Firenze: Vallecchi, 1966).

68 See B. Craxi, *Il rinnovamento socialista* (Venezia: Marsilio, 1981); and *L'Italia Liberata* (Milano: Sugarco, 1984).

69 *Mondo Operaio* under the editorship of Federico Coen played a crucial role in the new Craxi's course. See Degl'Innocenti (1993), on this, *op. cit.*, pp. 430ff.

70 See on this P. Farneti, *Il sistema dei partiti in Italia (1946–1979)* (Bologna: Il Mulino, 1983), pp. 64–6; and F. Cazzola, *Il Partito come organizzazione. Studio di un caso: il PSI* (Roma: Edizioni del Tritone, 1970), p. 280.

71 B. Craxi, *Un'onda lunga: articoli, interviste, discorsi, gennaio–dicembre 1988* (Imola: Galeati, 1988).

72 Degl'Innocenti (1993), *op. cit.*, p. 430.

73 *Ibid.*, pp. 436–8.

74 S. Holland, *The Socialist Challenge* (London: Quartet Books, 1975).

75 See, for example, Labour Party, *Labour's Programme 1982*, London 1982.

76 Sassoon (1996), *op. cit.*, p. 699.

77 *Ibid.*, p. 702.

78 See Labour Party, *Britain will Win*, General Election Manifesto 1987.

79 See Labour Party, *Social Ownership*, NEC Policy document, 1986.

80 Sassoon (1996), *op. cit.*, pp. 702–3.

81 See, for instance, G. Radice, *Labour's Path to Power: the New Revisionism* (London: Macmillan, 1989). Or B. Gould, *A Future for Socialism* (London: Cape, 1989), a book whose title clearly wanted to echo the title of Crosland's well-known earlier *The Future of Socialism* published in 1956. Another figure who played an important role in the reappraisal of the party's doctrine during the Kinnock years was Roy Hattersley: see for instance his *Choose Freedom: the Future for Democratic Socialism* (London: Penguin, 1987), a book where, in the footsteps of the radical utilitarian tradition, the author reasserted the importance of liberty as a social-democratic goal.

82 See, for instance, E. Hobsbawm, M. Jacques and F. Mulhern, *The Forward March of Labour Halted?* (London: Verso, 1981).

83 Labour Party, *Meet the Challenge, Make the Change*, NEC Policy document, 1989, p. 6ff.

84 Wright (1996), *op. cit.*, p. 135.

85 See, for instance, Tony Blair's, Speech to the Labour Party Conference (Brighton, 3 October 1995), in T. Blair, *New Britain. My Vision of a Young Country* (London: a New Statesman special selection, 1996), pp. 43–53, p. 49; or Blair's 'Speech to the Singapore Business Community on 8 January 1996', *Ibid.*, pp. 57–62.

86 See W. Hutton, *The State We're In* (London: Jonathan Cape, 1995); W. Hutton, *The Stakeholding Society* (Cambridge: Polity Press, 1999); and W. Hutton, *The State to Come* (London: Vintage, 1997).

87 See G. Mulgan and C. Leadbeater, *Mistakeholding: Whatever Happened to Labour's Big Idea?* (London: Demos, 1997).

88 See N. Thompson, 'Supply Side Socialism: The Political Economy of New Labour', *New Left Review*, no. 216 (1996), pp. 37–54, p. 38.

89 A. Giddens, *The Third Way. The Renewal of Social Democracy* (Cambridge: Polity Press, 1998).

90 See on this A. Asor Rosa, *La sinistra alla prova. Considerazioni sul ventennio 1976–1996* (Torino: Einaudi, 1996), p. 14.
91 G. Chiarante, *Da Togliatti a D'Alema. La tradizione dei comunisti italiani e le origini del PDS* (Roma-Bari, Laterza, 1996), p. 201.
92 See PCI, *Documenti per il XVII Congresso. Progetto di Tesi, Programma, Emendamento; Statuto, Criteri e Proposte*, in *Rinascita*, no. 5, 8 February 1986; and *Tesi, Programma, Statuto: i Documenti approvati dal XVII Congresso del PCI* (Roma: l'Unità, 1987).
93 Glotz (1986), *op. cit.*; see on this V. Fouskas, *Italy, Europe, the Left* (London: Ashgate, 1998), pp. 67ff.
94 *Ibid.*, p. 102.
95 See PCI, *Documenti per il Congresso Straordinario del PCI. Il Comitato Centrale della Svolta* (Roma: l'Unità, 1990); *Mozioni e Documenti del XX Congresso* (Roma: Fratelli Spada, 1990); *Idee e Proposte per la Costituente* (Roma: Fratelli Spada, 1990) and PDS, *Lo Statuto* (Roma: Fratelli Spada, 1991).

4 Shaping a 'Post-Fordist' Third Way

1   See R. Dahrendorf, *Reflections on the Revolution in Europe* (London: Chatto and Windus, 1990).
2   See, for instance, Bell (1960), *op. cit.*
3   Sassoon (1996), *op. cit.*, p. 285.
4   Hobsbawn (1994), *op. cit.*, p. 270.
5   Marquand (1988), *op. cit.*, p. 3.
6   See, for instance, N. Bobbio, *Destra e sinistra. Ragioni e significati di una distinzione politica* (Roma: Donzelli, 1994) and A. Giddens, *Beyond Left and Right. The Future of Radical Politics* (Cambridge: Polity Press, 1994).
7   F. Fukuyama, *The End of History and the Last Man* (London: Hamish Hamilton, 1992).
8   See, for instance, the well-known ex Marxist intellectual Lucio Colletti in 'Quale sinistra dopo il Muro', in *Corriere della Sera*, 20 marzo 1994, p. 24.
9   See on this Bobbio (1994), *op. cit.*
10 T. Blair, 'Third Way, phase two', in *Prospect* (March 2001), pp. 1–5, p. 1. See also Beppe Vacca, the President of the Gramsci Foundation and one of the closest advisers of Massimo D'Alema, in his preface in P. Borioni, *Socialismo postmoderno. La società aperta e il nuovo partito della sinistra* (Roma: Armando Editore, 1997), pp. 7–13, p. 12.
11 Wright (1996), *op. cit.*, p. 31. See also Labour Party, *Labour's Objects: Socialist Values in the Modern World* (London 1994).
12 This is the main argument underlying Bobbio's *Destra e sinistra, op. cit.*
13 See, for example, G. Pasquino, *Critica della sinistra italiana* (Roma-Bari: Laterza, 2001), p. 57.
14 T. Blair, *Socialism* (London: Fabian Society, 1994), p. 3; see also T. Blair, preface, in Wright (1996), *op. cit.*, pp. ix–x, p. ix.
15 T. Blair, 'The Radical Coalition', Speech at a Fabian Society Commemoration of the Fiftieth Anniversary of the 1945 General Election, 5 July 1995, in Blair (1996), *op. cit.*, pp. 1–18, p. 13.
16 Blair (2001), p. 2.

17   *Ibid.*, p. 4.
18   *Ibid.*, p. 2.
19   The resurgence of ethical socialism over other varieties that have exercised influence upon Labour in the past is evidenced by a selection of texts made in the collection edited by Antony Wright and Gordon Brown: *Values, Visions and Voices: An Anthology of Socialism* (Edinburgh: Mainstream, 1995).
20   Blair (1994), *op. cit.*, p. 3.
21   *Ibid.*
22   Crosland (1956), *op. cit.*; Jay (1962), *op. cit.*
23   Wright (1996), *op. cit.*, see section 'the mirage of Marxism', pp. 111–14.
24   See V. Spini (ed.), special issue 'La Nascita di un nuovo partito. Cronologia e documenti della costruzione dei Democratici di Sinistra', *Quaderni del Circolo Rosselli*, no. 12 (1998).
25   F. Bertinotti and A. Gianni, *Le idee che non muoiono* (Firenze: Ponte delle Grazie, 2000). See also the interview to Bertinotti by Marco Cianca, 'Bertinotti <<riscopre>> Marx: sì, credo nella rivoluzione mondiale', *Corriere della Sera*, Friday 20 October 2000, p. 13.
26   Walter Veltroni's Speech at the 1st DS Congress, Torino, 13–14 January 2000, in W. Veltroni, *I Care* (Milano: Baldini & Castoldi, 2000).
27   Fouskas (1998), *op. cit.*, p. 58.
28   On the weight of symbols in the PCI's transition into the PDS, see J. Dormagen, *I comunisti. Dal PCI alla nascita di Rifondazione Comunista. Una semiologia politica* (Roma: Koine Edizioni, 1996).
29   A. Occhetto, 'Il nuovo corso è discontinuità, non è demolizione del passato', *L'Unità*, 14 September 1989, p. 2. See also on this I. Ariemma, *La casa brucia. I democratici di sinistra* (Venezia: Marsilio, 2000), p. 43.
30   M. Mafai, *Dimenticare Berlinguer* (Roma: Donzelli, 1996).
31   See M. D'Alema (edited by Roberto Gualtieri), *La sinistra nell'Italia che cambia* (Milano: Feltrinelli, 1997), p. viii; and M. D'Alema, 'I pensieri lunghi di Enrico Berlinguer', in Paul Ginsborg and Massimo D'Alema (edited by Michele Battini), *Dialogo su Berlinguer* (Firenze: Giunti, 1994), pp. 23–49, p. 46. On the debate on the Berlinguer's legacy see also: G. Vacca, *Vent'anni dopo* (Torino: Einaudi, 1997); Walter Veltroni, *La sfida interrotta* (Milano: Baldini & Castoldi, 1994); P. Folena, *I ragazzi di Berlinguer* (Milano: Baldini & Castoldi, 1997); and C. Valentini, *Berlinguer. L'eredità difficile* (Roma: Editori Riuniti, 1997).
32   See, for instance, N. Bobbio, 'La democrazia nei *Quaderni*', in 'Gramsci dopo la caduta di tutti i muri', supplement of *l'Unità*, 15 January 1991. In this article Bobbio aimed at drawing the attention to the democratic and liberal elements present in Gramsci's thinking.
33   G. Liguori, *Gramsci conteso. Storia di un dibattito 1922–1996* (Roma: Editori Riuniti, 1996), p. XI.
34   *Ibid.*, pp. 249–55. See also Paolo Conti, 'Veltroni: sì a una sinistra che impari da Gramsci come dai fratelli Rosselli', *Corriere della Sera*, 26 October 2000, p. 11. The article appeared the day after the conference 'Gramsci e Rosselli. Il Socialismo, il Fascismo, la Storia d'Italia', organised by the Fondazione Istituto Gramsci, the Fondazione Circolo Fratelli Rosselli and the Istituto Socialista di Studi Storici (Rome, 25 October 2000).
35   P. Bagnoli (ed.), *La Nuova storia: politica e cultura alla ricerca del socialismo liberale* (Firenze: Festina Lente, 1992), p. 16.

36 P. Bagnoli, 'Il socialismo liberale e il futuro della sinistra', in *Ibid.*, pp. 129–34, p. 130. See also on this G. De Luna, *Storia del Partito d'Azione. La rivoluzione democratica (1942/1947)* (Milano: Feltrinelli, 1982), p. x.

37 N. Bobbio, 'Attualità del socialismo liberale', preface in C. Rosselli, *Socialismo Liberale*, (Einaudi: Torino, 1997, 1973a), pp. V–XIX, p. VIII.

38 *Ibid.* See also C. Pinto, *La fine di un partito. Il PSI dal 1992 al 1994* (Roma: Editori Riuniti, 1999).

39 Valdo Spini is also Editor of the *Quaderni del Circolo Rosselli*.

40 'Socialismo e libertà: ricordando Rosselli', Rome, Residenza di Ripetta, 27 February 1999 (the conference proceedings can be found in http://www.angon.it/laburisti/agenda).

41 See Walter Veltroni's Speech when he was elected party's secretary, in *l'Unità*, 6 November 1998.

42 Veltroni (2000), *op. cit.* See also Walter Veltroni's speech at the XXI Socialist International Congress (8 November 1999, Milan).

43 Veltroni (2000), *op. cit.*

44 P. Conti, 'Veltroni: sì a una sinistra che impari da Gramsci come dai fratelli Rosselli', *Corriere della Sera*, 26 October 2000, p. 11.

45 See for instance D. Cofrancesco, 'G.L. e il fattore F. Come non leggere Carlo Rosselli', in M. Degl'Innocenti (edited by), *Carlo Rosselli e il socialismo liberale* (Manduria-Bari-Roma: Piero Lacaita Editore, 1999), pp. 177–85, p. 179.

46 See John Rosselli, 'Introduction', in Rosselli, *Socialismo Liberale*, *op. cit.*, pp. XXI–LIII.

47 See F. Sbarberi, *L'utopia della libertà uguale. Il liberalismo sociale da Rosselli a Bobbio* (Torino: Bollati Boringhieri, 1999), pp. 12–14.

48 G. Brown, 'The Politics of Potential: a New Agenda for Labour', in D. Miliband (ed.), *Reinventing the Left* (Cambridge: Polity Press, 1994), pp. 113–22, p. 115. See also Blair (2001), *op. cit.*, p. 4.

49 Blair (2001), *op. cit.*, p. 13.

50 See, for instance, A. Etzioni, *The Spirit of Community: Rights, Responsibilities and the Communitarian Agenda* (New York: Crown Publishers, 1993) and his more recent *The Third Way to a Good Society* (London: Demos, 2000).

51 See T. Blair, 'Speech in Southwark Cathedral, 29 January 1996', in Blair (1996), *op. cit.*, pp. 63–75, pp. 65–6.

52 See on this D. Marquand, *The New Reckoning. Capitalism, States and Citizens* (Cambridge: Polity Press, 1997), p. 80.

53 M. Gervasoni, *L'intellettuale come eroe. Piero Gobetti e le culture del novecento*, (Firenze: La Nuova Italia, 2000), p. 441.

54 P. Flores D'Arcais, 'L'alternativa azionista', *Micromega*, no. 3 (1991), pp. 24–32. See also on this P. Sylos Labini, 'Sinistra e azionismo', *Micromega*, 2 (1999), pp. 158–64.

55 P. Flores D'Arcais, 'Gobetti, liberale del futuro', introduction in P. Gobetti (edited by Ersilia Alessandrone Perona), *La Rivoluzione Liberale* (Torino: Einaudi, 1995, 1st edn 1964), pp. vii–xxxii, p. xxvii.

56 A journal that over the past ten years has been playing a fundamental role in disseminating liberal thought into the Italian political–cultural debate is the left-leaning *Reset*. Contributions by authors such as Ronald Dworkin or Bruce Ackerman have been regularly published together with those by 'Third Way thinkers' such as Anthony Giddens, Will Hutton and Ulrich Beck.

200   *Notes*

57   See W. Veltroni, *Al Governo? Il Kennedy della sinistra italiana* (Bologna: Camenta ed., 1995) and W. Veltroni, *Il sogno spezzato. Le idee di Robert Kennedy* (Milano: Baldini e Castoldi, 1996).
58   F. Sbarberi, introduction in a L. T. Hobhouse, *Liberalismo* (Firenze: Vallecchi, 1995), p. 20. See also Bobbio (1997), *op. cit.*, p. VI.
59   See R. Dahrendorf, *Per un Nuovo Liberalismo* (Roma-Bari, Laterza, 1993).
60   K. Popper, *The Open Society and its Enemies* (1945) was translated in Italian in 1974 (K. Popper, *La società aperta e i suoi nemici* (Roma: Armando Editore, 1974). Moreover, it was only in the 1980s that Popper's thinking made real inroads within Italian political and cultural debate.
61   See Nadia Urbinati, 'Perché abbiamo bisogno di Amartya Sen', *Reset*, n. 63 (November–December 2000), pp. 54–7.
62   See, for example, L. Violante, *Le due libertà. Contributo per l'identità della sinistra* (Bari-Roma: Laterza, 1999), p. 19. The title of Violante's book echoes Isaiah Berlin's 'Two Concepts of Liberty', in *Four Essays on Liberty* (London-New York: Oxford University Press, 1969; Italian transl: I. Berlin, *Quattro Saggi sulla libertà* [Milano: Feltrinelli, 1989]).
63   S. Messina, 'Rutelli: <<Giuro, toglierò al Polo la bandiera della libertà>>, *Corriere della Sera*, 22 October 2000, p. 3.
64   D'Alema (1997), *op. cit.*, p. XIV. See also M. D'Alema, 'The Challenge of the New Right', *Policy Network*, issue 1 (Summer 2001), pp. 32–3.
65   Wright (1996), *op. cit.*, p. 140.
66   J. Meadowcroft, 'Is there a liberal alternative? Charles Kennedy and the Liberal Democrats' strategy', *Political Quarterly*, vol 71 (October–December 2000), pp. 436–42, p. 436.
67   T. Blair, *The Third Way. New Politics for the New Century*, Fabian pamphlet no. 588 September 1998, p. 1; see also N. Lawson and N. Sherlock (eds), *The Progressive Century: the Future of the Centre–Left in Britain* (London: Palgrave, 2001). The book edited by Neal Lawson, an early Labour moderniser, and Neil Sherlock, a former adviser to Paddy Ashdown, was published immediately after Labour's second landslide in 2001, and indeed testifies to the widespread revival of the notion of a natural alliance of progressives for a progressive century.
68   Meadowcroft (2000), *op. cit.*, p. 436.
69   J. Ashley, 'Interview to Paddy Ashdown', *New Statesman*, 9 July 2001, pp. 18–19.
70   *Ibid.*
71   R. Grayson, 'What is a Third Way?', in W. Wallace and N. Stockley (eds), *Liberal Democrats and the Third Way* (London: Centre for Reform, Paper no. 4, 1998), pp. 6–14, p. 6.
72   N. Stockley, "The Third Way: where do Liberal Democrats stand?' in Wallace and Stockley (eds) (1998), *op. cit.*, pp. 25–33, p. 25.
73   W. Wallace, 'The Third Way and the Fourth ...', in Wallace and Stockley (eds) (1998), *op. cit.*, pp. 15–24, p. 18.
74   Violante (1999), *op. cit.*, pp. 49–50.
75   Giddens (1994), *op. cit.*, p. 14.
76   Giddens (1998), *op. cit.*, pp. 36–7. See also U. Beck, *The Risk Society. Towards a New Modernity* (London: Sage Publications, 1992), pp. 127ff.

77 Giddens (1998), *op. cit.*, pp. 33–5.
78 Giddens (1994), *op. cit.*, p. 14.
79 Giddens (1998), *op. cit.*, pp. 72ff.
80 *Ibid.*, p. 66.
81 G. Mulgan, *Politics in an Antipolitical Age* (Cambridge: Polity Press, 1994). See also Mulgan's Italian correspondent A. Mastropaolo, *Antipolitica all'origine della crisi italiana* (Napoli: L'Ancora del Mediterraneo, 2000).
82 See, for example, G. Vacca, *Per una Nuova Costituente* (Milano: Bompiani, 1996); G. Cotturi, *La Lunga Transizione* (Roma: Editori Riuniti, 1997); M. D'Alema, *La Grande Occasione. L'Italia verso le riforme* (Milano: Mondadori, 1997). Or for similar books in respect to Great Britain, Tony Wright, *Socialism and Decentralisation* (London: Fabian Society, 1984) and S. Weir and W. Hall (eds.), *The Untouchables: Power and Accountability in the Quango State* (London: Scarman Trust, 1996). See also on this Marquand (1997), *op. cit.*, p. 43 and p. 81; and D. Marquand, 'Reinventing Federalism: Europe and the Left', in Miliband (1994), *op. cit.*, pp. 219–30.
83 Sassoon (1996), *op. cit.*, p. 736.
84 See, for example, P. Hewitt and D. Mattinson, *Women's Votes: the Key to Winning*, Fabian pamphlet no. 353, June 1989.
85 See Lipset and Rokkan (1967), *op. cit.*
86 G. Greer, *The Whole Woman* (London: Transworld Publisher, 1999).
87 S. Tindale, 'Sustaining Social Democracy: the Politics of the Environment', in Miliband (1994), *op. cit.*, pp. 192–206, pp. 192–3.
88 Giddens (1998), *op. cit.*, p. 62.
89 Tindale (1994), *op. cit.*, p. 194.
90 Sassoon (1996), *op. cit.*, p. 679.
91 See on this N. Fairclough, *New Labour, New Language?* (New York: Routledge, 2000).
92 D. Coates and P. Lawler, *New Labour in Power* (Manchester: Manchester University Press, 2000), p. 5.
93 T. Blair, 'Accepting the Challenge (Speech accepting the leadership of the Labour Party, London, 21 July 1994)', in Blair (1996), *op. cit.*, pp. 21–6, p. 21.
94 Blair (1998), *op. cit.*, p. 8.
95 T. Blair, 'New Labour, New Britain (Speech to the Labour Party conference, Blackpool, 4 October 1994)', in Blair (1996), *op. cit.*, pp. 27–42, p. 32.
96 *Ibid.*, p. 32. See also L. Byrne, *Information Age Government: Delivering the Blair Revolution* (London: Fabian Society, 1998).
97 Blair (1998), *op. cit.*, p. 10.
98 A. Bagnasco, *Le tre Italie* (Bologna: Il Mulino, 1977).
99 See D. Sassoon, *Contemporary Italy* (London: Longman, 1997, 1st edn 1986), p. 65.
100 M. D'Alema, *Un paese normale. La Sinistra e il futuro dell'Italia* (Milano: Mondadori, 1995). On the shortcomings of Italian capitalism see also Giulio Sapelli, *L'Italia di fine secolo. Economia e classi dirigenti: un capitalismo senza mercato* (Venezia: Marsilio, 1998).
101 Blair, 'New Labour, New Britain', *op. cit.*, p. 32.
102 Folena (1997), *op. cit.* See also on this P. Ignazi, *Dal PCI al PDS* (Bologna: Il Mulino, 1992), p. 116.

103   D'Alema (1997), p. xvii and p. 78; see also W. Veltroni, *Governare a sinistra* (Milano: Baldini & Castoldi, 1997), p. 94.

104   See R. Rossanda and P. Ingrao (eds), *Appuntamenti di Fine Secolo* (Roma: Manifestolibri, 1995); M. Revelli, *La sinistra sociale. Oltre la civiltà del lavoro* (Torino: Bollati Boringhieri, 1997); G. Lunghini, *L'età dello spreco. Disoccupazione e bisogni sociali* (Torino: Bollati Boringhieri, 1995). See also on the 'two Lefts', F. Bertinotti, *Le due sinistre* (Milano: Sperling & Kupfer, 1997).

105   *Marxism Today*, special issue (November–December 1998).

106   See G. Monbiot, *The Captive State: the Corporate Takeover of Britain* (Basingtoke: Macmillan, 2000).

107   This is the central thesis of books such as D. Coates, *Models of Capitalism. Growth and Stagnation in the Modern Era* (Molden Mass: Polity Press, 2000).

108   See, for example, D'Alema (1997), *op. cit.*, p. xii.

109   A. Giddens, *The Runaway World: how Globalisation is Reshaping our Lives* (London: Profile Books Ltd., 1999), p. 1.

110   A. Giddens, 'Brave New World: the New Context of Politics', in Miliband (1994), *op. cit.*, pp. 21–38. See also on this J. Gray, *False Down: the Delusions of Global Capitalism* (London: Granta Books, 1998).

111   R. Kuttner, 'Don't forget the demand side', in Miliband (1994), *op. cit.*, pp. 146–51, p. 147.

112   Wright (1996), *op. cit.*, p. 119.

113   *Ibid.*

114   C. Leadbeater, *Living on Thin Air* (London: Viking, 1999), p. viii.

115   D'Alema (1997), *op. cit.*, p. XII.

116   Giddens (1999), *op. cit.*

117   Giddens (1994), *op. cit.*, p. 10.

118   Giddens (1998), *op. cit.*, pp. 32–3.

119   See on this A. Turner, *Just Capital: the Liberal Economy* (with an introduction by Ralf Dahrendorf) (London: Macmillan, 2001).

120   See D. Sassoon *Social Democracy at the Heart of Europe* (London: Institute of Public Policy Research, 1996); Marquand (1997), *op. cit.*, and Mark Leonard, *Rediscovering Europe* (London: Demos, 1998).

121   Sassoon (1996), *op. cit.*, pp. 771ff.

122   D'Alema (1996), *op. cit.*, p. xxv.

123   See D. Sassoon, 'The Italian Communist Party's European Strategy', *The Political Quarterly*, Vol. 47 (1976), pp. 253–76.

124   The centrality of the European question in the shift from PCI to PDS is illustrated clearly by Vassilis Fouskas in his *Italy, Europe, the Left*, *op. cit.*, p. 141.

125   On Labour's past policy on integration see M. Newman, *Socialism and European Unity. The Dilemma of the Left in Britain and France* (London: Junction Books, 1983).

126   As an indication of New Labour's new more positive attitude towards Europe, see Peter Mandelson and Roger Liddle, *The Blair Revolution* (London: Faber and Faber, 1996) published one year before the 1997 election, pp. 157–82. See also Labour Party, 'Future of the European Union: Labour's Position in Preparation for the Intergovernmental Conference 1996', Interim Report, Labour Party, 14 September; and Labour Party, *New Labour: Because Britain Deserves Better*, General Election Manifesto 1997.

127   *Ibid.*

128 'The Future of Europe. Seven Leaders with Seven Visions', *The Guardian*, 30 May 2001, p. 12.
129 See P. Toynbee and D. Walker, *Did Things Get Better? An Audit of Labour's Successes and Failures* (London: Penguin, 2001), pp. 142–52.
130 Anon. author, 'Vote Conservative', *Economist*, 2 June 2001, p. 13.
131 T. Blair and G. Schroeder, *Europe: the Third Way – die Neue Mitte* (London: Labour Party and the SPD, 1999), p. 31.
132 See on this, Labour Party, *Made in Britain. New Markets, New Technology, New Government*, London 1991; and Labour Party, *A New Economic Future for Britain: Economic and Employment Opportunities for All*, London 1995.
133 Tony Blair, Interview in the *Guardian*, 8 April 1997, p. 1.
134 Blair (1998), *op. cit.*, p. 8.
135 Blair and Schroeder (1999), *op. cit.*, p. 31.
136 See Movimento per l'Ulivo, *Il Programma de l'Ulivo*, Aprile 1996, in www.democraticidisinistra.it/ulivo, section: 'Le buone regole dell'economia nazionale'.
137 Eurostat data, quoted in Sassoon (1996), *op. cit.*, p. 659.
138 C. Baccetti, *Il PDS. Verso un nuovo modello di partito?* (Bologna: Il Mulino, 1997), p. 252.
139 See Michael Contarino, 'Italy's December 1998 "Social Pact for Development and Employment": Towards a new Political Economy for a "normal country"?', in M. Gilbert and G. Pasquino (eds), *Italian Politics. The Faltering Transition* (New York, Oxford: 2000), pp. 170–84.
140 See on this T. Boeri, R. Layard, S. Nickell, *'Welfare to Work'*/Report to Prime Ministers Blair and D'Alema (London: Department for Education and Employment, 2000), section 'The Italian experience'.
141 Labour Party, *Meet the Challenge, Make the Change, op. cit.*, p. 133.
142 Kuttner (1994), *op. cit.*, p. 147.
143 See P. Bianchi, S. Cassese, V. della Sala, 'Privatisation in Italy: aims and constraints', *West European Politics*, Vol. 11 (October 1988), pp. 87–100.
144 Gruppi Parlamentari della Maggioranza L'Ulivo insieme per l'Italia (ed.), *I Governi di Centro–sinistra: Impegni mantenuti e cose da fare. Un bilancio del lavoro svolto e da svolgere fino alla fine della legislatura* (Roma: Ufficio Comunicazione del Gruppo DS-L'Ulivo della Camera dei Deputati, March 2000), p. 69. See also Sassoon (1997), *op. cit.*, p. 87.
145 My emphasis.
146 Labour Party, General Election Manifesto 1983, London 1983.
147 Wright (1996), *op. cit.*, p. 135.
148 Blair (1994), *op. cit.*, p. 4.
149 Miliband (1994), *op. cit.*, p. 5.
150 Wright (1996), *op. cit.*, p. 140.
151 Blair and Schroeder (1999), *op. cit.*, p. 28.
152 Blair (2001), *op. cit.*, p. 2.
153 Blair and Schroeder (1999), *op. cit.*, p. 29.
154 M. Taylor and G. Kelly, 'Diversity must serve its purpose across the public sector', in *Policy-Network*, 6 June 2001, www.epn.org.
155 See IPPR, *Building Better Partenrships* (London: IPPR Report, 2001).
156 See Labour Party, *Ambitions for Britain*, General Election Manifesto 2001, London 2001.

157   Giddens (1998), *op. cit.*, pp. 99–100.
158   Blair and Schroeder (1999), *op. cit.*, p. 30.
159   *Ibid.*, p. 27.
160   Blair (1998), *op. cit.*, p. 4.
161   *Ibid.*
162   Violante (1999), *op. cit.*, pp. 104–7.
163   The Institute for Fiscal Studies, 'Election 2001', www.ifs.org.uk/election, 4 June 2001.
164   Blair and Schroeder (1999), *op. cit.*, p. 328.
165   G. E. Andersen, 'Equality and Work in the Post-industrial Life-cycle', in Miliband (1994), *op. cit.*, pp. 167–85, p. 172.
166   Marquand (1997), *op. cit.*, p. 5.
167   *Ibid.*, p. 6.
168   M. Regini and I. Regalia, 'Employers, Unions and the State: the Resurgence of Concertation in Italy?', in M. Bull and M. Rhodes (eds), *Crisis and Transition in Italian Politics* (London: Frank Cass, 1997), pp. 210–30, pp. 215–17.
169   Blair (2001), *op. cit.*, p. 3.
170   G. Brown, 'Why Labour is Still Loyal to the Poor', *Guardian*, 2 August 1997, p. 9.
171   Violante (1999), *op. cit.*, p. 73.
172   Blair and Schroeder (1999), *op. cit.*, p. 28.
173   Giddens (1998), pp. 104ff.
174   Report of the Social Justice Commission (London: Vintage, 1994).
175   *Ibid.*, p. 79.
176   *Ibid.*, p. 104.
177   Giddens (1998), *op. cit.*, pp. 117ff.
178   Blair and Schroeder (1999), *op. cit.*, p. 35.
179   Movimento per l'Ulivo, *Il Programma de l'Ulivo*, Aprile 1996, in www.democraticidisinistra.it/ulivo, section: "Un'Italia che sa, un'Italia che vale'. See also on this S. Parker, 'The Government of the Ulivo', in R. D'Alimonte and D. Nelken, *Italian Politics. The Centre-Left in Power* (Colorado and Oxford: Westview Press, 1997), pp. 125–42.
180   Blair (1994), *op. cit.*, p. 5.
181   *Ibid.* See also Blair and Schroeder (1999), *op. cit.*, p. 33; and Labour Party, *New Labour: Because Britain Deserves Better, op. cit.*, which indicated education as New Labour's 'number one priority'.
182   Blair (1998), *op. cit.*, p. 4.
183   *Ibid.*, p. 5.
184   Giddens (1998), *op. cit.*, 1998, pp. 65ff.
185   See Boeri, Layard, Nickell (eds) (2000), *op. cit.*, section 'The British Experience'.
186   *Ibid.*
187   *Ibid.*
188   *Ibid.* Section 'The Italian Experience'
189   Coates and Lawler (2000), *op. cit.*, p. 41.
190   Blair and Schroeder (1999), *op. cit.*, p. 36.
191   Giddens (1998), *op. cit.*, p. 103.
192   A. Etzioni, 'The Third way is a Triumph', *New Statesman*, 25 June 2001, pp. 25–6, p. 26.

193 *Ibid.*
194 See, for example, R. Dahrendorf, 'Whatever happened to liberty', *New Statesman*, 6 September 1999, pp. 25–7.
195 P. Towsend, 'Persuasion and Conformity: An Assessment of the Borrie Report on Social Justice', *New Left Review*, no. 213 (1995), pp. 137–50, p. 145.
196 Crosland (1956), *op. cit.*
197 Marquand (1997), *op. cit.*, p. 4.
198 IPPR, *The Justice Gap* (London: IPPR, 1993), pp. 44–5.
199 The Institute for Fiscal Studies, 'Election 2001', www.ifs.org.uk/election, 4 June 2001. For a wide-ranging account on the first Blair government see also A. Seldon, *The Blair Effect* (London, Little, Brown & Co., 2001).
200 *Ibid.*

5 Moving to the Centre: Socialists Get Rid of the Cloth Cap

1 D. Kavanagh, *Election Campaigning. The New Marketing of Politics* (Oxford: Blackwell, 1997 [1st edn 1995]), p. 22.
2 See M. Paci, *Il mutamento della struttura sociale italiana in Italia* (Bologna: Il Mulino, 1992), pp. 278–9.
3 A. Occhetto, *Il sentimento e la ragione. Un'intervista di Teresa Bartoli* (Milano: Rizzoli, 1994), p. 84. See also P. Ginsborg, *L'Italia del tempo presente. Famiglia, società civile, Stato 1980–1996* (Torino: Einaudi, 1998), pp. 60ff.
4 R. Biorcio, 'Comunicazione politica e flussi elettorali', in M. Livolsi and U. Volli (eds), *Il Televoto. La Campagna Elettorale in televisione* (Milano: Franco Angeli, 1997), pp. 145–61, p. 155.
5 See Baccetti (1997), *op. cit.*, p. 159; and Ariemma (2000), *op. cit.*, p. 191.
6 See Istituto Cattaneo, Italian National Election Studies, May–June 2001, *La Repubblica*, 15 November 2001, p. 29. See also I. Diamanti, *Perché ha vinto il centro–destra* (Bologna: Il Mulino, 2001).
7 Kavanagh (1997), *op. cit.*, p. 23.
8 Bell (1962), *op. cit.*
9 See J. K. Galbraith, *The Culture of Contentment* (Harmondsworth: Penguin, 1992).
10 See Mulgan (1994), *op. cit.*
11 G. Sani, 'Il verdetto del 1992', in R. Mannheimer and G. Sani, *La rivoluzione elettorale. Tra la prima e la seconda repubblica* (Milano: Anabasi, 1994), pp. 39–70, p. 53.
12 Dahrendorf (1961, 1st edn 1959), *op. cit.*
13 See M. Franklin, *The Decline of Class Voting in Britain: Changes in the Basis of Electoral Choice, 1964–1983* (Oxford: Clarendon Press, 1985); on Italy see A. Accornero, *Era il secolo del lavoro* (Bologna: Il Mulino, 2000, 1st edn 1997), p. 123.
14 G. Sapelli, *L'Italia inafferrabile* (Venezia: Marsilio, 1989, p. 118); On the effects of post-Fordism on class relations see also J. Rogers and W. Streeck, 'Productive Solidarities: Economic Strategy and Left Politics', in Miliband (1994), *op. cit.*, pp. 128–45.

15   See on this Anthony Heath, Roger Jowell, John Curtice, *Labour's Last Chance: the 1992 Election and Beyond* (Aldershot: Dartmouth Publishing Company, 1994).
16   Kavanagh (1997), *op. cit.*, p. 23.
17   *Ibid.*, p. 107.
18   Heath, Jowell and Curtice (1994), *op. cit.*, pp. 275–95, p. 282.
19   R. Inglehart, *The Silent Revolution. Changing Values and Political Styles Among Western Publics* (Princeton University Press, 1977).
20   S. M. Lipset, *Political Man: the Social Bases of Politics* (New York: Doubleday, 1981 revised edn, 1st edn, 1960); Z. Bauman, *Memories of Class: the Pre-history and After-life of Class* (Boston-London: Routledge, 1982); A. Gorz, *Farewell to the Working Class: an Essay on Post-Industrial Socialism* (London: Pluto Press, 1982).
21   For a critical account of the 'classless society', see A. Adonis and S. Pollard, *A Class Act: The Myth of Britain's Classless Society* (London: Penguin, 1998), p. ix.
22   M. D'Alema, *Progettare il futuro*, 1996, Speech at the Pontignano Anglo-Italian workshop (Milano: Bompiani, 1996), p. 66.
23   M. D'Alema, 'Stralcio dell'intervento al Forum della Sinistra, Roma 19 dicembre 1996', *Quaderni del Circolo Rosselli*, special issue 'La Nascita di un Nuovo Partito', no. 12 (1998), pp. 48–55, p. 54.
24   See Labour Party, *Meet the Challenge, Make the Change, op. cit.*, p. 120.
25   See on this A. Heath, R. Jowell and J. Curtice, 'Can Labour Win?', in Heath, Jowell, Curtice (1994), *op. cit.*, pp. 275–95, p. 294.
26   A. Heath and R. Jowell, 'Labour's Policy Review', in Heath, Jowell, Curtice (1994), *op. cit.*, pp. 191–209, p. 201.
27   Heath, Jowell and Curtice, 'Can Labour Win?', *op. cit.*, p. 294.
28   A. Heath and B. Taylor, 'New Sources of Abstention', in G. Evans and P. Norris (eds), *Critical Elections. British Parties and Voters in Long-Term Perspective* (London: Sage Publication, 1999), pp. 164–80, p. 172.
29   Baccetti (1997), *op. cit.*, p. 203.
30   D'Alema, 'Stralcio dell'intervento al Forum della Sinistra, Roma 19 dicembre 1996', p. 50.
31   Kavanagh (1997), pp. 26–38.
32   See on this D. Butler and D. Kavanagh, *The British General Election of 2001* (London: Palgrave, 2001).
33   See M. Foley, *The British Presidency* (Manchester: Manchester University Press, 2000) and P. Hennessy, *The Prime Minister* (London: Penguin, 2001).
34   N. Jones, *Control Freaks* (London: Politico's Publishing, 2001).
35   Labour Party, *Ambitions for Britain*, General Election Manifesto 2001.
36   See on this R. Grandi, 'Strategie a confronto', in Livolsi and Volli (eds) (1997), pp. 83–106.
37   Veltroni (1997), p. 103.
38   I. Crewe, 'How the Suburbs Turned Red', *New Statesman*, 4 June 2001, pp. 19–20, p. 19.
39   Biorcio (1997), *op. cit.*, p. 155.
40   David Brooks, *Bobos in Paradise* (New York: Simon and Schuster, 2000).
41   See on this Pippa Norris, 'Gender: A Gender-Generation Gap?, in Evans and Norris (eds) (1999), *op. cit.*, pp. 148–63.
42   *Ibid.*, p. 148.
43   Sassoon (1996), *op. cit.*, p. 118.

44 G. Zincone, 'La donna è mobile ma non abbastanza', *Reset* (July–August 2001), pp. 18–19.
45 *Ibid.*, p. 19.
46 Toynbee and Walker (2001), *op. cit.*, pp. 29–32.
47 See C. Mouffe, *The Democratic Paradox* (London: Verso, 2000).
48 Kavanagh (1997), *op. cit.*, p. 12.
49 Labour History Archive and Study Centre (Manchester), Labour Party Archive, NEC minutes, June 1955.
50 M. Abrams, 'Why Labour has lost Elections' published in four parts, *Socialist Commentary* (May 1960), pp. 4–9; (June 1960), pp. 5–11; (July 1960), pp. 5–12; (August 1960), pp. 5–9. The articles were later published as Abrams and Rose (1960), *op. cit.*
51 See Labour History Archive and Study Centre (Manchester), Labour Party Archive, Home policy Sub-Committee minutes, 18 February 1957; Home policy Sub-Committee minutes, 17 June 1957; Home policy Sub-Committee minutes, 17 September 1959; Home policy Sub-Committee minutes, 28 October 1959; Home policy Sub-Committee minutes, 7 November 1959.
52 Kavanagh (1997), *op. cit.*, p. 52.
53 Sassoon (1996), *op. cit.*, p. 697.
54 Kavanagh (1997), *op. cit.*, p. 91. See also P. Norris, 'Labour Party Factionalism and Extremism', in Heath, Jowell, Curtice (eds) (1994), *op. cit.*, pp. 173–90, p. 173.
55 For a very critical assessment of the 'cosmetic exercises' carried out by New Labour see Fairclough (2000), *op. cit.*
56 Kavanagh (1997), *op. cit.*, p. 89.
57 Butler (1989), *op. cit.*, p. 98.
58 Labour History Archive and Study Centre (Manchester), Labour Party Archive, NEC minutes, October 1954, 'Report on the Light programme discussions on the Scarborough and Blackpool conferences'.
59 See for this P. Norris, 'New Politicians? Changes in Party Competition at Westminster', in Evans and Norris (eds) (1999), *op. cit.*, pp. 22–43, p. 25.
60 E. Vallini, 'Contributo per uno studio sulle tecniche elettorali', *Tempi Moderni*, Vol. I (July 1958), pp. 266–9, p. 268.
61 A. Spreafico and J. La Palombara, *Elezioni e Comportamento Politico in Italia* (Milano: Edizioni di Comunità, 1963).
62 See, for instance, E. Vallini, 'Contributo per uno studio sulle tecniche elettorali', *op. cit.*, pp. 266–9.
63 Spreafico and La Palombara (1963), *op. cit.* See introduction, pp. xiii, xxi and p. 265.
64 See on this F. Venturino, *Partiti, Leader, Tematiche. La formazione dell'opinione pubblica nelle elezioni del 1996* (Milano: Franco Angeli, 2000).
65 See Sani (1994), *op. cit.*, p. 64.
66 See on this Diamanti (2001), *op. cit.*
67 Venturino (2000), *op. cit.*, see introduction.
68 Baccetti (1997), *op. cit.*, p. 64.
69 Ariemma (2000), *op. cit.*, p. 190.
70 Baccetti (1997), *op. cit.*, p. 121. See also on this M. Pamini, 'From Militants to Voters: from the Pci to the PDS', in P. Ignazi and C. Ysmal (eds), *The Organisation of Political Parties in Southern Europe* (Westport, Conn.: Praeger, 1998).

71   Kavanagh (1997), *op. cit.*, p. 33.
72   Mandelson and Liddle (1996), *op. cit.*, pp. 211ff.
73   *Ibid.*
74   Ariemma (2000), *op. cit.*, p. 189; See also Baccetti (1997), *op. cit.*, p. 135.
75   J. Rentoul, *Tony Blair. Prime Minister* (London: Little, Brown & Co., 2000 revised edn, 1st edn 1995); J. Sapel, *Tony Blair: the Moderniser* (London: Michael Joseph, 1995); M. Perriman, *The Blair Agenda* (London: Lawrence & Wishart, 1996); D. Draper, *Blair's Hundred Days* (London: Faber and Faber, 1997); A. Marr, *Who is Tony Blair?* (London: Penguin, 1997).
76   Mandelson and Liddle (1996), *op. cit.*
77   Livolsi and Volli (eds) (1997), *op. cit.*, see introduction, p. 11.
78   Pasquino (2001), *op. cit.*, p. 15.
79   Volli (1997), *op. cit.*, p. 180.
80   See on this P. Ciofi e F. Ottaviano, *Un partito per il leader. Il nuovo corso del PSI dal Midas agli anni novanta* (Soveria Mannelli: Rubbettino, 1990).
81   Ariemma (2000), p. 162.
82   *Ibid.*, p. 194.

Epilogue

1   R. Jenkins, 'Equality', in Crossman (ed.) (1952), *op. cit.*, pp. 69–90, p. 73.
2   G. Sapelli, *Storia economica dell'Italia contemporanea* (Milano: Bruno Mondadori, 1997), p. 141.
3   A. Giddens, *The Third Way and its Critics* (Cambridge: Polity Press, 2000).
4   'Goldilocks Politics', *The Economist*, 19 December 1998, pp. 47–49.
5   S. Hall, 'The Great moving nowhere show', *Marxism Today* (November–December 1998), pp. 9–14.
6   Guiducci (1956), *op. cit.*, pp. 130–1.
7   *Ibid.*, pp. 157–8.

References

Abrams, Mark and Richard Rose, *Must Labour Lose?* (London: Penguin Books, 1960).
Abrams, Mark, 'The Future of the Left. New Roots of Working Class Conservatism', *Encounter* (May 1960), pp. 57–9.
—— 'Why Labour has lost Elections' published in four parts, *Socialist Commentary* (May 1960), pp. 4–9; (June 1960), pp. 5–11; (July 1960), pp. 5–12; (August 1960), pp. 5–9.
Abse, Toby, 'Italy: a New Agenda', in Perry Anderson and Patrick Camiller (eds), *Mapping the European Left* (London: Verso/New Left Review, 1994), pp. 189–232.
Accornero, Aris, *Era il secolo del lavoro* (Bologna: Il Mulino, 2000, 1st edn, 1997).
Acland, R., Barbara Castle, Richard Crossman, Ian Mikardo *et alia*, *Keeping Left* (London: New Stateman, 1950).
Adaris, A. and S. Pollard, *A Class Act: The Myth of Britain's Classless Society* (London: Penguin, 1968).
Ajello, Nello, *Il Lungo Addio. Intellettuali e PCI dal 1958 al 1991* (Roma-Bari: Laterza, 1997).
Alasia, Giovanni, 'Il PSI e il sindacato', *Mondo Operaio*, Vol. XVI (August–September 1963), pp. 2–6.
Alexander, Ken and John Hughes, *A Socialist Wages Plan*, New Left Discussion Pamphlet series (London: Universities and Left Review, 1959).
Amaduzzi, Ruggero, in 'Capitalismo contemporaneo e controllo operaio' (Round Table organised by *Mondo Operaio* on contemporary capitalism), *Mondo Operaio*, Vol. X (December 1957), pp. 10–21.
Amato, Paolo, *Il PSI tra Frontismo e Autonomia (1948–1954)* (Cosenza: Lerici, 1958).
anon., 'La partecipazione politica e i partiti in Italia', Round table organised by Tempi Moderni, *Tempi Moderni*, Vol. V (January–March 1962), pp. 29–76.
anon., 'Partecipazione politica a livello di base', *Tempi Moderni*, Vol. I (May–June 1958), pp. 150–66.
anon., 'Vote Conservative', *The Economist*, 2 June 2001, p. 13.
anon., 'Goldilocks Politics', *The Economist*, 19 December 1998, pp. 47–9.
Arfè, Gaetano (ed.), *Trent'Anni di Politica Socialista (1946–1976). Atti del Convegno organizzato dall'Istituto Socialista di Studi Storici, Parma, Gennaio 1977* (Roma: Mondo Operaio-Edizioni Avanti!, 1977).
Ariemma, Iginio, *La casa brucia. I democratici di sinistra* (Venezia: Marsilio, 2000).
Armstrong, Philip, Andrew Glyn, John Harrison, *Capitalism since 1945* (London: Basil Blackwell, 1991).
Arnaudi, Carlo, 'La ricerca scientifica in Italia', *Attualità*, no. 7, January 1956.
—— *Per una nuova organizzazione della ricerca scientifica*, Speech to the Senate, 18 July 1962 (Roma: tipografia Bardi G., 1962), pp. 1–35.
Artis, Michael, 'Balogh's Economic Policies', *New Left Review*, no. 22 (December 1963), pp. 106–11.
Ashley, Jackie, 'Interview to Paddy Ashdown', *New Statesman*, 9 July 2001, pp. 18–19.

Asor Rosa, Alberto, *La sinistra alla prova. Considerazioni sul ventennio 1976–1996* (Torino: Einaudi, 1996).

Baccetti, C., *Il PDS. Verso un nuovo modello di partito?* (Bologna: Il Mulino, 1997).

Bagnasco, Andrea, *Le tre Italie* (Bologna: Il Mulino, 1977).

Bagnoli Paolo (ed.), 'Liberalsocialismo', special issue of *Il Ponte*, Vol. XLII (January–February 1986).

—— (ed.), *La Nuova storia: politica e cultura alla ricerca del socialismo liberale* (Firenze: Festina Lente, 1992).

—— 'Il socialismo liberale e il futuro della sinistra', in Bagnoli (1992), *op. cit.*, pp. 129–34.

Balogh, Thomas, *Planning for Progress. A Strategy for Labour*, Fabian Tract no. 346, July 1963.

Barbadoro, Idomeneo, 'Sviluppo economico e lotta rivoluzionaria', *Mondo Operaio*, Vol. X (September 1957), pp. 13–15.

Barca, Luciano, 'Problemi del Capitalismo di Stato e della pianificazione', Istituto Gramsci (ed), *Tendenze del Capitalismo Italiano. Atti del Convegno di Roma*, *op. cit.*, pp. 65–106.

Barrat Brown, Michael, 'The Controllers', *Universities and Left Review*, no. 5 (Autumn 1958), pp. 53–61; no. 6 (Spring 1959), pp. 32–41; no. 7 (Autumn 1959), pp. 43–9.

Bartolini, Stefano, *The Political Mobilization of the European Left, 1860–1980. The Class Cleavage* (Cambridge: Cambridge University Press, 2000).

Bauman, Zygmunt, *Memories of Class: the Pre-history and After-life of Class* (Boston-London: Routledge, 1982).

Bean, J. M. W., (ed.), *The Political Culture of Modern Britain* (London: Hamish Hamilton, 1987).

Beck, Ulrich, *The Risk Society. Towards a New Modernity* (London: Sage Publications, 1992).

Bedani, Gino, *Politics and Ideology in the Italian Workers' Movement* (Oxford: Berg Publisher, 1995).

Bedeschi, Giuseppe, *La parabola del Marxismo in Italia, 1945–1983* (Roma-Bari: Laterza, 1983).

Bell, Daniel, *The End of Ideology* (New York: The Free Press, 1965 [1st edn 1962]).

Bellamy, Richard, 'Mr. Strachey's guide to contemporary capitalism', *Marxist Quarterly*, Vol. 4 (January 1957), pp. 21–30.

Berlin, Isaiah, 'Two Concepts of Liberty', in *Four Essays on Liberty* (London-New York: Oxford University Press, 1969; Italian transl: I. Berlin, *Quattro Saggi sulla libertà* (Milano: Feltrinelli, 1989)).

Bernstein, Eduard, *Evolutionary Socialism* (New York: Schocken Books, 1963).

Bertinotti, Fausto and Alfonso Gianni, *Le idee che non muoiono* (Firenze: Ponte delle Grazie, 2000).

Bertinotti, Fausto, *Le due sinistre* (Milano: Sperling & Kupfer, 1997).

Bestazzi, Edvige, *La Politica Scolastica del PSI discussa nel Convegno Nazionale sulla Scuola 'Politica Scolastica Integrata nella Politica di Sviluppo', Roma 26–27 maggio 1962* (Roma: Fratelli Palombi Editori, 1962).

Bevan, Aneurin, *In Place of Fear* (New York: Monthly Review Press, 1964 [1st edn London: Heinemann, 1952]).

Bianchi, P., Sabino Cassese, Vincent della Sala, 'Privatisation in Italy: aims and constraints', *West European Politics*, Vol. 11 (October 1988), pp. 87–100.

Bianciardi, Luciano, *L'Integrazione* (Milano: Bompiani, 1960).

—— *La Vita Agra* (Milano: Bompiani, 1962).

Biorcio, Roberto, 'Comunicazione politica e flussi elettorali', in Livolsi and Volli (1997) (eds), *op. cit.*, pp. 145–61.

Blair, Tony and Gerhard Schroeder, *Europe: the Third Way – die Neue Mitte* (London: Labour Party and the SPD, 1999).

Blair, Tony, *New Britain. My Vision of a Young Country* (London: a New Statesman special selection, 1996).

—— *Socialism* (London: Fabian Society, 1994).

—— *The Third Way. New Politics for the New Century*, Fabian pamphlet no. 588 September 1998.

—— 'New Labour, New Britain' (Speech to the Labour Party conference, Blackpool, 4 October 1994), in Blair (1996), *op. cit.*, pp. 27–42.

—— 'Speech in Southwark Cathedral, 29 January 1996', in Blair (1996), *op. cit.*, pp. 63–75.

—— 'The Radical Coalition', in Blair (1996), *op. cit*, pp. 1–18.

—— 'Third Way, phase two', *Prospect* (March 2001), pp. 1–5.

—— preface, in Wright (1996), *op. cit.*, pp. ix–x.

Bobbio, Norberto, *Politica e Cultura* (Torino: Einaudi, 1955).

—— *Destra e sinistra. Ragioni e significati di una distinzione politica* (Roma: Donzelli, 1994).

—— 'Attualità del socialismo liberale', preface in Carlo Rosselli, *Socialismo Liberale*, (Einaudi: Torino, 1997, 1973a), pp. V–XIX.

—— 'La democrazia nei *Quaderni*', in 'Gramsci dopo la caduta di tutti i muri', supplement of *l'Unità*, 15 January 1991.

Boeri Tito, Richard Layard and Stephen Nickell, *'Welfare to Work'*/Report to Prime Ministers Blair and D'Alema (London: Department for Education and Employment, 2000).

Bogdanor, Vernon and Robert Skidelsky, *The Age of Affluence 1951–1964* (London: Macmillan, 1970).

Bonazzi, Giuseppe, 'Prospettive dell'automazione e via italiana al socialismo', *Mondo Operaio*, Vol. XI (August 1958), pp. 9–18.

—— 'Prospettive dell'automazione e via italiano al socialismo', *Mondo Operaio*, Vol. XI (August 1958).

Bowen, James, *A History of Western Education*, Vol. III, *The Modern West* (London: Methuen & Co, 1981).

Brittan, Samuel, *Steering Economy: the Role of the Treasury* (London: Secker & Warburg, 1969, revised edition [1st edn Penguin, Harmondsworth, 1964]).

Brivati, Brian, *Hugh Gaitskell* (London: Richard Cohen, 1996).

Brooks, David, *Bobos in Paradise* (New York: Simon and Schuster, 2000).

Brown, Gordon, 'The Politics of Potential: a New Agenda for Labour', in Miliband (1994) (ed.), *op. cit.*, pp. 113–22.

—— 'Why Labour is Still Loyal to the Poor', *Guardian*, 2 August 1997, p. 9.

Bruno, Groppo and G. Riccamboni (eds), *La Sinistra e il '56 in Italia e in Francia* (Padova: Liviana, 1987).

Bruno, Groppo, 'Il 1956 nella cultura politica del PCI', in Groppo and Riccamboni (eds) (1987), *op. cit.*, pp. 189–218.

Burnham, James, *The Managerial Revolution* (London: Putnam, 1942).

Butler, David and Dennis Kavanagh, *The British General Election of 2001* (London: Palgrave Macmillan, 2001).

Butler, David, *British General Elections since 1945* (Oxford: Basil Blackwell, 1989).

Byrne, Liam, *Information Age Government: Delivering the Blair Revolution* (London: Fabian Society, 1998).

Cafagna, Luciano, 'Fine della "classe generale"', in Luciano Cafagna *et alia, Classe Operaia, partiti politici e Socialismo nella Prospettiva Italiana* (Milano: Feltrinelli, 1966), pp. 228–38.

—— *C'era una volta ... Riflessioni sul comunismo italiano* (Venezia: Marsilio, 1991).

—— *La grande slavina. L'Italia verso la crisi della democrazia* (Venezia: Marsilio, 1993).

Cairncross, Alan, *The British Economy since 1945* (Oxford: Basil Blackwell, 1992).

Calvino, Italo, 'La Bonaccia delle Antille' (originally published in *Città Aperta* in 1957), in Mughini (ed.) (1975), *op. cit.*

Carabba, Manin, *Un ventennio di programmazione* (Bari: 1977).

Cattani, Venerio, 'Ancora sul Programma', *Mondo Operaio*, Vol. XII (October 1959), pp. 43–7.

Cazzola, Fabio, 'Elettori e Iscritti al PSI', in Sivini (ed) (1969), *op. cit.*, pp. 189–212.

Cazzola, Franco, *Il Partito come organizzazione. Studio di un caso: il PSI* (Roma: Edizioni del Tritone, 1970).

CGIL-Ufficio Studi Economici e Ufficio Stampa e Propaganda (ed.), *CGIL e Programmazione economica* (Roma: 1964).

Chesi, Marco, 'Rassegna di interpretazioni sullo sviluppo economico italiano nel secondo dopoguerra', *Società e Storia*, no. 41 (July–September 1988), pp. 669–91.

Chester, Norman, *The Nationalisation of British Industry 1945–51* (London: HMSO, 1975).

Chiarante, Giuseppe, *Da Togliatti a D'Alema. La tradizione dei comunisti italiani e le origini del PDS* (Roma-Bari: Laterza, 1996).

Chun, Lin, *The British New Left* (Edinburgh: Edinburgh University Press, 1993).

Cianca, Marco, 'Bertinotti "riscopre" Marx: sì, credo nella rivoluzione mondiale', *Corriere della Sera*, Friday 20 October 2000, p. 13.

Ciofi, P. and F. Ottaviano, *Un partito per il leader. Il nuovo corso del PSI dal Midas agli anni novanta* (Soveria Mannelli: Rubbettino, 1990).

Coates, David and Peter Lawler, *New Labour in Power* (Manchester: Manchester University Press, 2000).

Coates, David, *Models of Capitalism. Growth and Stagnation in the Modern Era* (Molden Mass: Polity Press, 2000).

Codignola, Tristano, 'La battaglia socialista per la scuola', *Mondo Operaio*, Vol. XIV (January–February 1961), pp. 19–22.

—— 'La Riforma Controriformistica', *Mondo Operaio*, Vol. XII (November 1959), pp. 1–7.

—— *Nascita e morte di un Piano. Tre anni di battaglia per la scuola pubblica* (Firenze: La Nuova Italia, 1962).

Coen, Federico and Giuseppe Tamburrano, 'Sulla funzione e la struttura dello Stato nella moderna società capitalistica', in Istituto Gramsci (edited by), *Tendenze del Capitalismo Italiano. Atti del Convegno di Roma, op. cit.*, pp. 171–90.

Coen, Federico, 'La nuova politica laburista', *Mondo Operaio*, Vol. XIII (October–November 1960), pp. 6–9.

—— 'Temi e problemi della nostra politica', *Mondo Operaio*, Vol. XII, no. 12 (December 1959), pp. 7–12.

—— 'Le elezioni americane e il programma democratico', *Mondo Operaio*, Vol. XIII (September 1960), pp. 22–5.

—— 'Le due anime del laburismo', *Mondo Operaio*, Vol. XIII, no. 3, March 1960, pp. 34–9.

—— 'Scienza e politica al Congresso Laburista', *Mondo Operaio*, Vol. XVI (October 1963), pp. 11–24.

—— 'Sindacati, programmazione e politica dei redditi', *Mondo Operaio*, Vol. XVII (November–December 1963), pp. 59–62.

Cofrancesco, Dino, 'G.L. e il fattore F. Come non leggere Carlo Rosselli', in Maurizio Degl'Innocenti (ed.), *Carlo Rosselli e il socialismo liberale* (Manduria-Bari-Roma: Piero Lacaita Editore, 1999), pp. 177–85.

Colarizi, Simona (ed.), *Riccardo Lombardi, Scritti Politici 1945–1963. Dalla resistenza al Centrosinistra* (Venezia: Marsilio, 1978).

Cole, G. D. H., *What's Wrong with the Trade Unions*, Fabian Tract no. 301, September 1956.

Colletti, Lucio, 'Quale sinistra dopo il Muro', *Corriere della Sera*, 20 March 1994, p. 24.

Conti, Paolo, 'Veltroni: sì a una sinistra che impari da Gramsci come dai fratelli Rosselli', *Corriere della Sera*, 26 October 2000.

Cook, Chris and Ian Taylor (eds), *The Labour Party* (London and New York: Longman, 1980).

Coopey, Richard, Steven Fielding, Nick Tiratsoo (eds), *The Wilson Governments 1964–1970* (London and New York: Pinter Publishers, 1993).

Cotturi, Giuseppe, *La Lunga Transizione* (Roma: Editori Riuniti, 1997).

Craig, F. W. S. (ed.) *British General Election Manifestos, 1900–1974* (London: Macmillan, 1974).

Craxi, Bettino, *Il rinnovamento socialista* (Venezia: Marsilio, 1981).

—— *L'Italia Liberata* (Milano: Sugarco, 1984).

—— *Un'onda lunga: articoli, interviste, discorsi, gennaio–dicembre 1988* (Imola: Galeati, 1988).

Crewe, Ivor, 'How the Suburbs Turned Red', *New Statesman*, 4 June 2001, pp. 19–20.

Crosland, Anthony, *The Future of Socialism* (London: Jonathan Cape, 1956).

—— 'The Transition from Capitalism', in Crossman (ed.) (1952), *op. cit.*, pp. 33–69.

—— *Can Labour Win?*, Fabian Tract no. 324, May 1960.

—— *The Conservative Enemy: a Program of Radical Reform for the 1960s* (London: Jonathan Cape, 1962).

Crossman, Richard (ed.), *The New Fabian Essays* (London: Turnstile Press, 1952).

—— (ed.), *Planning for Freedom* (London: Hamish Hamilton, 1965).

—— 'Scientists in Whitehall' (1963), in Crossman (ed.) (1965), *op. cit.*, pp. 134–47.

—— 'Towards a New Philosophy of Socialism', in Crossman (ed.) (1952), *op. cit.*, pp. 1–32.

—— *Labour and the Affluent Society*, Fabian Tract no. 325, June 1960.

—— *Socialism and the New Despotism*, Fabian Tract no. 298, November 1955.

D'Alema, Massimo (edited by Roberto Gualtieri), *La sinistra nell'Italia che cambia* (Milano: Feltrinelli, 1997).

—— *La Grande Occasione. L'Italia verso le riforme* (Milano: Mondadori, 1997).

—— *Progettare il futuro*, 1996, Speech at the Pontignano Anglo–Italian workshop (Milano: 1996).

D'Alema, Massimo *Un paese normale. La Sinistra e il futuro dell'Italia* (Milano: Mondadori, 1995).

—— 'I pensieri lunghi di Enrico Berlinguer', in Paul Ginsborg and Massimo D'Alema (edited by Michele Battini), *Dialogo su Berlinguer* (Firenze: Giunti, 1994), pp. 23–49.

—— 'The Challenge of the New Right', *Policy Network*, issue 1 (Summer 2001) pp. 32–3.

D'Almeida, Fabrice, *Histoire et politique en France et en Italie: l'esemple des socialistes 1945–1983* (Roma: Ecole Française de Rome, 1998).

D'Apice, C., *L'Arcipelago dei Consumi. Consumi e Redditi delle Famiglie Italiane dal Dopoguerra a Oggi* (Bari: De Donato, 1981).

Dagnino, Virgilio, *Obsolescenza delle ideologie: per una morale socialista e libertaria* (Milano: Azione Comune, 1967).

Dahrendorf, Ralf, *Class and Class Conflict in Industrial Society* (Stanford, California: Stanford University Press, 1961 (1st German edition 1957; 1st British edition by Routledge and Kegan Paul, London, 1959; Italian edition: Ralph Dahrendorf, *Classi e Conflitti di Classe nella Società Industriale*, prefaced by Alessandro Pizzorno, Rome and Bari: Laterza, 1963)

—— *Reflections on the Revolution in Europe* (London: Chatto and Windus, 1990).

—— *Per un Nuovo Liberalismo* (Roma-Bari: Laterza, 1993).

—— 'Whatever happened to liberty', *New Statesman*, 6 September 1999, pp. 25–7.

Daneo, Camillo, *La Politica economica della ricostruzione 1945–1949* (Torino: Einaudi, 1975).

De Luna, Giovanni, *Storia del Partito d'Azione. La rivoluzione democratica (1942/1947)* (Milano: Feltrinelli, 1982).

De Martino, Francesco, 'Ancora dello Stato', *Mondo Operaio*, Vol. IX (July 1956), pp. 423–6.

—— 'Pretese questioni di teoria intorno ai problemi dello Stato', *Mondo Operaio*, Vol. IX (October 1956), pp. 563–6.

Degl'Innocenti, Maurizio, *Storia del PSI dal dopoguerra ad oggi* (Roma-Bari: Laterza, 1993).

Diamanti, Ilvo, *Perché ha vinto il centro–destra* (Bologna: Il Mulino, 2001).

—— 'Dossier: DS, quel piccolo PCI', *La Repubblica*, 15 November 2001, pp. 28–9.

Diebold, John, *Automation – The Advent of the Automatic Factory* (New York: Van Nostrand, 1952).

Dobb, Maurice, 'Some Economic Revaluations', *Marxist Quarterly*, Vol. 4 (January 1957), pp. 2–7.

Dogan, Mattei, 'Europa. Comportamento elettorale degli operai dell'industria', *Tempi Moderni*, Vol. III (July–September 1960), pp. 91–4.

—— 'La stratificazione sociale dei suffragi', in Spreafico and La Palombara (ed.) (1963), *op. cit.*, pp. 407–74.

Dormagen, Jean-Yves, *I comunisti. Dal PCI alla nascita di Rifondazione Comunista. Una semiologia politica* (Roma: Koine Edizioni, 1996).

Draper, Derek, *Blair's Hundred Days* (London: Faber and Faber, 1997).

Drucker, Peter F., *The Practice of Management* (London: Heinemann, 1955 [1st edn, New York: Harper & Row, 1954]).

Durbin, Elisabeth, *New Jerusalem: the Labour Party and the Economics of Democratic Socialism* (London: Routledge and Kegan Paul, 1985).

Elliot, Gregory, *Labourism and the English Genius; the Strange Death of Labour England* (London and New York: Verso, 1993).

Ellison, Nicholas, *Egalitarian Thought and Labour Politics* (London: LSE/Routledge, 1994).

Esping-Andersen, Gosta, 'Equality and Work in the Post-industrial Life-cycle', Miliband (1994), *op. cit.*, pp. 167–85.

Etzioni, Amitai, *The Spirit of Community: Rights, Responsibilities and the Communitarian Agenda* (New York: Crown Publishers, 1993).

—— *The Third Way to a Good Society* (London: Demos, 2000).

—— 'The Third Way is a Triumph', *New Statesman*, 25 June 2001, pp. 25–6.

Evans, Geoffrey and Pippa Norris (eds), *Critical Elections. British Parties and Voters in Long-term Perspective* (London: Sage Publication, 1999), pp. 164–80.

Fairclough, Norman, *New Labour, New Language?* (New York: Routledge, 2000).

Farneti, Pietro, *Il sistema dei partiti in Italia (1946–1979)* (Bologna: Il Mulino, 1983).

Favretto, Ilaria, 'La svolta autonomista del PSI vista oltremanica: il partito laburista, il Foreign Office e il centro–sinistra', *Italia Contemporanea*, no. 202 (March 1996), pp. 5–44.

Fielding, Steven, ' "White Heat" and White Collars: the Evolution of Wilsonism', in Coopey, Fielding and Tiratsoo (eds) (1993), *op. cit.*, pp. 29–47.

Flora, Peter, F. Kraus, W. Pfenning, *State Economy and Society in Western Europe 1815–1975*, Vol. I–II, *The Growth of Industrial Societies and Capitalist Economies* (Frankfurt: Campus Verlag; London: Macmillan Press; Chicago: St James Press, 1987).

Flores D'Arcais, Paolo, 'Gobetti, liberale del futuro', introduction in P. Gobetti (edited by Ersilia Alessandrone Perona), *La Rivoluzione Liberale* (Torino: Einaudi, 1995, 1st edn 1964), pp. VII–XXXII.

—— 'L'alternativa azionista', *Micromega*, no. 3 (1991), pp. 24–32.

Foa, Vittorio, 'Il socialismo per un'Italia moderna', *Mondo Operaio*, Vol. X (February–March 1957), pp. 69–71.

—— 'L'industria di stato e i monopoli', *Mondo Operaio*, Vol. IX (May 1956), pp. 286–9.

Folena, Pietro, *I ragazzi di Berlinguer* (Milano: Baldini & Castoldi, 1997).

Foley, Michael, *The British Presidency* (Manchester: Manchester University Press, 2000).

Foot, John, 'The Family and the "Economic Miracle": Social Transformation, Work, Leisure and Development at Bovisa and Comasina (Milan), 1950–1970', *Contemporary European History*, no. 4 (1995), pp. 327–38.

Fortini, Franco, *Dieci Inverni 1947–1957* (Bari: De Donato, 1973).

Fouskas, Vassilis, *Italy, Europe, the Left* (London: Ashgate, 1998).

Franklin, Mark, *The Decline of Class Voting in Britain: Changes in the Basis of Electoral Choice, 1964–1983* (Oxford: Clarendon Press, 1985).

Fuà, Giorgio and Paolo Sylos Labini, *Idee per la programmazione economica* (Roma-Bari: Laterza, 1963).

Fukuyama, Francis, *The End of History and the Last Man* (London: Hamish Hamilton, 1992).

Gaitskell, Hugh, 'The Ideological Development of Democratic Socialism in Great Britain', *Socialist International Information*, Vol. V (24 December 1955), pp. 921–51.

—— *Socialism and Nationalisation*, Fabian Tract no. 300, 1956.

Galbraith, John K., *The Affluent Society* (London: Hamish Hamilton, 1958 (Italian transl.: *Economia e benessere*, Milan: Ed. di Comunità, 1959 or *La società opulenta*, Milan: Etas Kompass, 1967).

—— *The New Industrial State* (London: Hamish Hamilton, 1967).

—— *The Culture of Contentment* (Harmondsworth: Penguin, 1992).

Galli, Giorgio, *Storia del socialismo italiano* (Roma-Bari: Laterza, 1980).

—— 'Tre anni di Revisionismo', *Tempi Moderni*, Vol. III (April–June 1960), pp. 56–69.

—— *I partiti politici italiani* (Milano: Rizzoli, 1991).

Gerratana, Valentino (ed.), *Antonio Gramsci. Quaderni del Carcere*, Vol. 3 (Torino: Einaudi, 1977).

Gervasoni, Marco, *L'intellettuale come eroe. Piero Gobetti e le culture del novecento* (Firenze: La Nuova Italia, 2000).

Giddens, Anthony, *The Third Way. The Renewal of Social Democracy* (Cambridge: Polity Press, 1998).

—— *The Third Way and its Critics* (Cambridge: Polity Press, 2000)

—— (ed.), *The Global Third Way Debate* (Cambridge: Polity Press, 2001).

—— *Beyond Left and Right. The Future of Radical Politics* (Cambridge: Polity Press, 1994).

—— *The Runaway World: How Globalisation is Reshaping our Lives* (London: Profile Books Ltd., 1999).

—— 'Brave New World: the New Context of Politics', in Miliband (1994), *op. cit.*, pp. 21–38.

Gilbert, Mark and Gianfranco Pasquino (eds), *Italian Politics. The Faltering Transition* (New York-Oxford: Berghann, 2000).

Ginsborg, Paul, *A History of Contemporary Italy* (Harmondsworth: Penguin Books, 1990).

—— *L'Italia del tempo presente. Famiglia, società civile, Stato 1980–1996* (Torino: Einaudi, 1998).

Giolitti, Antonio, *Riforme e Rivoluzione* (Torino: Einaudi, 1957).

—— *Un socialismo possibile* (Torino: Einaudi, 1968).

—— *Lettere a Marta. Ricordi e riflessioni* (Bologna: Il Mulino, 1992).

—— 'Alcune osservazioni sulle riforme di struttura', *Passato e Presente*, no. 6 (November–December 1958), pp. 677–91.

—— 'L'operaio, la grande fabbrica e il monopolio', *Mondo Operaio*, Vol. XIII (March 1960), pp. 23–6.

—— 'Politica ed economia nella lotta di classe. Un'intervista con Antonio Giolitti', *Mondo Operaio*, Vol. X (September 1957), pp. 2–4.

—— 'Programma e formule', *Mondo Operaio*, Vol. XII (July 1959), pp. 6–9.

—— *Programmazione economica e progresso civile. Discorso pronunciato alla Camera dei Deputati nella seduta del 24 maggio 1962* (Roma: Camera dei Deputati Tipografia, 1962).

Glotz, Peter, *Manifesto per Una Nuova Sinistra Europea* (Milano: Feltrinelli, 1986).

Goldthorpe, John, *The Affluent Worker: Political Attitudes and Behaviour* (Cambridge: Cambridge University Press, 1968).

Gorz, André, *Farewell to the Working Class: an Essay on Post-Industrial Socialism* (London: Pluto Press, 1982).

Gould, Brian, *A Future for Socialism* (London: Cape, 1989).

Gozzano, Francesco, 'Un governo socialista in Inghilterra', *Mondo Operaio*, Vol. XVII (November–December 1964), pp. 10–17.

Grandi, Roberto, 'Strategie a confronto', in Livolsi and Volli (1997) (ed.), *op. cit.*, pp. 83–106.

Gray, John, *False Down: the Delusions of Global Capitalism* (London: Granta Books, 1998).

Grayson, Richard, 'What is a Third Way?', in Wallace and Stockley (1998) (eds), *op. cit.*, pp. 6–14.

Greer, Germain, *The Whole Woman* (London: Transworld Publisher, 1999).

Groppo, B., 'Il 1956 nella cultura politica del PCI', in B. Groppo and G. Riccamboni, *La Sinistra e il '56 in Italia e in Francia* (Padova: Liviana, 1987), pp. 189–213.

Gruppi Parlamentari della Maggioranza L'Ulivo insieme per l'Italia (ed.), *I Governi di Centro–sinistra: Impegni mantenuti e cose da fare. Un bilancio del lavoro svolto e da svolgere fino alla fine della legislatura* (Roma: Ufficio Comunicazione del Gruppo DS-L'Ulivo della Camera dei Deputati, March 2000).

Guiducci, Roberto and Fabrizio Onofri (eds), *Costituente Aperta. Le nuove frontiere del socialismo in Italia* (Firenze: Vallecchi, 1966).

Guiducci, Roberto, *Socialismo e Verità* (Torino: Einaudi, 1956).

—— (ed.), *New Deal Socialista. Valori e strumenti per un piano a lungo periodo* (Firenze: Vallecchi, 1965).

—— 'Il mito dell'industria e programma alternativo' (July–August 1959), in Guiducci (ed.) (1965), *op. cit.*, pp. 32–54.

—— 'Un piano di riforme democratiche' (May–October 1957), in Guiducci (ed.) (1965), *op. cit.*, pp. 19–31.

Hall, Stuart, 'The Great Moving Nowhere Show', *Marxism Today* (November–December 1998), pp. 9–14.

Harvey, Audrey, *Casualties of the Welfare State*, Fabian Tract no. 321, 1960.

Haseler, Stephen, *The Gaitskellites: Revisionism in the British Labour Party, 1951–1964* (London: 1964).

Hattersley, Roy, *Choose Freedom: the Future for Democratic Socialism* (London: Penguin, 1987).

Hayward Jack and M. Watson (eds), *Planning, Politics and Public Policy: the British, French and Italian Experiences* (Cambridge: Cambridge University Press, 1975).

Heath, Anthony and Bridget Taylor, 'New Sources of Abstention', in Evans and Norris (eds) (1999), *op. cit.*, pp. 164–80.

Heath, Anthony, Roger Jowell and John Curtice, *Labour's Last Chance: the 1992 Election and Beyond* (Aldershot: Dartmouth Publishing Company, 1994).

Heath, Anthony and Roger Jowell, 'Labour's Policy Review', in Heath, Jowell, Curtice (eds) (1994), *op. cit.*, pp. 191–209.

Heath, Anthony, Roger Jowell and John Curtice, 'Can Labour Win?', in Heath, Jowell, Curtice (eds) (1994), *op. cit.*, pp. 275–95.

Heffer, Eric S., 'L'Avvenire del Laburismo Inglese', *Mondo Operaio*, Vol. XII (July 1959), pp. 46–7.

Hennessy, Peter, *The Prime Minister* (London: Penguin, 2001).

Hennessy, Peter and Anthony Seldon (eds), *Ruling Performance: British Governments from Attlee to Thatcher* (Oxford: Blackwell, 1987).

Hobsbawm, Eric, *Age of Extremes* (London: Michael Joseph, 1994).

Hobsbawm, Eric, Jacques, M. and Mulhern, F., *The Forward March of Labour Halted?* (London: Verso, 1981).
Holland, Stuart, *The Socialist Challenge* (London: Quartet Books, 1975).
Hughes, John, 'An Economic Policy for Labour', *New Left Review*, no. 24 (March–April 1964), pp. 5–31.
Hutton, Will, *The State We're In* (London: Jonathan Cape, 1995).
—— *The State to Come* (London: Vintage, 1997).
—— *The Stakeholding Society* (Cambridge: Polity Press, 1999).
Ignazi, Piero, *Dal PCI al PDS* (Bologna: Il Mulino, 1992).
Inglehart, Ronald, *The Silent Revolution. Changing Values and Political Styles Among Western Publics* (Princeton NJ: Princeton University Press, 1977).
IPPR, *Building Better Partnerships* (London: IPPR Report, 2001).
Istituto Cattaneo, Italian National Election Studies, *La Repubblica*, 15 November 2001, p. 29.
Istituto Gramsci (edited by), *I Lavoratori e il Progresso Tecnico*, Proceedings of the conference held at the Gramsci Institute, 30 June–1 July 1956, 'Le trasformazioni tecniche ed organizzative e le modificazioni del rapporto di lavoro nelle fabbriche italiane' (Rome: Editori Riuniti, 1956).
—— (edited by), *Tendenze del Capitalismo Italiano. Atti del Convegno di Roma* (Rome: 1962).
Jay, Douglas, *Socialism in the New Society* (London: Longman, 1962).
Jenkins, Roy, 'Equality', in Crossman (ed.) (1952), *op. cit.*, pp. 69–90.
Jones, Nicholas, *Control Freaks* (London: Politico's Publishing, 2001).
Jones, Tudor, *Remaking the Labour Party. From Gaitskell to Blair* (New York and London: Routledge, 1996).
Kavanagh, Dennis (ed.), *Politics and Personalities* (Worcester: Billing & Sons, 1990).
—— *Election Campaigning. The New Marketing of Politics* (Oxford: Blackwell, 1997 [first edition, 1995]).
—— 'Must Labour Lose Again', in Kavanagh (ed.) (1990), *op. cit.*, pp. 91–104.
Kavanagh, Dennis and P. Morris (eds), *Consensus Politics. From Attlee to Major* (Oxford: Blackwell, 1994 [first edition, 1989]).
Koestler, Arthur, *Suicide of a Nation? An Enquiry into the State of Britain* (London: Vintage, 1994) (first published in Great Britain by Hutchinson, 1963).
Labour Party–Labour Research Department (ed.), *Twelve Wasted Years*, September 1963.
Labour Party, *Labour Believes in Britain*, London 1949.
—— *Labour and the New Society*, London 1950.
—— *Challenge to Britain*, London 1953.
—— *Personal Freedom: Labour's Policy for the Individual and Society*, London 1956.
—— *Towards Equality: Labour's Policy for Social Justice*, London 1956.
—— *Industry and Society: Labour's Policy on Future Public Ownership*, London 1957.
—— *Public Enterprise: Labour's Review of Nationalised Industries*, London 1957.
—— *Learning to Live: a Policy for Education from Nursery School to University*, London 1958.
—— *Planning for Progress*, London 1958.
—— *Labour's Educational Policy*, London 1959.
—— *Labour in the Sixties*, London 1960.
—— *Signposts for the Sixties*, London 1961.

—— *Labour and the Scientific Revolution*, London 1963.

—— *Labour's Programme 1982*, London 1982.

—— *Social Ownership*, London 1986.

—— *Britain Will Win*, General Election Manifesto 1987.

—— *Meet the Challenge, Make the Change. A New Agenda for Britain, Final Report of Labour's Policy Review for the 1990s*, London 1989.

—— *Made in Britain. New Markets, New Technology, New Government*, London 1991.

—— *Labour's Objects: Socialist Values in the Modern World*, London 1994.

—— *A New Economic Future for Britain: Economic and Employment Opportunities for All*, London, 1995.

—— 'Future of the European Union: Labour's Position in Preparation for the Intergovernmental Conference 1996', Interim Report, Labour Party, 14 September 1996.

—— *New Labour: Because Britain Deserves Better*, General Election Manifesto 1997.

—— *Ambitions for Britain*, General Election Manifesto 2001.

Lama, Luciano, 'I Sindacati e la programmazione economica', *Mondo Operaio*, Vol. XV (August–September 1963), pp. 12–17.

Lanaro, Silvio, *Storia dell'Italia Repubblicana. Dalla fine della guerra agli anni novanta* (Venezia: Marsilio, 1992).

Landolfi, Antonio, 'Partito Socialista Italiano: struttura, organi, dirigenti, correnti', *Tempi Moderni*, Vol. V (January–March 1962), pp. 3–45.

Lawson, Neal and Neil Sherlock (eds), *The Progressive Century: the Future of the Centre–Left in Britain* (London: Palgrave, 2001).

Leadbeater, Charles, *Living on Thin Air* (London: Viking, 1999).

Leonard, Mark, *Rediscovering Europe* (London: Demos, 1998).

Leonardi, Silvio, *Progresso tecnico e Rapporti di lavoro* (Torino: Einaudi, 1956).

Leruez J., *Economic Planning and Politics in Britain* (London: Martin Robertson, 1975).

Liguori, Guido, *Gramsci conteso. Storia di un dibattito 1922–1996* (Roma: Editori Riuniti, 1996).

Lipset, Seymour Martin, *Political Man: the Social Bases of Politics* (New York: Doubleday, 1981 revised edition, [first edition 1960]).

—— 'The Changing Class Structure and Contemporary European Politics', in *Daedalus. Journal of the American Academy of Arts and Sciences*, Vol. 93 (Winter 1964), Special issue 'A New Europe?', pp. 271–303.

Lipset, Seymour Martin and Reinhard Bendix, *Social Mobility in Industrial Society* (London: Heinemann, 1959 (American edition by University of California Press, Berkeley, 1959).

Lipset, Seymour Martin and Stein Rokkan (eds), *Party Systems and Voter Alignments* (London: Collier Macmillan, 1967 (American edition, New York: Free Press, 1967).

Livi, Alfredo, 'Per una politica della corrente sindacale socialista', *Mondo Operaio*, Vol. XVII (April 1964), pp. 21–5.

Lombardi, Riccardo, 'La conquista democratica dello Stato' (Riccardo Lombardi's speech to the 34th PSI National Congress, Milan, 28–30 March 1961), in Colarizi (ed.) (1978), *op. cit.*, pp. 337–66.

Lombardi, Riccardo, 'La nuova politica delle alleanze' (Speech to the 33rd PSI National Congress, Naples, 15–19 January 1959), in Colarizi (ed.) (1978), *op. cit.*, pp. 293–6.

Lombardi, Riccardo, 'Schema di relazione introduttiva al Convegno delle Partecipazioni Statali', in PSI-Sezione Economica, *Convegno delle Partecipazioni Statali, op. cit.*, pp. 7–44.

Longo, Luigi, *Revisionismo nuovo e antico* (Torino: Einaudi, 1957).

Lowe, Roy, *Education in the Post-War Years: a Social History* (London and New York: Routledge, 1988).

Lunghini, Giorgio, *L'età dello spreco. Disoccupazione e bisogni sociali* (Torino: Bollati Boringhieri, 1995).

Maddison, Angus, *Phases of Capitalist Development* (Oxford: Oxford University Press, 1982).

—— *The World Economy in the 20th Century* (Paris: Organisation for Economic Co-operation and Development, 1989).

Mafai, Miriam, *Lombardi* (Milano: Feltrinelli, 1976).

—— *Dimenticare Berlinguer* (Roma: Donzelli, 1996).

Maglietta, Clemente, 'I Laburisti di fronte alla Rivoluzione Tecnologica', *Nord e Sud*, no. 50 (February 1964), pp. 47–51.

Mallet, Serge, *La Nuova Classe Operaia* (Torino: Einaudi, 1976 [first edition 1963]).

Mandelson, Peter and Roger Liddle, *The Blair Revolution* (London: Faber and Faber, 1996).

Mannheimer, Renato and Giacomo Sani, *La rivoluzione elettorale. Tra la prima e la seconda repubblica* (Milano: Anabasi, 1994).

Marquand, David *The Unprincipled Society. New Demands and Old Politics* (London: Jonathan Cape, 1988).

—— *The New Reckoning. Capitalism, States and Citizens* (Cambridge: Polity Press, 1997).

—— 'Reinventing Federalism: Europe and the Left', in Miliband (1994), *op. cit.*, pp. 219–30.

Marr, Andrew, *Who is Tony Blair?* (London: Penguin, 1997).

Mastropaolo, Alfio, *Antipolitica all'origine della crisi italiana* (Napoli: L'Ancora del Mediterraneo, 2000).

McKenzie, Robert and Allan Silver, *Angels in Marble: Working Class Conservatives in Urban England* (London: Heinemann, 1968).

Meadowcroft, John, 'Is there a liberal alternative? Charles Kennedy and the Liberal Democrats' strategy', *Political Quarterly*, Vol. 71 (October–December 2000), pp. 436–42.

Menichelli, Alessandro, 'Cultura e lotta operaia', *Mondo Operaio*, Vol. IX (August–September 1956), pp. 492–4.

Mercer, Helen, Neil Rollings and Jim Tomlinson (eds), *Labour Governments and Private Industry: the Experience of 1945–1951* (Edinburgh: Edinburgh University Press, 1992).

Messina, Sebastiano, 'Rutelli: <<Giuro, toglierò al Polo la bandiera della libertà>>', *Corriere della Sera*, 22 October 2000, p. 3.

Middlemas, Keith, *Power, Competition and the State*, Vol. II, *Threats to the Postwar Settlement: Britain, 1961–1974* (London: Macmillan, 1990).

Mikardo, Ian, 'Trade Unions in a Full Employment Economy', in Crossman (ed.) (1952), *op.cit.*, pp. 143–60.

Miliband, Ralph, *Parliamentary Socialism. A Study in the Politics of Labour* (London: Merlin Press, 1972 [first edition Allen & Unwin, London, 1961]).

Minkin, Lewis, *The Labour Party Conference. A Study into Politics of Intra-Party Democracy* (London: Allen Lane, 1978).

Mitchell, B. R. *European Historical Statistics 1750–1975*, 2nd revised edition (first published in 1975) (London: Macmillan Press, 1981).

Momigliano, Franco and Alessandro Pizzorno, 'Consumi in Italia', in Franco Momigliano and Alessandro Pizzorno, *Aspetti e Problemi Sociali dello Sviluppo Economico in Italia* (Roma-Bari: Laterza, 1959).

Momigliano, Franco, *Sindacati, progresso tecnico, programmazione economica* (Torino: Einaudi, 1966).

Monbiot, George, *The Captive State: the Corporate Takeover of Britain* (Basingtoke: Macmillan, 2000).

Mondolfo, Rodolfo (ed.), *Bilancio del Marxismo* (Bologna: Cappelli, 1965).

Morgan, Kenneth O., *The People's Peace. British History 1945–1990* (Oxford: Oxford University Press, 1992 [1st ed. 1990]).

Mouffe, Chantal, *The Democratic Paradox* (London: Verso, 2000).

Movimento per l'Ulivo, *Il Programma de l'Ulivo*, Aprile 1996, in www. democraticidisinistra.it/ulivo, section: 'Le buone regole dell'economia nazionale'.

Mughini, Giampiero (ed), *Il revisionismo socialista. Antologia di testi 1955–1962* (Roma: Nuova Serie dei Quaderni di Mondo Operaio, 1975).

Mulgan, Geoff and Charles Leadbeater, *Mistakeholding: Whatever Happened to Labour's Big Idea?* (London: Demos, 1997).

Mulgan, Geoff, *Politics in an Antipolitical Age* (Cambridge: Polity Press, 1994).

Myrdal, G. *Beyond the Welfare State* (London: 1960).

Nenni, Pietro, *Diari (1943–1971)*, 3 Vols. (Milano: SugarCo, 1981-3).

—— 'Luci e ombre del congresso di Mosca', *Mondo Operaio*, Vol. IX (March 1956), pp. 146–54.

—— 'La polemica sul revisionismo', *Mondo Operaio*, Vol. XII, no. 7, July 1959, pp. 40–3.

—— 'Le prospettive del Socialismo Europeo', *Mondo Operaio*, Vol. XIII, no. 6, June 1960, pp. 32–4.

—— 'Relazione al Comitato Centrale del PSI, 17 ottobre 1962', *Avanti!*, 18 October 1962.

—— (edited by G. Tamburrano), *Il Socialismo nella democrazia. Realtà del presente* (Firenze: Vallecchi, 1966).

Newman, Michael, *Socialism and European Unity. The Dilemma of the Left in Britain and France* (London: Junction Books, 1983).

Norris, Pippa, 'Labour Party Factionalism and Extremism', in Heath, Jowell, Curtice (1994), *op. cit.*, pp. 173–90.

—— 'New Politicians? Changes in Party Competition at Westminster', in Evans and Norris (eds) (1999), *op. cit.*, pp. 22–43.

Occhetto, Achille, *Il sentimento e la ragione. Un'intervista di Teresa Bartoli* (Milano: Rizzoli, 1994).

—— 'Il nuovo corso è discontinuità, non è demolizione del passato', *l'Unità*, 14 September 1989.

OEEC National Account Statistics, 1955–1965, Paris, 1964.

Onofri, Fabrizio, 'La via sovietica (leninista) alla conquista del potere e la via italiana, aperta da Gramsci', *Nuovi Argomenti*, (November 1956–February 1957), pp. 48–85.

Osborne, John, *Look Back in Anger* (London: Faber, 1957).

Paci, Massimo, *Il mutamento della struttura sociale italiana in Italia* (Bologna: Il Mulino, 1992).

Padget, Stephen and William E. Paterson, *A History of Social Democracy in Postwar Europe* (London and New York: Longman, 1991).

Pamini, M., 'From Militants to Voters: from the PCI to the PDS', in P. Ignazi and C. Ysmal (eds), *The Organisation of Political Parties in Southern Europe* (Westport, Conn.: Praeger, 1998).

Panzani, Luciano, 'L'esperienza inglese: il dilemma nazionalizzazione – azionariato pubblico', in Cottino (ed.) (1978), *op. cit.*, pp. 145–87.

Panzieri, Renato, (edited by Stefano Merli), *Dopo Stalin. Una stagione della sinistra* (Venezia: Marsilio, 1986).

—— 'Sette tesi sul controllo operaio', *Mondo Operaio*, Vol. XI (February 1958), pp. 11–15.

—— 'Tredici tesi sulla questione del partito di classe', in R. Panzieri (1986) *op. cit.*, pp. 122–52.

—— column 'Filo Rosso', *Mondo Operaio*, Vol. X (April 1957).

Panzieri, Renato and Lucio Libertini, 'Sette tesi sul controllo operaio', *Mondo Operaio*, Vol. XI (February 1950), pp. 11–15.

Parenti, Alberto, 'Programmazione e ricerca scientifica', *Mondo Operaio*, Vol. XIX (June–July 1966), pp. 33–5.

Pasquino, Gianfranco, *Critica della sinistra italiana* (Roma-Bari: Laterza, 2001).

PCI, *Documenti per il XVII Congresso. Progetto di Tesi, Programma, Emendamento; Statuto, Criteri e Proposte*, in *Rinascita*, no. 5, 8 February 1986.

—— *Tesi, Programma, Statuto: i Documenti approvati dal XVII Congresso del PCI* (Roma: l'Unità, 1987).

—— *Documenti per il Congresso Straordinario del PCI. Il Comitato Centrale della Svolta* (Roma: l'Unità, 1990).

—— *Mozioni e Documenti del XX Congresso* (Roma: Fratelli Spada, 1990).

—— *Idee e Proposte per la Costituente* (Roma: Fratelli Spada, 1990).

PDS, *Lo Statuto* (Roma: Fratelli Spada, 1991).

Pedone, Franco, *Novant'anni di pensiero socialista attraverso i congressi del PSI 1957–1966* (Venezia: Marsilio, 1984).

Perriman, Mark, *The Blair Agenda* (London: Lawrence and Wishart, 1996).

Pesenti, Antonio and Vincenzo Vitello, 'Tendenze attuali del capitalismo italiano', in Istituto Gramsci (edited by), *Tendenze del Capitalismo Italiano. Atti del Convegno di Roma*, *op. cit.*, pp. 13–96.

Petronio, Giuseppe, 'La riforma della scuola', *Mondo Operaio*, Vol. IX (January 1956), pp. 32–7.

Picciurro, Giuseppe, 'Funzione Pubblica della Ricerca Scientifica', *Mondo Operaio*, Vol. XVII (April 1964), pp. 17–24.

Pimlott, Ben, *Harold Wilson* (London: Harper Collins, 1992).

Pinto, Carmine, *La fine di un partito. Il PSI dal 1992 al 1994* (Roma: Editori Riuniti, 1999).

Pizzorno, Alessandro, *I soggetti del pluralismo, classi-partiti-sindacati* (Bologna: Il Mulino, 1980).

—— 'I tolemaici, ovvero i migliori anni della nostra vita', *Passato e Presente*, no. 3 (May–June 1958), pp. 1–3.

—— 'The Individualistic Mobilization of Europe', in *Daedalus. Journal of the American Academy of Arts and Sciences*, Vol. 93 (Winter 1964), special issue 'A New Europe?', pp. 199–224.

Pollock, Frederick, *Automation. The Economic and Social Consequences of Automation*, translated from the first German edition 1956 (Oxford: Basil Blackwell, 1957).

—— *Automazione. Conseguenze economiche e sociali* (Torino: Einaudi, 1976 [1st Italian edn 1956]).

Popper, Karl, *La società aperta e i suoi nemici* (Roma: Armando Editore, 1974).

Porter, Dilwyn, 'Downhill all the way: thirteen Tory years 1951–1964', in Coopey, Fielding, Tiratsoo (eds) (1993), *The Wilson Governments 1964–1970* (London and New York: Pinter, 1993, pp. 10–28.

Przeworski, Adam, *Capitalism and Social Democracy* (Cambridge: Cambridge University Press, 1985).

PSI, *Resoconto stenografico 32° Congresso Nazionale PSI, Venezia 6–10 febbraio 1957* (Milano–Roma: Edizioni Avanti!, 1957).

—— *Resoconto stenografico 33° Congresso Nazionale PSI, Napoli 15–18 gennaio 1959* (Milano-Roma: Edizioni Avanti!, 1959).

—— *Resoconto Stenografico 34° Congresso Nazionale PSI, Milano 15–20 marzo 1961* (Milano-Roma: Edizioni Avanti!, 1961).

PSI-Commissione nazionale scuola, *Il Piano Medici per la scuola dell'Obbligo* (Firenze: Tipografia Coppini, 1960).

PSI-Sezione Economica, *Il PSI per la Scuola Oggi e Domani* (Firenze: Tipografia STIAV, 1963).

—— *Nota sull'attuale congiuntura economica in Italia e sulle politiche per fronteggiarla* (Roma: SETI, 1963).

PSI-Sezione Economica, *Convegno delle Partecipazioni Statali* (Milano: Edizioni Avanti!, 1960).

Pugliese, Orazio and Daniele Pugliese (eds), *Da Gramsci a Berlinguer. La via italiana al socialismo attraverso i congressi del partito comunista italiano* (Milano: Edizioni del Calendario, 1985).

Radice, Giles, *Labour's Path to Power: the New Revisionism* (London: Macmillan, 1989).

Ramsden, John, *The Making of Conservative Policy: the Research Department since 1929* (London: Longman, 1980).

Rapone, Leonardo, 'Il planismo nei dibattiti dell'antifascismo italiano', *Storia Contemporanea*, no. 3 (June 1979), pp. 571–86.

Recuperati, Giuseppe, 'La politica scolastica dal centro–sinistra alla contestazione studentesca', *Studi Storici*, no. 1 (1990), pp. 235–60.

Rentoul, John, *Tony Blair* (London: Little, Brown & Co., 1995).

Report of the Social Justice Commission (London: Vintage, 1994).

Revelli, Marco, *La sinistra sociale. Oltre la civiltà del lavoro* (Torino: Bollati Boringhieri, 1997).

Rogers, Joel and Wolfgang Streeck, 'Productive Solidarities: Economic Strategy and Left Politics', in Miliband (1994), *op. cit.*, pp. 128–45.

Roggi, Piero, *Scelte politiche e teorie economiche in Italia nel quarantennio repubblicano* (Torino: Giappichelli, 1988).

Rollings, Neil, ' "The Reichstag method of governing"? The Attlee Government and Permanent Economic Controls', in Mercer, Rollings, Tomlinson (eds) (1992), *op. cit.*, pp. 15–36.

Rossanda, Rossana and Pietro Ingrao (eds), *Appuntamenti di Fine Secolo* (Roma: Manifestolibri, 1995).

Ruffolo, Giorgio, *La Grande Impresa nella Società Moderna* (Torino: Einaudi, 1971, 1st edn 1965).

Rusconi, Gian Enrico, 'L'ultimo azionismo', *il Mulino*, n. 4 (luglio–agosto 1992), pp. 575–93.

Salsano, Alfredo, *Il Neocapitalismo. Progetti ed ideologia*, in *Storia d'Italia*, Vol. 5, part 1 (Torino: Einaudi, 1972), pp. 888–909.

Sani, Giacomo, 'Il verdetto del 1992', in Mannheimer and Sani (eds) (1994), *op. cit.*, pp. 39–70.

Sapel, Jon, *Tony Blair: the Moderniser* (London: Michael Joseph, 1995).

Sapelli, Giulio, *L'Italia di fine secolo. Economia e classi dirigenti: un capitalismo senza mercato* (Venezia: Marsilio, 1998).

—— *L'Italia inafferrabile* (Venezia: Marsilio, 1989).

—— *Storia economica dell'Italia contemporanea* (Milano: Bruno Mondadori, 1997).

Sassoon, Donald, *One Hundred Years of Socialism* (London: I. B. Tauris, 1996).

—— *La via italiana al socialismo. Il PCI dal 1944 al 1964* (Torino: Einaudi, 1980).

—— 'The Italian Communist Party's European Strategy', *The Political Quarterly*, Vol. 47 (1976), pp. 253–76.

—— *Contemporary Italy* (London: Longman, 1997, [first edition, 1986]).

—— *Social Democracy at the Heart of Europe* (London: Institute of Public Policy Research, 1996).

Sbarberi, Franco, Introduction in L. T. Hobhouse, *Liberalismo* (Firenze: Vallecchi, 1995).

—— *L'utopia della libertà uguale: il liberalismo sociale da Rosselliy Bobbio* (Torino: Bollati Boringhień, 1999).

Schneer, Jonathan, *Labour's Conscience. The Labour Left 1945–1951* (London: Unwin Hyman, 1988).

Seldon, Anthony, *The Blair Effect* (London, Little, Brown & Co., 2001).

Shanks, Michael, *Planning and Politics. The British Experience 1960–1976* (London: George Allen & Unwin, 1977).

—— *The Stagnant Society* (London: Penguin Books Ltd, 1964 [first edn, 1961]).

Shonfield, Andrew, *Modern Capitalism. The Changing Balance of Public and Private Power* (Oxford: Oxford University Press, 1965).

Sivini, G., *Partiti e Partecipazione Politica in Italia* (Milano: Giuffrè, 1969).

Snow, C. P., *The Two Cultures and the Scientific Revolution*, the Rede Lecture 1959 (Cambridge: Cambridge University Press, 1959).

Socialist Union (edited by), *Twentieth Century Socialism*, Penguin Special, Harmondsworth, 1956.

Spini, Valdo, 'Il dibattito sulla programmazione agli inizi degli anni '60', in Arfè *et alia* (1977), *op. cit.*, pp. 187–225.

—— (ed.), special issue 'La Nascita di un nuovo partito. Cronologia e documenti della costruzione dei Democratici di Sinistra', *Quaderni del Circolo Rosselli*, no. 12 (1998).

—— *La Rosa e l'Ulivo. Per il nuovo partito del socialismo europeo in Italia* (Milano: Baldini & Castoldi, 1998).

Spreafico, Alberto and Joseph La Palombara, *Elezioni e Comportamento Politico in Italia* (Milano: Edizioni di Comunità, 1963).

Spriano, Paolo, *Le Passioni di un Decennio (1946–1956)* (Roma: Ed. L'Unita, 1992).

Stockley, Neil, 'The Third Way: where do Liberal Democrats stand?' in Wallace and Stockley (eds) (1998), *op. cit.*, pp. 25–33.

Strachey, John, *Contemporary Capitalism* (London: Gollancz, 1956 (Italian transl.: *Il capitalismo contemporaneo* (Milan: Feltrinelli, 1957)).

Street, Sarah, 'The Conservative Party Archives', *Twentieth Century British History*, Vol. 3 (1992), pp. 103–11.

Strinati, Valerio, *Politica e cultura nel Partito Socialista Italiano, 1945–1978* (Napoli: Liguori, 1980).

Sylos Labini, Paolo, *Saggio sulle classi sociali*, Laterza, Rome and Bari, 1974.

——'Sinistra e azionismo', *Micromega*, 2 (1999), pp. 158–64.

Taddei, Francesca, *Il socialismo italiano del dopoguerra: correnti ideologiche e scelte politiche (1943–1947)* (Milano: Franco Angeli, 1984).

Tamburrano, Giuseppe, *Storia e Cronaca del Centro-Sinistra* (Milano: Rizzoli, 1984).

——'Marx, Engels, Lenin e lo Stato', *Mondo Operaio*, Vol. IX (October 1956), pp. 566–72.

——'Per un programma socialista di governo', *Mondo Operaio*, Vol. XII (April–May 1959), pp. 21–4.

Therborn, Goran, *European Modernity and Beyond. The Trajectory of European Societies 1945–2000* (London: Sage, 1995).

Thompson, E. P., *Out of Apathy* (London: Verso, 1989 [first edition, 1960]).

Thompson, Noel, *Political Economy and the Labour Party* (London: UCL Press, 1996).

——'Supply Side Socialism: The Political Economy of New Labour', *New Left Review*, no. 216 (1996), pp. 37–54, p. 38.

Thompson, Willy, *The Long Death of British Labourism* (London: Pluto Press, 1993).

Tindale, Stephen, 'Sustaining Social Democracy: the Politics of the Enviroment', in Millband (1994), *op. cit.*, pp. 192–206.

Titmuss, Richard, *The Irresponsible Society*, Fabian Tract no. 323, April 1960, pp. 1–20.

Townsend, Peter, 'Persuasion and Conformity: An Assessment of the Borrie Report on Social Justice', *New Left Review*, no. 213 (1995), pp. 137–50, p. 145.

Toynbee, Polly and David Walker, *Did Things Get Better? An Audit of Labour's Successes and Failures* (London: Penguin, 2001).

Treneman, Joseph and Denis McQuail, *Television and Political Image: a study of the impact of television on the 1959 General Elections* (London: Methuen, 1961).

Turner, Adair, *Just Capital: The Liberal Economy* (with an introduction by Ralph Dahrendorf) (London: Macmillan, 2001).

Turone, Sergio, *Storia del sindacato in Italia. Dal 1943 al crollo del comunismo* (Roma-Bari: Laterza, 1992).

Urbinati, Nadia, 'Perché abbiamo bisogno di Amartya Sen', *Reset*, n. 63 (November–December 2000), pp. 54–7.

Vacca, Giuseppe, *Politica e teoria nel Marxismo Italiano* (Bari: De Donato, 1972).

——*Gli Intellettuali di sinistra e la crisi del 1956* (Roma: Editori Riuniti, 1978).

——preface in Paolo Borioni, *Socialismo postmoderno. La società aperta e il nuovo partito della sinistra* (Roma: Armando Editore, 1997), pp. 7–13.

——*Per una Nuova Costituente* (Milano: Bompiani, 1996).

——*Vent'anni dopo* (Torino: Einaudi, 1997).

Valentini, Chiara, *Berlinguer. L'eredità difficile* (Roma: Editori Riuniti, 1997).

Vallauri, Carlo, 'La crisi del '56 e il PSI', in *Arfè et alia* (1977), *op. cit.*, pp. 73–105.

Vallini, Edio, 'Contributo per uno studio sulle tecniche elettorali', *Tempi Moderni*, Vol. I (July 1958), pp. 266–9.

Vasetti, Fernando, 'Partito e tecnici', *Mondo Operaio*, Vol. X (February–March 1957), pp. 72–7.

Veltroni, Walter, *La sfida interrotta* (Milano: Baldini & Castoldi, 1994).
—— *Al Governo? Il Kennedy della sinistra italiana* (Bologna: Camenta edn, 1995).
—— *Il sogno spezzato. Le idee di Robert Kennedy* (Milano: Baldini & Castoldi, 1996).
—— *Governare a sinistra* (Milano: Baldini & Castoldi, 1997).
—— *I Care* (Milano: Baldini & Castoldi, 2000).
Venturino, Franco, *Partiti, Leader, Tematiche. La formazione dell'opinione pubblica nelle elezioni del 1996* (Milano: Franco Angeli, 2000).
Violante, Luciano, *Le due libertà. Contributo per l'identità della sinistra* (Bari-Roma: Laterza, 1999).
Walker, David, 'The First Wilson Governments 1964–1970', in Hennessy and Seldon (eds) (1987), *op. cit.*, pp. 186–215.
Wallace, William and Neil Stockley (eds), *Liberal Democrats and the Third Way* (London: Centre for Reform, Paper no. 4, 1998).
Wallace, William, 'The Third Way and the Fourth…', in Wallace and Stockley (eds) (1998), *op. cit.*, pp. 15–24.
Weir, S. and W. Hall (eds.), *The Untouchables: Power and Accountability in the Quango State* (London: Scarman Trust, 1996).
Wilson, Harold, *The New Britain* (Harmondsworth: Penguin Special, 1964).
—— *Purpose and Politics. Selected Speeches* (London: 1964)
—— 'A Four Year Plan', *New Stateman and the Nation*, Vol. LXI (26 March 1961), pp. 462–8.
—— 'Speech opening the Science Debate at the Party's Annual Conference, Scarborough, 1963', in Wilson (1964), *op. cit.*, pp. 14–27.
—— 'Wilson Defines British Socialism' (article written for the *New York Times*, September 15, 1963), in Wilson (1964), *op. cit.*, pp. 263–70.
—— *In Place of Dollars* (London: Tribune Monthly Publications), 1953.
—— *Post-War Economic Policies in Britain*, Fabian Tract, no. 309, September 1957.
—— *The Labour Government 1964–1970. A Personal Record*, Weidenfeld & Nicolson, London, 1971.
Woodward, Nicholas, 'Labour's Economic Performance 1964–70', in Coopey, Fielding, Tiratsoo (eds) (1993), *op. cit.*, pp. 72–101.
Wright Mills, Charles, *The Power Elite* (Oxford: Oxford University Press, 1956).
Wright, Antony and Gordon Brown, *Values, Visions and Voices: An Anthology of Socialism* (Edinburgh: Mainstream, 1995).
Wright, Antony, *Socialism and Decentralisation* (London: Fabian Society, 1984).
—— *Socialisms Old and New* (New York and London: Routledge, 1996).
Zincone, Giovanna, 'La donna è mobile ma non abbastanza', *Reset* (July–August 2001), pp. 18–19.
Zweigg, Ferdinand, *The Worker in an Affluent Society: Family, Life and Industry* (London: Heinemann, 1961).

Manuscript collections

Labour History Archive and Study Centre (Manchester), Labour Party Archive.
Archivio Centrale dello Stato (Rome), Nenni Papers.
Fondazione di Studi Storici 'Filippo Turati' (Florence), PSI Archive.
Fondazione Istituto Gramsci (Rome).

Index